Finally Meeting
PRINCESS MAUD

Finally Meeting PRINCESS MAUD

SEAMUS DUNLEAVY
and SHIRLEY THOMPSON

BREWIN BOOKS

First published by
Brewin Books Ltd, 56 Alcester Road,
Studley, Warwickshire B80 7LG in 2006
www.brewinbooks.com

ISBN 1 85858 284 9

A Cataloguing in Publication Record
for this title is available from the British Library.

Typeset in New Baskerville
Printed in Great Britain by
Cromwell Press Ltd.

CONTENTS

Dedication   vii

Acknowledgements   viii

Foreword by Professor Carl Chinn MBE   ix

Chapter 1   Barrack Street   1

Chapter 2   An American Dream   11

Chapter 3   Christmas in Charlestown   13

Chapter 4   Looking for 'Makes'   19

Chapter 5   The Jelly Thieves   31

Chapter 6   Eureka   43

Chapter 7   Leaving for Liverpool   50

Chapter 8   Birkenhead Sunsets   57

Chapter 9   The Empress   66

Chapter 10   Cycling under the Mersey   69

Chapter 11   Carol in Litherland   76

Chapter 12   Innocents Abroad   82

Chapter 13   Wars of the Roses   89

Chapter 14   Sparkhill Landlords   100

Chapter 15   Mary Griffin   107

Chapter 16   A Carrycastle Funeral   117

Chapter 17   From 'Talk' to The Liffey   125

Chapter 18   A Blinding Flash   141

Chapter 19   Shay and Rue   147

Chapter 20   Copperfield and Homer   165

Chapter 21   Lovelace in Splendour   185

Select Bibliography   203

This book is dedicated to my wife, Mary, and to my three children, Tracey, Shamus and Russell, without whose love and support this story might have had a completely different ending. Also, to the memory of those millions of Irish immigrants, who have struggled, down through the years, to build a new life for themselves, far from their native land. God bless them all!

ACKNOWLEDGEMENTS

The authors are indebted to the following people, companies and organisations for their valuable contributions, various favours and support, which have been of great assistance in the publication of this book:

The Dunleavy Family: Mary, Tracey, Shamus and Russell; Mickey Dunleavy.

Gordon and Richard Bragg; Brendan Breslin; Carl Chinn; Sean McQuade; Oliver Muldoon; Muriel Waters. Also, Ian Boyle, for supplying photographs of the 'Princess Maud'.

Sports Personalities: Bill (Wayne) Bridges; Pete Roberts; Ray Robinson.

Newspapers: The Solihull Times (Editor Enda Mullen), Poppy Brady of the *Birmingham Mail.*

Publishers: Alan and Alistair Brewin.

Thanks are also due to the author of our opening poem - *The Pride of the County Mayo*, whose identity is currently unknown to us.

FOREWORD

A land of magnificent and rugged scenery is Mayo. Belonging to the sea, lakes and skies as much as to the land, it is a many coloured place with its alluring shades of green, blue, grey and brown. Almost as far west as you can go in Europe, Mayo reaches out to the New World as much as it lies within the Old. In the same wise its past, present and future are not broken by time but are interwoven by a profound timelessness. Neolithic fields, Iron Age forts, Medieval castles, round towers and abbeys, and nineteenth-century cottages call out of those who have gone before – and their lives live on in ancient stories handed down by generations of seannachai, skilled storytellers who were the keepers of the folk memory.

Stand, listen and feel in Mayo and it as if you are close to the dreamland of Tir na nOg, the lovely land of youth where the leaves never died, the sun always shone, the flowers bloomed all the year, and the people were forever young and happy. But as beautiful as Mayo is, its people did not live in a rural idyll. With their land taken by foreign lords and their Catholic faith penalised, Mayo was a hard place to get by in the nineteenth century and from the 1820s many of its men, women and children were pushed away from their homes in search of work and food.

This great and unhappy migration was forced upon them by deteriorating economic conditions. A growing population meant that many families had to farm marginal land that could not support them. Benefiting from a high demand, landlords pushed up rents at a time when bad harvests led to famine conditions that blighted the already unhappy lives of the rural poor.

Added to this cauldron of hardship were the attempts of many landlords to bring in large farms that were worked by landless labourers. Agrarian warfare erupted in the west and south of Ireland, as working people banded together in secret societies to protect the oppressed. When landlords sought to seize the goods of tenants in rent arrears, large numbers of neighbours assembled by night with carts and horses to carry off the whole produce of the farm; whilst people combined to force landlords to employ local men and to try and keep up wages.

As an Irish priest exclaimed to the French visitor Alexis de Tocqueville, if a starving man sought help from his landlord he would be met by "liveried lackeys, or dogs better nourished than he, who will roughly drive him away". But if he presented himself at the door of a cottage he would do so without fear and would be "sure to receive something to appease his present hunger". It was the poor who prevented the poor from starving to death in Ireland.

Little is known of those first Irish pioneers to the West Midlands and the route they took is uncertain. Some may have trudged towards Sligo town and caught a boat there; whilst others may have slogged across the Irish Midlands to Dublin. Here they would have taken the cattle boat to Liverpool, paying 3d (just over 1p) for a rough passage on deck. Those long and uncomfortable sailings must have been frightening when the winds blew fiercely and the waves of the Irish Sea surged powerfully.

Writing in 1892, John Denvir explained that 'the hardy Connaughtmen generally passed through Liverpool on their way to the English agricultural counties. It was a sight to remember – the vast armies of harvest men, clad in frieze coats and knee breeches, with their clean white shirts with high collars and tough blackthorns . . . marching literally in their thousands from the Clarence Dock, Liverpool and up the London Road to reap John Bull's harvest'.

From Liverpool, these spalpeens, seasonal agricultural labourers, spread out across Lancashire, Cheshire, Staffordshire and Warwickshire in search of crops to bring in, farmers needing labour, and cash to earn. Sometimes these men and women stayed on the farms but often they rented a bed in dreary, dank and low lodging houses in the poorest areas of Stafford, Wolverhampton and Birmingham.

Each day they would rise early and tramp out to their labour in the fields. At night these Connacht folk would traipse back to dark streets and dismal rooms shared with many others. No doubt they sang of their homeland and of the families that they had left behind, and no doubt many of them slept fitfully, beset as they were with melancholic hearts.

But even though they must have missed the bogs, mountains, waters and cliffs of Mayo, and even though they must have thought longingly of their friends and kin, still some of these folk made up their minds not to return home after the bringing in of the harvest in the English Midlands. Instead, they sent for their families to join them in settling in a foreign land where nobody but they spoke the Irish and where they were marked out further by their Catholicism and their ways. And come they did – in their many, many thousands during the terrible years of the Great Hunger of the late 1840s when the potato crop failed and famine, diseases and death stalked the land and preyed upon the poor.

No-one knows the names of those first Mayo folk to leave their county west of the Shannon – nor of those of their fellow Connacht men and women from Roscommon, Galway and Sligo. Difficulties and hard times they faced in Birmingham and the Black Country, but strong of mind and character they stayed and made their mark upon Birmingham and the West Midlands in a host of ways.

One hundred years later, a new migration from the West of Ireland began. Once again the people of Mayo were prominent and once again they made their mark on the building, in factories, as nurses, in business, on the buses, in sport and in many other powerful ways. Amongst those who made their mark so resolutely was Seamus Dunleavy. With the strength of an ancient warrior yet has he the speech of the seannachai. His tales about his Charlestown days, about the donkeys and fleas, teachers and characters, handball and tossing school draw us to an older world whilst his stories about his wrestling, night clubs, pubs and hotels take us into a newer and more tangible world. Like the county from which he hails, Seamus stands in the present, beckons to the future and harks to the past. And as a proud as he is to be a Mayoman he is as proud to be an Irish Brummie.

Professor Carl Chinn MBE

The Pride of the County Mayo

(Air: 'Eileen McMahon')

The boys from the County of Mayo
  Sparkled on many a field
When the lads in the red and green shirts
  Forced the champions of Ireland to yield
Now the West is awakened to brothers
  Whose daring exploits we all know
At wrestling they have taken top honours
  The Dunleavys from County Mayo.

The Dunleavys brought glory to Ireland
  And champions they did overthrow
But the greatest on show at the Spin, Whip or Throw
  Was Seamus the pride of Mayo.

Came rough-house Alf Cadman from Salford
  Saying, "These Irish a lesson I'll show",
But the lesson he showed was a thrashing
  From the Pride of the County Mayo.

Now Scotland sent for wild Ian Campbell
  This giant who feared not a foe
He had beaten the overseas champions
  And had sixty-six wins in a row
Oh, fierce was the struggle that followed
  Between these great men of renown
Campbell the champion from Clydeside
  And Dunleavy from old Charlestown.

Round after round went to Campbell
  Whose great strength was clearly on show
But Dunleavy came back with a knock-out
  Bringing victory to him and Mayo.

Now they have crumbled the might of all Europe
  From Belgrade to far off Moscow
They have beaten the French and the Germans
  and the terrible Russians also.

The Dunleavys brought glory to Ireland
  And champions they did overthrow
But the greatest on show at the Spin, Whip or Throw
  Was Seamus the pride of Mayo.

Chapter One

BARRACK STREET

It was past midnight, on a biting cold November night. She could hear Nora's voice urging her on. Although clear, it sounded far away. She thought she drifted to unconsciousness, but she could not be sure. Plenty of pain and agony. They say births are easier after two or three, but she would not agree. From a distance she heard Nurse Healy's soothing voice: "One last push Mary Kate. Come on! The women of Mayo are made of good stuff!"

The year is 1934, in rural Western Ireland. Mrs. Dunleavy is giving birth to a fifth son, in a small village town, deep in County Mayo. As her friend, the local nurse ascends the stairs, to the tiny bedroom that serves as surgery and hospital, Mary Kate recalls the other births of her four sons and eldest daughter. They had all been different, but she hopes that this will be the last. But in rural Catholic Ireland, this is not to be.

Her friend was a big, jolly, chatty woman: "How many have you now, Mary Kate?" Although she had delivered all of Mary Kate's children, she could not remember exactly how many. She'd known Mary Kate all her life, but it seemed as though she had delivered most of the children in Charlestown, so she was hardly likely to remember how many children her friend had! Nora was a tall, heavy, rosy-cheeked woman, and always good-humoured; everyone liked her, around the town.

It was midnight or past when Mary Kate's labour began. Beads of sweat appeared and rolled off her pallid skin, as she endured the now familiar pain of childbirth. She pushed and pushed. But she was a woman who was worn and bruised by the harsh life of poverty and hardship, in rural Ireland. She exerted one last Herculean effort, arched her back, tensed every muscle in her body and pushed and prayed and screamed aloud. Then, what seemed an eternity, at last came to an end. A great shout of joy: "It's here Mary Kate!" – then boiling water and towels and the cutting of the cord. Shortly afterwards, another excited shout: "Mary Kate, it's a boy – a fine boy! Without the scales to weigh him, I would say he's at least eight to nine pounds."

Mary Kate collapsed back onto the pillow, her pain-wracked body drenched in sweat and blood. She felt totally drained and faint with the loss of blood; but she was euphoric. All of a sudden, a bundle of wet soggy humanity was placed in her arms. A feeling of calm and serenity descended upon her. He was definitely a fine punch of a boy. Mary Kate cuddled the baby close to her and smelled him. The bond between mother and son was complete. She felt so proud. Her husband would be proud as well.

A front window, to her left, looked out onto the darkness of Barrack Street. She expected great things of all her sons. Maybe this was the one who would do the best? Or perhaps bring shame and sorrow to her. Who knows? Nora's strong hands took the boy from Mary Kate and said: "Now sleep. The doctor will call in later and I'll stay for the rest of the night." Slowly, as the days passed, she regained her strength. Her baby was fine and healthy and the other children loved him, and looked after him, in their own way.

Charlestown straddles the County Sligo border and we were just on the border. A railway track divided County Mayo from County Sligo. It was more of a town than a village, in our eyes, and consisted of three streets: Barrack Street, where I was born, Main Street and then Chapel Street, where our main church or chapel was to be found. Barrack Street was so called because we had a Police Barracks directly opposite our house.

There were approximately thirty terraced houses altogether; fifteen on each side of the road – all joined together. In the fifteen houses on our side of Barrack Street, there were the Parsons, the Dunleavys, the Blakes, Tom MacDonald, the Co-op, Mrs. Cassidy, 'Baby' Frain, and the cinema – the *Eureka*. Then there was Tom Hopkins, Johnny O'Donnell, Pat McLoughlin and the Tunneys next to them. Finally, Joe Rogers; James Parsons, Kathleen Gannon; Martin Dunn; Jack Payton – fifteen houses each side Shirley.

We had a shop, but also a separate hall door, which took you into our back kitchen, where there was an open fire. We ate in the kitchen, because it also served us as a small dining room: roughly twelve-foot by twelve foot. Above that, we had another room, with a kitchen range, which I very rarely saw lit. But I believe before I came along, it was a very *warm* range. We burned turf on the open fire below, and cooked on it. My mum, or 'Mammy', as we called her, had a three-cornered, triangular stand, which she put her saucepans on and her iron pots. We made our own bread, which was flour, buttermilk and so forth. We had a 'crook' – I still have one as an ornament here, in England. We hung the main pots for potatoes and cabbage on that. It was always in the hearth, over the fire.

There were three bedrooms altogether. We had no toilets upstairs, but there was one outside. There were lots of people in our street who had no toilets at all. We were fortunate to have one, but we filled a bucket or chamber pot upstairs, and took them down to the toilet. But, often-as-not, we kicked one over Shirley, and there'd be a fair old stink – off and on!

Mammy was a short woman; a very pleasant, jolly woman, and she was supposed to have been very strong – physically. It was said that she could lift a two-stone weight – on her little finger! She had grey hair, all her life, and died at sixty-four, in 1959. My eldest sister was called Mai, then the first son, Paddy; a son, christened Luke, who we called Louie; a son Tommy; then she'd a son, Mickey, and I was the fifth son. After me came Angela, Kathleen, then Monica, the youngest. We must have been of strong stock, because none of my brothers or sisters died in infancy.

Things were very bad financially. We were living on my dad, Michael's earnings, which were very meagre at the time. After seeing the *Ma and Pa Kettle* films at the *Eureka*, we began to call him 'Pa', and continued to do so, throughout his lifetime. Pa was a carpenter, a very good one, and was working away at Tuam, in Galway, during the period when I was born. He used to actually cycle from Charlestown to Tuam, (pronounced Chewm) – the place where Pat Roach's great grandparents were from. Pat Roach was a good friend of mine, whom I helped to train, in his early days of wrestling – but I'll tell you more about that – in a later chapter.

Tuam was a helluva distance to cycle – forty miles from there to Charlestown. I can't remember if he used to come home weekly; but even if he did, it was a long distance. We would see him off, at the bottom of our backway. We'd a back way into Charlestown as well. The town was very well laid out, in so far as you had the streets and then you had a back way, which your horses and carts came up and down. You could bypass the centre of the town if you wanted to and put things, for the various jobs, in the back of your cart.

Everyone in town had a parcel of bog land, a mile out, on the outskirts of town, which they could cut. That was their fuel for the year. But we cut our turf when we were very small, with my oldest brother, Paddy. So we'd borrow a donkey and cart for the day, from a man called Sonny O'Donnell. He'd lend it to you for a day or two, but he'd want to use the donkey and cart himself, most of the time.

The cart was in fairly good condition. We'd load it up with turf and take it back to the shed at home. The donkey was fully trained and quite reliable. We had a stick to control it. After we'd taken a few cartloads of turf back home, we'd unyoke the donkey and go and have a ride on him. We shouldn't have done it, because the poor old animal was tired himself!

My older brother Paddy would drive the donkey all day, but then we'd have a practice on him later. It was a *huge*, big adventure for us younger ones, if we got together on the donkey. But we had to be sure that he was quiet – that he wasn't going to buck us! Paddy was in charge. There was a six-year age gap between us. Sadly, he died about three years ago... but I'm over-running my story.

I'm going home to Charlestown, this Thursday. The town is exactly the same as when we left it really. You know when you went to Birmingham Shirley? You might have known it when you were a kid, but you wouldn't know it all now. Well, in the typical little town in Ireland – this or that person may be dead, but the town itself remains the same. But where you grew up here, everything's changed; they've knocked houses down – demolished them, but my town is the same as the day I left. I can go through the whole town and say: "Mrs. Salmon is dead, Tom Hopkins is dead," and so on. But the Charlestown houses remain the same.

Barrack Street ran straight down. In the middle was what they called the 'Centrebox'. It was like a gazebo, a conical building, with a pointed roof on it. I'll draw it for you: this is exactly the picture. There's Barrack Street up here. That's Main Street, that's Chapel Street and that was the railway. Mayo's there and Sligo's there. There was a town there, called Bellaghy, which was in County Sligo. The railway's just there – there's the track. It was Charlestown Railway Station of course; it's closed down now. You could go to Dublin from there.

But the thing is, they used to have a market in the town square, every Wednesday. The Centrebox stood in the heart of the square. They would bring out big weighing scales, which were kept for the rest of the week in the Centrebox. If you wanted a hundredweight of potatoes, there was a man there who'd say: "Throw them on the scales!" Then he'd say: "There's not a hundredweight there – there's seven stone in that bag." So you'd buy seven stone of potatoes, or whatever it happened to weigh.

The farming community was all around us. When I grew up, there were rings in the street, so you could tie your horses to them, exactly like you see in the cowboy pictures! Everyone outside the town had a horse or a donkey. I remember people coming from the country and riding their horses into town. Being townspeople ourselves, we didn't have anywhere to stable a horse, although, in any case, we had no use for one.

I was born into a small public house called *Dunleavy's*. But when I say that Shirley, we used to sell absolutely nothing, although there always seemed to be *somebody* in. Customers would come in through the separate entrance to the pub. It was the shop. It's still there. It's a restaurant now – and a very good one. I'll be in it this time, when I'm visiting. It's strange like. It's about the size of this dining room. There was a counter there, with an old corkscrew bolted to it. But don't get the idea that we were making any money! Half the time the people who came in would pay you the next time they got the dole. They'd refer to that as having it 'on the slate', or 'on the tick'.

Jim Irwin lived ten houses away from us, in a cottage at the top end of Barrack Street. We were the nearest pub to him, so he'd have his first pint in our house about 10 am and his last, around eleven o'clock at night. He used to sell herring and cockles from a basin. When Mammy asked: "Are they fresh?" Jim would reply: "Mary Kate, they're alive. Just look at those red heads – straight from the sea!" Mammy would cook them on the tongs, over the kitchen fire. On his late-night visits he would say: "That's my twentieth pint today" – and I believed him! We used to see him at football matches, where he sold fruit from a tray, which hung around his neck.

Years later, I met him at Fort Dunlop, in Birmingham. He had a filthy job, working in the infamous 'Black Hole', where he had to mix chemicals with jute, to give the tyres their colour. On returning home to Charlestown, one year, I heard that Jim had sadly passed on.

Although we were poor I don't remember being hungry at all, because there was always plenty of bread that Mammy used to make, and soda cakes made with buttermilk. But we never had much meat. At Christmas, we always had a goose, never a turkey. I never had turkey until I came to England. The first time I ever remember eating peas, was at the Christmas Dinner. It was the first tin of peas I'd ever tasted– and I still love peas to this day – the big marrowfat peas. We had a spoonful each in those days, but I have a big tin to myself now! We'd have one goose between the lot of us for Christmas, which was absolutely nothing, because there's nothing on a goose – but a goose now can cost fifty quid! Well, you'd get two turkeys for that. A normal meal would be a mug of tea and a slice of bread and butter or jam. All the farmers used to make their own butter, so they'd come in from the countryside and sell us a roll of butter. Mrs. Regan, from a village about three miles away, would visit our house, from time to time. Her main claim to fame was that she could read tealeaves. Mammy was very superstitious, so her curiosity would get the better of her. She would say: "Great to see you Kathleen – I'll just put the kettle on, and we'll have a good strong cup of tea!" Then she'd say: "Kathleen you read my cup, but you won't tell me anything bad if you see it?"

She'd reply: "Oh Mary Kate, what badness could I see about you and your family – and you all God-fearing people?" Later, after Pa was obliged to seek employment in England, she'd study the leaves in the cup and say: "See that big clump of leaves? It's a load of money... and it's coming from across the water!" "Will it be soon?" Mammy would ask anxiously. Kathleen would be a bit evasive here and say that the leaves were a bit *hazy* and that it would be best to refill the teapot. This would go on and on. Kathleen would never see anything bad – only riches and money galore! But Mammy never saw any of it – it never came to her. Mrs. Regan was either a very clever woman, who enjoyed hours of drinking tea and a few biscuits... or she was completely daft. Or was Mary Kate daft?

There were very few clothes about. There was a crowd who came around to the market selling clothes, maybe from England. They'd be selling them off the back of a wagon, but they'd have curtains around at the back, to make it like a sort of room. They'd display the clothes on racks. I remember buying a jacket there – which was the first one that I ever had. There was a man there called Sonny Whittington. Sonny is what you'd call a young lad in the family – like 'son'. So it was an affectionate term – a nickname.

Sonny Whittington had a second-hand shop. He used to sell all the *Army & Navy* gear. So we all ended up looking like little soldiers! Every poor person in the town had this gear on then! But I was mad to get a tunic. When I got one, I thought: 'This is lovely gear.'

We had a clock in the house, but when I grew up in Ireland, nobody cared if you were half an hour late, or twenty minutes early – it was the done thing, like. You could either come tomorrow or the day after – whatever – and no one was too bothered. But now, it's different, because the whole of Ireland is progressive and up-market.

As a five-year-old lad, I'd be up for school: it started at nine, so Mammy would get us up. That was quite a thing – all the gang – tea and bread for the start of the day. I slept three in a bed: Mickey, myself and Tom. I was in the middle. We all slept the same way around – the right way up. Being the youngest of the three, I was always in the middle; they each claimed the outside of the bed. On the frame of the bed we had timber slats, going across. So off and on, with us messing about in the bed, one of the slats would collapse, so the mattress would go down. We would sleep like that for maybe two or three days, before Mammy would get the mattress up. We were too young to have the sense to do it! The timbers were cut too short to span the frame; there was only about an inch on either side. Whoever had cut them, if they'd left five or six inches, they'd have never fallen off. We had the same mattress throughout. We stayed that way until Tom went to England. There was another bed in the same room. Paddy and Louie were in one bed and the three of us in the second. When Paddy went to England, Louie had the bed to himself. But when Louie went off, Tom took over their bed, so Mickey and I had more room.

We had plenty of fleas – oh God yes, the fleas were rampant! Until DDT powder came in, which you shook all over the place; that eradicated them. There were two types: there was a black flea, which could hop; then there were the white fleas, which were more docile. But you'd get them in the creases of everything. It seems bizarre now, with people showering every day, and baths and lotions for your body – and after-shave.

But to think that you could be walking around and suddenly... Fleas would certainly be in your hair and in all the creases of your clothes. Off and on, you'd get a flea in your ear, in bed – and the noise it would make! It just seems funny – but it was absolutely true. We'd an old decanter, without a top to it, full of Holy Water – because it was all religion in Ireland. When the thunder and lightning came – out came the Holy Water – so that we were safe.

I remember vividly, getting the decanter of Holy Water. You would put your head to one side, then Mickey and myself, or one of the other lads, would fill your ear up, and of course, the flea would come to the top. But the *noise* it made Shirley! Well I'd have to put a flea in your ear, for you to understand what I'm talking about! He was so small and he was trying to get out, you see? The girls were in another room – and such-a-one might have a flea in her ear during the night. Well you'd have to, wouldn't you? Because they're hopping all around! They must have been all round the town at the time – or maybe it was just us? But when DDT came in, it was shaken all over the blankets and everything; so eventually, they disappeared.

Now another great hardship for us was the paying of rates. As we lived in a licensed house we had to pay a higher rate than the normal domestic payment. Sometimes we only sold a case of stout a week, but we still had to pay £7 a half year. It may as well have been £77 because there was not a penny to spare. The Rate Collector was a man called Harry Payton. He came from a village outside the town, called Madue. He was a big man who wore a long coat and a hat. We knew him, although we were only young. The very minute I spotted him, I would run to Mammy as quickly as possible and tell her. She would fly into a panic and if the rates were due, and they always were, she would close the doors. If he knocked for any length of time, Mammy would say: "Go out and tell him that I'm not in," although Harry Payton knew full well that she was. Where else could she be with a houseful of kids! He got his rates eventually but I grew up with the idea that Harry Payton was an evil ogre, even though he was simply doing his job. Years later, I met some of his family, in England. Sadly, I could not warm to them, because my mind was set in stone from my younger years – the die was cast.

Our local school was Lowpark National School. Lowpark was just the name of a local area. There was no park of that name there. My first teacher was Mrs. Coleman. It's funny, when you're a lad, because she used to wear what to us was very expensive perfume and powder. I can still sort of smell it. I was very aware of the smell of it, when she was close to me; she smelled very nice. She was very ancient – thirty-five! Horribly ancient. She used to wear rimless glasses, which again, were very attractive. She was pretty, with black hair – and the rimless glasses – which added to the sexiness, I should imagine. She had a pleasant manner about her. We were there for three years in that room. Then we went into a second room. There were three rooms in the school altogether. Two of them had interconnecting doors, which you pulled across. That was the big main room.

The school wasn't adjacent to the church, although we were *under* the church, because the priest would come. We were a Catholic community. The second teacher I had was Tom Gallagher. He was from the parish of Curry, which was about three or four miles outside of the town. He used to cycle to school on a big Raleigh bike. Tom was aggressive. He'd catch you by the locks, although I got on alright with him. But then he went off and was replaced by another teacher called Mick Swords, who had two sons in the classroom with us – Colum and Aidan. They had an older brother, named Kevin, who was at university. There were also two daughters, Bernie and Attracta, who attended another school, where their mother taught.

Bernie Swords and myself are now next-door-neighbours, when I'm in Charlestown. She's a terrific person! Aidan, Colum and Kevin were fantastic athletes, and between them represented the County at football, handball, boxing and running. Colum is a dentist in London, at the present time; Kevin is a retired doctor; sadly, Aidan has passed away.

I got to the Sixth Class in this local National School. Seventh would have been better, like, but I was very bad at Mathematics. It's funny, because I'm very good at Maths now. But then, I suppose I had to learn pretty quickly, as an adult. If I hadn't, I'd have gone broke!

I *was* good at Composition. The teacher would say: "Now we'll write a composition today on A Fall of Snow," and you'd have to write 'I was sitting inside the window and all of a sudden I saw the snowflakes coming down.' He'd say: "I want a page on that." But no matter what the composition was I'd end up writing at least two pages. On several occasions, Johnny Cassidy, the Principal Teacher, or occasionally Mick or Tom, would hold up my essay and say: "Seamus Dunleavy has written two pages." Then they'd read it out to the class. Without wanting to sound conceited, my compositions were good.

The way I'd work it out Shirley would be, I'd write, 'I came home from school, had something to eat, then all of a sudden, I looked out and the snowflakes were landing on the window.' Then I'd develop it by writing: 'So we all went out snowballing...' and so on; the story would be about what we did when the snow arrived – the games we played and how we'd interact with each other. How to have snow there was totally different to the times without it. That's how I'd build my story up, with all the different people and characters. And how your hands would be numb with the cold; we'd warm them up by the fire – then go out again. I'd really become involved, imagination-wise, in whatever situation I happened to be writing about. So, composition I was good at – everything else – no good! Compositions, I could write all day long.

Johnny Cassidy the Principal Teacher, was definitely apt to use corporal punishment, or the 'batta', as we called the stick. We had to be *very* careful and mind our 'Ps and Qs', particularly on a Monday morning! But punishment was meted out as a matter of course – it was like Victorian England.

Although we never brought turf to school, because we were too young to work our bog, in winter, there was always a roaring fire in the fireplace at school – and the headmaster was always perched in front of it, or standing with his backside to it. Now when he went out of the door there was a porch that he had to pass through, so somebody always stood up on a desk, (the windows were high), so that we knew where he was going. Well, this one day when he went out, Sean Brett hopped up on a desk, but he said: "I can't see him lads." Meanwhile, Mr. Cassidy had doubled back, and was standing behind him! "I can't see him lads," repeated poor Sean Brett. I'll leave it to your imagination what happened next!

Johnny Cassidy had a son in school as well. His son and Reggie Dooney, his nephew went on to Further Education. Reggie was the son of Johnny's sister, who taught next door in the Girls' School. Joe Cassidy and Reggie Dooney had a desk of their own. Joe Cassidy became a bishop – Bishop of Connaught – a very studious man. I've met him since and I said: "Joe, what do I call you?" He said: "Joe will do – you've known me long enough!" He retired within the last two or three years. I've heard him on the radio several times, when he's given his theologies on different subjects.

I remember Johnny catching him by the lapels one day and pulling them up. Joe must have had his feet caught in the desk, so the desk came with him! Reggie was seated alongside Joe, so the two of them came out – with the desk on the floor! His dad gave him plenty of stick, but it turned out well in the end. He became what he wanted him to be, I suppose. You can't get much higher than a bishop!

Chapter Two

AN AMERICAN DREAM

Mammy's brother Tom, and a second brother, whom they lost touch with, left for the Americas, long years before, together with her sister Bridget. The plan had been that she would join them. But marriage intervened – plus looking after the old people. She remembered her brothers again – the dance before they left, the promises, the expectations… the excitement. Surely they wrote at first, as did Bridget… and they were doing well. Wouldn't she be there with them soon? But the years rushed by. Now, all she seemed to get was an odd card at Christmas, or sometimes on St Patrick's Day.

None of the three made it home – when the old people died. For Mary Kate it was one of the blackest times in her life. The neighbours asked about them and were polite. But she knew that the dreams had sort of died, as time passed. She was on her own now – Bridget and her brothers… living in America… maybe dead. Her parents were now long gone. But God is good, and apart from the grinding poverty, which was widespread in the whole of Mayo, Mary Kate's five sons and a daughter were all healthy. Indeed, wouldn't they bring her fame and riches when grown? They would be different. All her dreams and aspirations focused on them.

It was estimated that from the late 1850s onwards, following the Great Potato Famine in Ireland, 80% of infants born to Irish immigrant families in New York didn't make it, past the age of one. However, conditions were even worse in Ireland, where nearly one million people died, (a quarter of the population), as a result of the Famine of 1845.

According to some historians, the experience of the 4.5 million Irish immigrants in the nineteenth and twentieth century, was typical of the American Immigrant experience in general. The *American Immigration Law Foundation* stated that 'Irish immigration to America represented the first mass immigration to the United States and set the stage for all future immigrating ethnic minorities.' By 1847, nearly one quarter of a million Irish were emigrating annually.

Mammy's siblings and Pa's sister had already 'hit off' for America, by the time I was born, in 1934; so I've not met them at all, but my brothers in

Ireland have. Mammy never talked about the fact that she would have like to have gone to America. Her brothers and sister never returned for the holidays... or anything else, for that matter.

But when my brother Louie was twenty-one or twenty-two, he went off to America. In Brooklyn, he found Bridget Coogan, Mammy's sister. She had married Dan Coogan, from Sligo, a county very close to Mayo. Louie lived near them for a while. As the years went by, we made contact with all their offspring. There are two first cousins.

Mammy had a first cousin named Johnny Gallagher, who lived three miles out of the town. He'd come in and visit us, maybe two or three times a year, and always bring us a big bottle of milk – and a soda cake – a very generous sort of a man. He didn't have much money himself, but he'd always bring my mother something. He had a family and *they* all went to America. A terrific number of Irish left for the 'New World'. In our town it was every other one – either England or America.

I remember that when people went to America, from the period just after the end of the First World War onwards, it was almost like a death sentence! When I was growing up there were people older than me who were going off (they'd probably be dead now of course). The fear was – maybe it was suggested to them – that many of them would never *ever* return.

The boat crossing was an ordeal in itself. The American Dream never turned out for many, and it was too far to travel, to come home again; they just hadn't got the money. Many would have felt that they had no choice, other than to go there. 'Wakes' were held for people, before they left, because it was nearly a guarantee that you wouldn't see them again. It was a very sad occasion, as they set off, into the Unknown. The fact that they weren't from college, and were often poorly educated, made it particularly hard. A certain percentage went to Night School and educated themselves when they were over there, and became successful as a result. That's *some* of them – it's the same in England. Some fell by the wayside, others didn't; that's the way it goes.

Chapter Three

CHRISTMAS IN CHARLESTOWN

When Michael Dunleavy, Seamus' carpenter father, returned home for the holidays, he had been working in Liverpool for most of the year, from approximately 1940 onwards, due to a shortage of work in Ireland. Ironically, this was the country that he'd fought, 'tooth-and-nail' against, in his youth, in an effort to help Ireland break free.

The pattern of coming and going to England then continued for years; a lifetime, it seemed. At Christmas the family were made particularly aware of it, because that was when their dad made his yearly visit back to them. As the years went by and successive brothers and sisters also went to work in England, they too would return home for Christmas, whenever they could. Although the family had a small shop in Charlestown, with poverty all around them it was impossible to make a living. The Dunleavys had expanded to five boys and four girls. Seamus was the last-born boy, with three sisters younger.

The expectation of your dad coming home was absolutely amazing – for all of the kids! The bus stop was in the centre of Charlestown, outside *Henry's Hotel*. We'd be waiting there. As well as Pa, there'd be thirty of forty spalpeens, agricultural labourers, getting off the bus. They were living in and around Charlestown. We used to think that Pa was so strong, carrying his case. We were only little kids. We'd try and lift his suitcase – and we couldn't budge it! Then we'd all troop up Barrack Street with him – maybe four or five of us kids: the boys anyway. It was a great time.

When you were in the grip of poverty, the old people would say: "If it's hard in this life, it will be easier in the next." I wonder if my mother ever got her reward?

Mammy was a religious woman, as was Pa. But in those far off days there was an aspect of the Clergy that I found embarrassing, revolting and diabolical, and that was the collection of the Church Dues – that awful, degrading process of reading out the names of people and their contributions. I still feel the shame of it all. It started at the top – the largest contributions:

John McIntyre, of the Mineral Water Factory – 5 guineas; Luke Mulligan – 5 guineas; Tom Tunney – shoe shop proprietor – 5 guineas. Then the priest moved to the three-pound people, then to the two-pound people, and finally, down the line, until he came to the half a crown, or 2/6d people. He seemed to pause, and in the *loudest* tones possible, would boom, "The following paid 2/6d!" He did not need to boom it out, because you could hear a pin drop.

There were only about three or four people in what I now call that 'Shit Street'. But *we* were there. You left the church with a lot of resentment in your heart. Mammy never went to church on the Sunday when the names were called out; eventually she stopped going altogether, although she said the Rosary with us, for most of our young life.

There wasn't a Protestant in the town, although there was a fair amount in the surrounding towns. There was never any particular friction between us and them, although for some strange reason, the Protestants always owned the best businesses. We were at the bottom rung of the ladder.

When Frank McCourt wrote about the Protestant girls in Limerick, he said they were always the better-looking ones! That was his perception, through the eyes of a child, of course. Well, they were a bit different you see, so you're *looking* at them differently. And they didn't mix. So what you can't have, you see – that's the best!

When Pa opened the big suitcase up, there'd always be something for each of us, which was absolutely amazing; maybe a little jack-in-the box, or some toy. We were just absolutely delighted. Then Himself and Mammy, obviously, renewed relations; they were both very happy to see each other.

Despite a perpetual shortage of money, Christmas was still a marvellous time. The 24 December, Christmas Eve, was a Fast Day, so there was no meat that day. It was the children's main night, because you had sweet cakes and sponge cakes galore, a bit of Swiss Roll, maybe biscuits, and the Irish 'brack'. Also we would have jelly, and a bottle of raspberry and blackcurrant cordial. That's what we liked when we were kids – the sweet stuff. So in fact, the Christmas Day goose didn't matter that much at all – to us! On the Continent, as in Ireland, Christmas Eve is a more important part of the celebrations than Christmas Day.

We would have a turf fire upstairs and this was gorgeous; mainly, because our fire in the downstairs kitchen smoked: if you opened one door, it caused a downdraft and you would have fire and ashes all over the kitchen. So we all had red eyes from the turf smoke, for many a year! The kitchen would be full of smoke, all the time. We tried everything. Pa was a good tradesman, but he couldn't solve the problem, because the chimney wasn't high enough. It would be the same effect as if there were ten people in here, smoking cigarettes – like a permanent fog.

We had no covering at all on the kitchen floor: no lino – just a concrete floor. Mammy kept a flock of chickens and a couple of geese. The geese were reared for killing at Christmas. The chickens roamed around our kitchen. If the back door was left open, often you would lose your cut of bread to them. You could be roaming around the kitchen, eating a piece of bread, then all of a sudden it would be gone – the chicken would have it. Up the back yard it would go!

Mickey was the Goose Executioner. I couldn't kill a goose Shirley – I was too frightened to! First we'd catch the goose and put it between his legs. Then we'd tie the legs and catch its neck and beak, so that it was bent like an 'S'. Mickey would pull the feathers off, where its neck bends, then get the knife and saw across the goose's head. I'd be underneath, with the bowl containing Mammy's mixture of oatmeal, cloves and spices, salt and onions, ready to catch the blood. Now when the blood ran, you had to keep mixing as quickly as you could, so that you ended up with a soggy, but firm mixture, until the last drop of blood had come. I'd take the mixture into her. It produced the most delicious pudding I had ever tasted. I don't mean pudding as an after dinner treat, but pudding as in Black Pudding – Pig's Pudding.

When the goose was plucked and cleaned, it would be singed, by lighting newspapers and drawing it over the flame – that way you got rid of the down. Mammy then cut the neck off. Down near the shoulder, she took the head off, which left her with a long neck. She'd pull the skin off the neck: it came off in one piece, about four or five inches in length. Then she sewed one end with a strong thread and put the soggy mixture mass in the open end, packed it tightly and sewed the other end. She put the mixture in a saucepan, over the fire, and boiled it. You can't get goose pudding in England, but you can get it in France, because the French make it that way. Until this day, I can still taste it. Beautiful. We would boil that on Christmas Eve. If we were up past 12 o'clock midnight, she would give us a slice or two. It was absolutely gorgeous. If I close my eyes, I can still taste it!

We had one room in our house, which we called the 'parlour' and that was an upstairs room. It was the only room in the house that had a carpet, although it was threadbare. But in those far off days, it was luxury at its best. We spent Christmas Day in the parlour. It was a 'squareish' room with an open fire in it. We used to have a turf fire (called peat, in England) not a coal one, and that was lovely, because as I've said earlier on, the chimney upstairs never smoked. There was a King Chair and a Queen Chair – and the threadbare carpet, of course. There was a chaise longue too – a proper matching set of three pieces of furniture. My parents must have had it in their younger days.

The parlour was like a Victorian room, as such; there were faded photographs around the room; maybe of their parents and different things. We always felt lovely and cosy with this fire. Two of us could fit in the one chair. We used to be absolutely delighted to get up there. We'd wrestle on top of them – and all that; but they were well sprung.

All three pieces, including the chaise longue, were upholstered in a sort of mottled greenish-grey colour. The threadbare carpet matched the chairs. We had a dining table up there too, with five or six chairs and that's where we'd eat our Christmas meal. It was a good-sized room. So we ate our dinner up there and thoroughly enjoyed it.

Christmas Day was a very enjoyable day. We did not have much goose. There were nine of us (plus), and Mammy and Pa, if he made it home for Christmas, so you would not have a lot. I remember peas being introduced to our household for the first time, at Christmas. We got a tin of Batchelors Peas and had a large spoonful each. I still love peas to this day, but now I eat a whole *tin* to myself – with a slice of bread.

With poverty around us, for the rest of the year, Christmas was quite a contrast, although, as I said before, we were never hungry, but we had very little meat. Mind you, we didn't get much off the Christmas goose – with eleven of us! Although there wasn't a great deal of food about, there were plenty of home-baked cakes and bread, which Mammy baked – constantly. As well as that, we used to have another great day, which was January 6th. That was very good in our house too: again, it was the sponge cakes and biscuits and all that: the equivalent of Twelfth Night.

There were times when Pa didn't make it home for Christmas. Being a ship's carpenter, he was sometimes stuck on a job, having to get the ship ready. It happened quite a few times, over the years. It was miserable for us, as children, when he didn't make it. But he'd come back home then, maybe two or three months after. We never knew what his situation was – and whether he could get enough money together, to come home. It wasn't easy. He rented a house in Liverpool for nine shillings a week.

Christmas Dinner was mainly just for the family, although there was a man who used to come and visit us – a bit: Tom Doherty – Pa's brother-in-law. He appeared for a few Christmases – to eat with us; but he'd be the only other one that I'd ever see, around the table.

We'd have a relaxing day, all sitting round; we might have a game of 'Snakes-and-Ladders' going, for us kids – or something like that. My parents didn't go out that much. Pa didn't go out to pubs; although he had one of his own, he never drank much. I think they were just glad to see each other again. Our pub was closed for Christmas Day, of course.

I never remember crackers or party hats. It wasn't like the pictures that you see on Christmas Cards – with hot chestnuts and so on. On Christmas Day we'd have a new toy each and we'd all head out of the house. All the kids of the town would be out with their new toys, Christmas Day. I remember plenty of snow, at different times. If there was snow, we'd definitely be out, snowballing, and trying to make a snowman, and this-that-and-the-other.

Pa was home for a week, or sometimes ten days, so it would give us a chance to get to know him again. His three brothers lived close by – Jim, Patrick and Tom. Luke was dead. They were all within a radius of twenty miles of each other, so it was easy enough for them to visit each other. They'd come and see Pa, because they knew that he'd be home. We were always very sad when he left. It was a happy family get-together at Christmas.

Although my book is bleak, in places, there *were* some very happy times. Charlestown was a very happy place. As opposed to what Frank McCourt said about his town, I couldn't say a bad word about Charlestown. During my childhood, there were no Christmas decorations around town, but it's as good as Birmingham now – all lit up.

We knew Father Christmas was about, like. We'd always get something. We used to leave our shoes out – not our socks! Just one of the shoes you'd been wearing – and something would be put in you shoe. You'd have an orange and maybe the equivalent of a Mars Bar. I can vividly remember a jack-in-the-box.

There were two toyshops in the area. We used to love them. They'd decorate their windows, around the 1st December. One of them, *O'Rourke's*, was on the Square, in Charlestown, the other was *Duffy's*, in Bellaghy. But there were all sorts of toys in them, so you'd be clamouring to look in the window.

I remember there was a little oil tanker. But it cost a half-a-crown. I saw it on display in *O'Rourke's* shop window. I had to earn half-a-crown, in order to buy it, in the time between when I saw it on display and Christmas. So I was selling jam pots and empty porter bottles and everything. I got close to it anyway; maybe Mammy helped me, but I bought it. I was the proudest boy with this tanker! It was about shoebox size. I had it for ages. So I didn't have that off Santa Claus – I bought it myself. It's always difficult, with younger brothers and sisters, trying to keep the idea of Santa Claus going. But I think they should keep that myth going as long as they can, because it's part of your childhood – a very good part of it.

There was always a fair amount of festive storytelling. We used to have several people who would come in. But when they started telling ghost stories, you'd be absolutely petrified. You'd have nightmares when you went to bed! They'd tell you that they were walking out from the town and there was a mysterious man walking with them, who never said a word. And of course, they'd be half drunk while they were telling it!

There was a black pig, which was reported to have been seen, just fifty yards above our house, but heading out of town into the country, on the Dublin Road. Lots of people claimed to have seen this black pig. And the black pig had crossed the road, in front of them and this-and-that-and-the-other. You'd be petrified!

There was another story about a Card School Shirley. A man had come in while the game was in progress. One of the players dropped a card; in stooping to pick it up, he noticed that the stranger had a hoof. So of course – it was the Devil. And that petrified you too!

Then there were great stories from people who had been working in England, then came back; especially if they'd been working for the farmers – which was really *rough* work. They'd tell how they were picking the spuds, all day long, and then in the evening, the farmer would give them a load of hay, in the barn, for them to sleep on. And you'd be thinking: 'That was desperate hard!' They'd say that there was no grub at all, because the rationing was on, during the war. And you'd think, 'Is there any tea or potatoes? How would you manage?' There'd naturally be a fair amount of drinking: mainly Guinness; it was all porter. So they'd tell you all *sorts* of stories about living in England – and then there'd be the haunted ghost stories, which were legendary, at home.

I remember one *particular* story about a coach that used to come through Charlestown. A dead coach – with no driver. It used to come at the dead of night; no one ever saw it – but you could *hear* it. It was wrapped in chains – with no driver at all! So you'd wonder: 'How would the coach get through the town, without a driver – without crashing into anything?' Oh, the *Dead Coach* was legendary!

Chapter Four

LOOKING FOR 'MAKES'

There was a story going round, that there was a man, years and years ago, who was a travelling man, and a great violin player; he'd go from town to town. The fairies heard him playing, as he went through the fort. They gave him plenty to drink, but he had to keep playing. He played and played, all through the night. When morning came he was very drunk and he fell asleep. He woke up, and when he came to, ten years had passed. So he went to the house where he was supposed to have played for the wedding and discovered that the wedding had taken place ten years earlier, in his absence. The house was now occupied by entirely different people, but they remembered the violin player who hadn't turned up!

We were always very sad when Pa left, but it had to be done. We all went barefooted in my youth. We would kick our shoes off in March and would not put a shoe on again until September or October. I remember going to school on frosty mornings, barefooted. There was a boy down the street who used to slide on ice… barefoot.

Johnny Clark was the boy's name and he went barefooted – winter and summer. He came from a very poor background; even poorer than we were – and that's saying something!

He came to this country Shirley, and I met him years and years ago. It was in Sparkhill, at a dance club called *The Harp*, in Walford Road. We only spoke briefly, because he was leaving the dance when I met him. He said: "I'll talk to you again." The years went by and I didn't see him for years and years and years. I own a pub here in the Bull Ring Birmingham, called *The Royal George*.

The *Royal George* was a famous Man O' War. There was a big replica of it, on the outside wall of the pub – hence the name. We've taken the ship down and we're trying to put an advertising hoarding up there, which *can* be very lucrative.

On this particular day, we were open on the Sunday afternoon. This fella came in and he had an Irish scarf on, in green, white and gold, and a hat with shamrocks on it. He was walking a bit unsteadily. I said: "What sort of a man are you? Are you going to cause me any trouble?" He said: "No trouble." I weighed him up, and I thought, 'Well he's not a young fellow really.' So in he goes. On the way out we spoke for a while. He said: "Do you remember John Clark?" Now I knew a fella called John Clark, who lived in Kings Heath, so I asked him if he came from there. He said: "No, this John Clark is from Charlestown." I said: "Sparkety Clarkety?" He said: "That's right." And it was Johnny Clark, after all those years. We talked for hours. He frequented the pub every day after that.

He'd been in the army, but he'd got some sort of a bullet hole in his leg, so he'd been invalided out. He must have had a good pension, because he was never ever broke. He didn't have *much* money, but he'd never ask you for any, and he was a good customer. He was always well dressed, which must have come from his army training. If it was raining he'd always have an umbrella with him, and smart shoes, which were always very clean.

He'd never been back home, since he left. When he got a bit drunk, he used to romance a bit about Charlestown. We'd sit on seats outside the pub in the summer. There were about twelve or so tables and chairs on a little car park area, at the front, adjacent to the pub. The *Royal George* is actually in Park Street, where the buses come round. We're directly opposite the new *Selfridges*. The Bull Ring is there – and we're at the start of Digbeth. I could shout to the stall-holders in the Bull Ring. That's how close we are!

Anyway, Clark had never been home since he left. I said: "I'll take you home, one of the days I'm going." He said: "Would you cove?" He used to live in Barrack Street too, but in a sort of a Rowton House, for men down on their luck, (and a few hard cases!). The Rowton House here in Birmingham was started by Lord Rowton. It's a big hotel now. He opened this huge place for men who'd come from the army, were perhaps disabled, and had no visible means of support. It became very well known. It was there for between eighty to a hundred years. It's now the *Chamberlain Hotel* – a good three-star hotel. So there was a little Rowton House in Charlestown, for men who walked from town to town; that was where Johnny Clark lived for many years.

His dad was an ex-army man, so Johnny had a 'rough-and-ready' upbringing you see? It's funny, because when he came to this country, *he* joined the army. We all used to say: "Oh – fighting for England – how could you do that?" But he went down the mines and when came back from doing that, he was conscripted. He did well out of it, because he got his pension. So he was a military man for a few years, but was eventually invalided out, when he was still a fairly young man He showed me the bullet hole in his leg.

Around 1995/96 he began giving me money in installments, for his plane ticket. When he'd given me £102 I said: "That's enough Johnny. That will take you there and back again very comfortably." We arranged to meet at Birmingham Airport, at seven o'clock in the morning. He said: "I'll be there at six o'clock." But believe it, or believe it not, something happened. He missed the plane. My sons, Russell and Shamus, were running the *Royal George*, so when I reached Charlestown, I rang them at the pub. Russell said: "Johnny's here!" He had arrived at the airport an hour early and he went to the *Ryanair* desk. But they won't give any information out. They wouldn't tell him whether Seamus Dunleavy was on the plane or not. So he thought that I was winding him up about going there. He said: "I went out there, but I didn't see you."

Because he couldn't see me and he was given no information at the Flight Desk, he had decided to head for the pub, and eventually, to get the next plane. He asked Russell where I was and Russell explained that I was already in Charlestown. Johnny asked if Russell would loan him the fare, because I had both tickets. I was sitting in Charlestown, with my brother, in his kitchen, when Russell phoned, to let me know the time that Johnny would be arriving in Dublin, within the next few hours. So I jumped back in my car again, and drove the 150 miles back to Dublin, to pick Johnny Clark up! He never spoke much on the way down to Mayo, because he was feeling so emotional.

When we got there, we started on the edge of Charlestown and visited every house. It was thirty-seven years, since he'd been there. Not one person in Charlestown knew him – not *one*. The first person he met was Tommy Joe Maloney. I said: "Tommy Joe, do you know this man?" He said: "I don't." I said: "You *should* know him. He's from here. You played handball with him and football." "God," he said, "I don't know him." And it transpired that Tommy Joe Maloney, his brother Sean, and Clark all left for England the same day! We met Sean at the other end of the town. But Tommy Joe had told him that Johnny Clark was in the town, so he knew in advance. But other than that, nobody knew him. He had lost most of his hair and he had a moustache, so how would they know? He said: "I left, a barefooted lad." But he totally enjoyed the visit.

Johnny was a very good handballer and he won an All Ireland Medal. Handball is a bit like Squash – but without a racquet! After he won the medal, he left for England, for the first time, just a few days later. Jack O'Donnell was a chemist in Charlestown, and also the Chairman of the Charlestown Handball Society, so he collected the medal for Clark. Through the years, I used to say to him: "Have you still got Clark's medal?" And he'd say to me, over the years, "Do you ever see Johnny Clark?" So we arrived at Jack O'Donnell's.

Remember that thirty-seven years had elapsed. We got to Jack's chemist shop. Sadly, he'd had a stroke and was in a wheelchair, but out he comes; perfectly lucid and 'with it', but he couldn't walk. He was a well-known man: one of the pillars of the town. I said: "Jack, do you know this man here?" "I don't know him Seamus." I said: "You *should* know him. You've had something of his for years and years." He said: "Johnny Clark – I don't believe it!" And Clark started crying. Then Jack started – and the two of them were crying like banshees – they nearly got meself going! I said: "Jack, you wouldn't have the medal after all this time?" He said: "Seamus, we moved – I haven't got it."

That night, I'd gone across to Mary's people, in another part of Mayo. When the townspeople found that Clark was at home, they got a photographer from Ballina, and they all gathered in the centre of the town and presented him with a lovely plaque of a Handballer, as he didn't have his medal; and he had his picture in the paper. He was absolutely delighted, and every year since then, he'd gone back home, on his own steam.

Every year on the 15 August, that's the anniversary of the apparition of Our Lady, at Knock, Clark is there. He's stayed in the same guesthouse every year since, and brings back a bottle of Holy Water, from Knock. So that's the story of John Clark – the man who used to slide on the ice in his bare feet and kick a football with his bare feet. I used to meet him at the *Royal George*, when I was there, because he used it every single day. I last saw him four or five months back. We let the pub now, so I'm no longer there on a regular basis.

Back in those early days, every year we would get the stone bruise. I don't know what caused them: whether it was an infection from a cut and the bare feet. But Mammy would put a big poultice of boiling hot bread on the stone bruise – as hot as you could bear; that drew the puss out. You would have it on for a week or so. Then with us growing up, we all had problems to keep shoes on our feet. Very little money, so we ended up wearing clogs, which were a lot cheaper.

There was a little clog factory in our town. They employed about five people, so we could get the clogs from them. Then, when we wore all the tips or irons off the clogs, through sliding in the winter, we covered the soles with thick rubber, cut from old car tyres. We were banned from the slides because the rubber thaws the slides. After the clogs, my mother would try and get us a pair of Sunday shoes. Most lads in the town had some, but we had not. When we eventually did get a pair, it was a long, drawn out ritual – a real game of 'Cat and Mouse'.

One shop in the town, which sold shoes, was called *Tunney's*. Mammy would send me down to *Tunney's*... size six or whatever, then I would get the price of them. No money with me whatsoever. The price might be 27/6d. I would take the shoes up to Mammy, who would look them over and would *always* say: "The leather is like paper. They're a bad pair of shoes – them. Go down to Tom Tunney" – and she might give you a pound – and she'd commandeer the shoes. You'd have five or six trips, up and down.

Down the street again with the shoes. "Mammy wants better leather." Tom Tunney would say: "If your mother wants better leather, she will have to pay a better price." Up again with another pair – 34/6d. Mammy would say: "Tom Tunney is the biggest robber in town," and she would curse him – "and all belonging to him!"

After various excursions up and down, she would settle on a pair. If the shoes were 34/6d, my mother would give us 14/6d. She would keep the shoes and say: "Tell him to knock a pound off!" Up again. "He wants the shoes and will knock two shillings off." Down again. "My mother will give you a pound and no more." We eventually got the shoes and used to get more off than we should. But it was tough going. It was a ritual – the shoes. I think poor Tom Tunney used to go weak every time he saw us coming!

It was good business training though, especially the bargaining side of it: that whatever you're doing, you never give them the asking price. Even to this day, Mary will go to the best hotel, in England, Ireland or anywhere, and she'll always say: "Could you do a room a bit cheaper?" And nine times out of ten, they'll say: "Well, that very unusual, but we'll knock five per cent off." She always does it. People get overawed and they're embarrassed to ask. They'll say: "Well, we've never been asked that before ... 'could you knock a bit off?' " It's the people with the most money who will ask – because that's how they became wealthy in the first place!

Back in Charlestown, we were all at school now. We walked there. No heating in the building. All the pupils had to pay for a cart of turf to be delivered to the school. We never did. We had a bog, but with Pa away we were too small and young to work it, yet. So not contributing to the school heating was not conducive to great popularity with the teachers, or the clergy, who were in charge of schools.

After mass, on Sunday, we kids all assembled round the Ball Alley. This is a *huge* game, in the West of Ireland mostly, although it is played throughout. It has four concrete walls and a smooth concrete floor. It is played like Fives in England, or like squash, without the racquets. The fellow who serves is in charge, until the other player gets him out. The points are called 'aces'. You start even, toss for the serve and it goes up in aces.

The main alley would be taken over by the big lads, aged fourteen to sixteen years, so we would play on the side-walls until we could get a game. Sometimes half a dozen or a dozen arrived near enough together, and could not decide who should have a game; (we all wanted one!). So, to decide, we had a game called 'Calling Names', or 'Bowler'.

This was a line of boys, ranked in file. We tossed a coin to decide who would be Server. He would toss a ball or 'serve' and he would go down along the line, until he lost his serve. He would count his aces and the first four boys who got to eleven would take over the ball alley and have a game of doubles – two against two. There'd be four very high walls, including a front and back wall. We'd all head for the Ball Alley, but the bigger lads would commandeer it. So we'd go there, although we'd play *outside,* against the main wall of the Ball Alley. But that had no floor. It was grass. So the ball could bounce in any direction.

You'd be playing sometimes and the big lads would come along and you'd have to scarper away – they'd take over – "Go on lads – let the big lads play!" If half a dozen of us arrived together, you see, and we couldn't decide who would play, four would play on the court at the same time, (two against two). Sometimes we'd play against the front wall of the alley, sometimes against the side. If there were six or seven of us there we'd form a queue, which is what I've described as 'Calling Names', or 'Bowler'. One man would serve and the first man to score five aces or seven, he'd step out, because his place was guaranteed.

It's the same as 'Fives' in England. So the first four to reach at least five aces would have a game in the alley. There'd be a line of lads there and if I'm serving and I get one ace off you, the next lad steps forward, I beat him; third lad and so forth, until I've got my five aces. But you could knock me out, in which case I'd go to the back of the queue, and you'd be serving *me.* You might only get three aces during your serving session, but if nobody got a five, when you came back again you'd have three aces in hand.

You'd build up a cumulative score, but if somebody got a five, your score was cancelled out. There could be as many as ten boys in the line, so you might stand there all day and not get a game! You could play singles or doubles, once you got a game. It could be that only half the boys in the line would get a game that day. The finish of the game was when somebody scored twenty-one. It was great fun!

When Pa came back from England, he had a workshop in our backyard, where he did all sorts of other timberwork, including the making of carts and wheelbarrows. There was a bellows and an anvil in our yard, so it *looked* like a smithy. Pa had plenty of work, because everyone had timber carts and wheelbarrows. Whilst he was working there we could hear the ball in the Ball Alley – the echo of it – of a fine evening. Pa would see me listening, while he was doing something, and he'd say, "Seamus, I don't know what you'll do when you go to England; you'll have no trade!" – because I wanted to get away – up to the Ball Alley. But it kept us active – we were 'fit as fleas'.

A real luxury would be if there were about twenty boys waiting, because sometimes there was a penny a man on the games, in which case they took on a very competitive edge. If you understand handball you will know what I mean – a lot of skinned knuckles and plenty of skin on the walls! Sometimes, you might say: "I'll play you for a penny." Well, I'll tell you, that was *very* serious. The big lads would play for a shilling and you'd see the money on the floor. You'd say: "God – have you seen the money?" Often we'd go up to the Ball Alley and on an odd time you might get sixpence or a threepenny bit left there, which they'd forgotten to pick up. But there were skinned knuckles, because although the ball sometimes went very close to the wall, you wouldn't be put off by that – you still tried to play the shot.

You could play very low shots, like you do in squash, so they'd be very difficult to return too. There's a mark on the alley wall, and if you get below that line, it's very hard to return the ball. But with the money involved you'd risk leaving your skin on the wall!

Happy days – and in the long summer evenings after all the ball games were over, because the darkness nudged the daylight into oblivion, the older boys had a Toss School. This was held at the back of the old Town Hall. Here I watched in awe, as two pennies were tossed in the air, to decide who would claim £3, £5, or maybe £10. This was an *amazing* sum of money. Candles were brought and flashlights and the excitement was breathtaking!

There was a legendary gambler called Tom Carroll. Tom would never bet on 'heads'; it was always 'harps' for Tom. Never ever changed. He always called against the Crown. But Tom was a harmless soul and now, looking back over fifty-six or fifty-seven years, I am sure that he had not much bad feeling for the Crown or Royalty in general. I said the older boys gambled, but in fact, it was the businessmen who *really* gambled.

Tom was a very likeable fella. His job was to take the goods from the station and distribute them round the town, to the merchants, in a flat-bottomed cart. He knew everyone in town, because he was employed by the railway. If there was a big box come in, maybe for the Clog Factory, he'd deliver it to them. Once he'd dropped the stuff off, we'd all jump on the cart. A spin on the cart was great and he had a horse, of course. There'd be about half a dozen of us sitting on it. Tom would let you ride all day with him, if you wanted to.

There was a well-known butcher's, called *Webb's*; Gerry Walsh who owned *Walsh's Garage*; John McIntyre (factory owner), Luke Collerar (chemist), and of course, a few of the Tinker people as well.

I saw plenty of fights over wrong calls... and bad losers! Plenty of blood and snot, which we, as kids, loved. We had a few very good fighting men in Charlestown and eventually it always seemed to end up as Charlestown versus the Tinkers. Charlestown always won! But you would get plenty of fights for a few days after. Then the Tinkers would leave town, usually after one or two were locked up, and for a few nights things would be OK. But there was still some trouble between the townsfolk, with the tossing. Sometimes you would hear if someone won a fair bit, or if a stranger won a bit, that the two-headed penny was being used. I have never seen any, in my time.

We used to get up very early in the morning, after the Toss School, the night before. The Toss School began on Saturday evening and continued on through Sunday morning. So on Monday morning we would be up at the crack of dawn and would rake the Toss School area, looking for 'makes' – and we nearly always got some. 'Makes', Shirley, was the word we used for money. You'd say to your friend, "Have you got any makes cove?" which meant, "Have you got any money?"

I remember once, one of my older brothers, Tom, found a florin. We were shaking with excitement. Usually it was pennies, or an odd sixpence, but a florin was worth two shillings. Mammy immediately confiscated it. Tom would get a penny or twopence, but he would buy an ice cream and we would all have a lick. We seemed to notice a change in our mother, just by getting a two-shilling piece.

"Looking for Makes," was part of the unusual lingo that we had in Charlestown – I *still* don't know where it comes from. But if another boy came to our town or street, we would revert to this Cant; that's what we used to call it. If a stranger came round we would say: "Stall me own bakes," which was "Look at this fellow." We all called each other "Cove." "Luke's Cove," meant "Watch out." And Luke's sometimes meant 'nothing'. We would call Gards "The Shaids", so "Any Shaids about?" was "Any Gards about?" A hat or a cap was a Keady. A sixpence was a sprazzy; a penny was a wing. We seemed to be the only town around that used words like that. I never knew where it came from. Even to this day, if I said that to someone from Charlestown, he'd know exactly what I'm talking about!

Although 'Lukes' sometimes meant nothing, it could be used in several different ways. You could say: "I've got Lukes." If somebody was telling you a story, and you didn't believe them you'd say: "Ah – Lukes Cove!" I don't know how it came about. With the Toss School, you might say: "Are there any Shaids coming?" Because they'd disband it if they caught you doing that, for some reason; which is difficult to understand now, because you can gamble all day if you want to – it's your money. But then it was against the law: they'd break up the school and send everyone home.

Ironically, living opposite the Police Barracks, the key that opened our hall door would open the Barracks too. Often as not, they'd come across: "Mick, give us your key. One of the Gards hasn't turned up yet." This continued for years, without any thought of us rifling files. Another ironic part of Charlestown life!

I used to do little jobs around the town and get a penny or two, so I always had a few pence in my pocket. I remember Mammy saying: "That fella will always have money."

I always had schemes going – I always seem to have been like that. When we were kids, we used to get a quart (two pints) of milk off the milkman, Martin Brennan, but we never had enough milk; we'd have to pinch a half-cup of milk, because the quart wouldn't go round. And I'd think: 'I'll buy a pint of milk for myself.' So I started buying milk, with the few bob, that I'd got for myself, (when I'd sell a few jam pots and porter bottles). But Mammy knocked it on the head. She said, "You can't do that," although it was *my* money.

Maybe she should have said, "Well, you've bought this yourself Seamus," – and let the other lads do the same. My brothers were all older than me. Hardly the best way to reward initiative! But there's the old saying that you can't make the weak strong by making the strong weak. In years to come, when we started with the one property, I always thought that we should have an office at the boat. Then immediately they came off the boat, if they were coming to Birmingham and they wanted accommodation, we could supply it, couldn't we? But then we went in other directions, so we never did that. I've always tried to plan well ahead and spot the potential in a whole variety of situations.

I'd run a few errands too, for people like shopkeepers, for example, and make a few shillings that way. Someone would maybe want you to go down to the station for them, get the early morning or evening paper; or perhaps unload a cart of turf. Just a range of jobs; maybe take a bottle of tea out to the bog.

The McGowans for instance, had land just out of the town. 'Bea' (short for Beatrice) McGowan would ask me to take tea, or a dinner, out to her brother Pake. We have a friend called Pake O'Donnell. It's short for Patrick. Another name for Patrick was Paud (but we call it Paugin). There's a great football manager called Paudi O'Shea, although his proper name would be Patrick O'Shea; 'Paudi' is his nickname. I also had a monthly job, looking after Regan's yard, on Cattle Market Day, where I made between three to four shillings. I had to let the cattle into the yard and then mind them, while the farmers went for a few pints. The amount you were paid depended upon the generosity of the man whose cattle you were guarding.

Mammy had no opportunity to plan ventures, because of the sheer hard work of raising the family and the austerity of the times. But Pa sometimes had schemes in mind, which never came to fruition, because he had a large family to keep. He and his brothers were from a long line of entrepreneurs, who were a little above the rest, having had the first car in Glanntaverne. They were also expert stonemasons and owned a dancehall and a shop, in their village. But Pa's fortunes had declined, with the arrival of a huge family.

Whereas my local river was the Mullaghanoe, pronounced 'mullanahoe', Frank McCourt's river in Limerick, in *Angela's Ashes*, was the River Shannon. His alcoholic father blamed the Shannon for all of their illnesses. We'd sometimes find coins and other items in our river. It runs right through the centre of Charlestown, and remains a major feature of the town; there's a bridge there too. The town part of it was a bit rough, stony, and full of rubbish, but about a half mile out of the town, you'd see a lot of people fishing in it. It starts about three miles out of town at Mullaghanoe, and flows through Charlestown, then on into the River Moy, (a famous salmon fishing river that every fisherman knows), which eventually flows into the sea.

Although it was normally about a foot deep, you could end up getting cut, by broken bottles for example. People would throw all sorts of things into it – boxes and so on. It was a good width – the width of this room here, so we're talking about a good twelve feet. After a flood, as a kid, it would be way above your knees, and you'd have to try to keep your balance, walking through it. You'd be walking like this… just holding your balance and going along, step by step. After heavy rainfall it would be fairly fast-flowing, so potentially hazardous at times. Why there was no one ever drowned in it I never will know!

We were only little children, so we made our short pants shorter, as we went down into it –like swimming trunks. There might be half a dozen of us in it. Although I've never heard of anyone drowning in it, Sylvester Cassidy fell in, and was carried away for a few feet. I don't know who fished him out! The river never flooded the town itself, but the fields were sometimes flooded, a few miles beyond the town. A river, in Ireland, can be rather mystical; in some circumstances, taking on an almost magical quality – especially with children. I've a photo of it somewhere – on the bridge. A picture, after all, is worth a thousand words.

There were places on the outskirts of Charlestown, like a copse with trees, where the fairies were supposed to live and all those forts are now preserved areas; you cannot build a house on or around them. They were in runs and in dells and sheltered by trees, and could be found on Anthony Mulligan's land. If you walked out of town the fort was there. As I'm driving around Ireland, I can see where these forts are, because there are quite a few of them. That's where the fairies are supposed to come out, at the dead of night, and sing; and you can hear the fairy music. The grass growing on these areas always seems to be of a deeper green – for some strange reason.

As I said, there was one on Anthony Mulligan's land and we'd often go up there as kids – as coves. We were always a bit apprehensive, because we thought we might meet the fairies; for that was where they were supposed to live. We'd be between the ages of six and eleven at the time. There was a huge, flat stone there. Underneath the stone there was reputed to be a tunnel, which was supposed to lead from that stone, into Anthony Mulligan's house. Whether that was true, I don't know, but we always *thought* that. It was a huge stone – half the size of this table!

So it was feasible that it could be concealing a tunnel entrance. We *believed* that there was a secret tunnel there, which led into Anthony Mulligan's house. The trees were always bent and twisted – weird shapes, rather like Japanese Bonsai trees. That's why I could spot a fairy fort; there were hills and hollows too. They were very romantic places really.

You wouldn't go there at night – let's put it that way! We always thought that the fairies came out at night, and danced and so forth. If you were caught watching them, they'd put a spell on you. The enchanted violinist story, at the beginning of this chapter, is rather like the tale of Rip Van Winkle, but on a shorter time scale. It's typical of the sort of stories we would hear about the forts. The musician was entirely fictitious; it didn't derive from something that had actually happened to a fiddler. It wasn't a man we knew at all. It occurred during just on one night. The 'Little People' loved music – weird fairy music.

The more cynical amongst us might suggest that there's something in the soil or the atmosphere around the forts, which produces this effect. But the countryside in Ireland, if you're on your own, is indeed rather haunting. The foliage is totally different from England – everything is kept so neat and trim here; whilst in Ireland, things are allowed to grow more wild.

Because everything is so haunting and romantic, you could imagine people living under the ground, whereas you couldn't imagine it happening so much in England. A field over here is just that, but in Ireland, it might have a different feel about it altogether.

And if ever you heard the Banshee, well… you were gone… totally! The Banshee is a fairy woman. I've met people who've sworn black was white – that they've heard the Banshee. She is the harbinger of death, and once you've heard her wailing, then a death is imminent!

You might say: "Could it not simply be the wind howling?" Well, the Banshee is very well documented, in all sorts of stories. Again, if someone supposedly heard the Banshee on a Yorkshire farm, for example, you'd probably laugh. But in Ireland, if you look around you, the country leads you towards that sort of notion. You could *believe* that you'd heard it! Especially if you heard it while you were walking through the Fort; you'd say: "Well… that's the Banshee!"

Chapter Five

THE JELLY THIEVES

Summertime was the best; the fine weather seemed to eliminate their worries for a while. You always felt better on a sunny day, than you did on a wet, misty morning, or a foggy day. Everyone went barefooted in the town, although the better-off lads put their shoes on earlier than Seamus and his coves: they kept theirs off to the bitter end – literally – until there was snow and frost on the ground. No shoes in the summer gave them the exhilarating freedom of running around in bare feet. If you are by the seaside, on a day out, running up and down the soft, golden sand you feel great! The old feet feel better and if you've any corns, they get a good rinsing in the sea.

The summer holidays were a great time! Handball was the main game – they all played that – and 'Cowboys and Indians': half of the gang would be cowboys and the other half were Indians. Another favourite was *Block*. A crowd of lads would gather together, then one poor unfortunate would be chosen to be in what they called the 'Den', denoted by a stone on a windowsill. But nobody wanted that job! The other kids would scamper off, and even if the lad in the Den saw you go in one particular direction, he'd still got to catch you. If you made it back to the windowsill before him, you shouted: "Block 123!" Then you were free. The last one to be caught then had to guard the Den. But nobody wanted that job – you wanted to be away – hiding in different places.

We'd be playing around the Town Hall; the Ball Alley was just behind that. So we'd be behind the Ball Alley, and the fella would be looking for us – it might take him five or ten minutes, before he'd come across one of us. We'd stacks of places to hide in. Two of us might get back to the Den and shout "Block 123!" So if he couldn't find anyone and he saw three or four of us there, he knew that we'd reached safety. He'd probably operate from a windowsill on the Town Hall. So there we were, just trousers and short sleeves – barefooted – feeling, literally, 'footloose and fancy free'. And we'd never come back indoors until we were starving with the hunger! There was an old sandpit there as well. We didn't take any food or drink with us because our house was within easy reach. Eddie Tunney's was a little further down. We were all around the town. Johnny Fitzpatrick was around the corner from Barrack Street, but, again, you could 'spit to his house' from there. Our group of friends also included Gerald Healy, Mikey O'Donnell, Peader Frain, Sparkety Clarkety, Colum Swords and Frank O'Connor.

You didn't need many clothes on you. Winter – you had stone bruises on your feet, and you'd be looking for the overcoat. I never owned a coat until I came to England. But still, summer was far ahead of winter. I think maybe I had one pair of shoes, and then I graduated to clogs. As I got a bit bigger I probably had a Sunday pair. But everyone in the house hadn't a new pair of shoes – that's for sure!

In the summertime nowadays, you'd be having salads and fruit drinks and life would be altogether more pleasant than the times we're talking about. But in those days Mammy always baked cakes, and our staple diet was tea and bread. As I've said before, the amount of meat we had was very small. We used to get a shilling's worth of boiling beef and a bone. It was a mug of tea when you went in, from playing with the lads, and a slice of bread. We'd have soup two or three times a week, but very little meat.

In the winter, it was in early, but in the summer we'd do a lot of bird nesting, out in the fields. You'd come across birds' nests. If there was a lark hovering overhead, you'd know that there was a nest there. It was great going over the bog, to find a nest, with maybe four or five speckled-blue eggs. We tended to know the different birds, which I don't know now: the lark, the linnet, the corncrake, and so forth.

There was an abundance of corncrakes around the town. They made an unusual rasping sound. Like the bittern, they are now a protected species, across the United Kingdom and Southern Ireland. Sadly, most of them have disappeared, with the advent of the Combine Harvester. But the sound of the corncrake has stayed with me, all my life – hence the future name of one of my companies.

There was always a crowd of us. A woman named Mrs. Salmon had a house in Barrack Street, which was also an ice cream and sweetshop. That was a great place for us young lads to meet up, some evenings. She was in America for years, and she was a bit eccentric. But you could always get lovely sweets there and an ice cream, for a penny; depending upon what humour she was in, you could get a thick ice cream; if she was in a bad mood, you'd get a very thin one! You could have a tuppenny one, which was a full wafer. It depends; you could be chatting away, and she'd put a bit of extra on. Someone would say: "God, look how thin this ice-cream is!" Then another would say: "Look at the thickness of mine!"

Mrs. Salmon had grey hair, pulled back in a bun and was actually a very nice woman – I liked her. She'd stick up for herself and she'd a bit of a temper, but she'd been to America in her youth and would often tell us yarns. Like how she'd worked for big families over there, (she'd probably been in service), and about how she'd got to America, and so forth. But I was enthralled to hear her talk. I remember one story vividly. She'd found the man of the house and he'd shot himself in the head. She described the pool of blood and his brains all shot out! We thought about the pictures – Humphrey Bogart shooting James Cagney and so on. So we'd be thinking: 'If ever I go to America, I'd better watch out!' Years later you'd remember her story – did it really happen? I *suppose* it did.

But they were long summer evenings. Sometimes we'd make a bicycle. We'd get a bicycle frame and two wheels, and try and make a bike that you could cycle on. It was nearly impossible, but if you were going downhill, somebody would give you a push.

Everybody had a bicycle when we were growing up, because there were no cars. There was at least one bicycle shop in Charlestown, so you could get wheels and spokes and this-that-and-the-other from there. My eldest brother Paddy was good at putting things together, and all of a sudden you'd have a bicycle that could run down a hill. There'd be no brakes, so it was a case of jumping off, before a wheel came off! But we'd be tinkering around with things like that. Then we'd have Scraw Fights, between the Barrack Street lads: digging up a piece of turf or lawn with your heel; if it was a bit wet, we'd have these fights between ourselves, get plastered with clabar (mud), and end up with black faces!

We used to play football but only the senior lads in the town had a proper football. So the older brothers would get a pig's bladder, and after many attempts to inflate it by mouth, would manage to get it reasonably hard. I wouldn't touch it by mouth, but my oldest brother, Paddy, with the help of Johnny Clark, would do the job. That's the same 'Sparkety Clarkety', from Chapter 4 – who went barefoot, winter or summer, as a lad, and won the All Ireland Medal for handball.

We would get the bladder off the Giblins or Hubert Cregg. I remember one day going to the slaughterhouse, which was just down our back way. The Giblin brothers were about to operate on a large pig. They were *delighted* to see me because it took three people to assist in making the pig immobile. First they tied a rope onto each of the front legs. Mike Giblin and I caught hold of a rope each and pulled in opposite directions. Then Mike's brother Josie, picked up a fourteen-pound sledgehammer…

That's the way they used to knock the pigs out. It's amazing. We have a thing now called the Humane Killer – where a blade comes out of a gun, and they put it into the pig or cow's head and it goes straight into the brain and kills it. But those times, they had to knock them out with a sledgehammer, before they could stick them, with a knife. Josie aimed the first blow, as hard as he could, at the pig's head. We were a long way off the Humane Killer, back then. Joe Giblin had a very bad squint, and held his head to one side. There is a name for his condition, but I did not know it at the time. The first blow hit the pig on the snout. He was aiming for the part of his head between his ears. So you can imagine the squealing, the roaring and the struggling of this pig! And me terrified! The second shot of the sledge hit the concrete floor and sent sparks flying. After what seemed eternity, he managed to clock the pig a ferocious blow, just above the eyes, on the forehead.

The sound of a sledgehammer on a pig's scull is with me yet! He administered a few more fatal blows, but the pig had gone limp and stopped the desperate squealing of terror. "The bastard is done for Josie!" says Mike. "Hold on awhile Mike, till I get the sharp scion," (pronounced 'skeen').' The Scots have the scion dubh, the black knife, in their socks; scion means knife. Josie got the scion, turned the pig sideways and drove it between the pig's two front legs. Oh my God – the blood was squirting everywhere! Then he retracted the scion and cut the pig's throat. I was walking in blood – smelly hot blood. I nearly fainted!

I'd be about eleven or twelve: they just wanted someone to keep the pull on the rope. And yet it was brutal – and in a funny way – exciting. How a man could kill a mighty pig. When I recovered, I asked for the bladder. "Now Sheamin," (pronounced 'Sheameen' or sometimes Sheamey), says Mike, "you'll have the bladder tomorrow, and a bit of pork for your mother. You are making a fine punch of a young fellow." I swore I would never eat a bit of pig for the rest of my life. But today, my favourite meal is bacon, egg and sausages. So my belly got the better of my ambivalence to the pig!

When I came up the backway, I felt a bit like the famous English hangman, Pierpoint. He had hanged all the Irish patriots, and all the English murderers. I felt as if I had assisted in a killing, but, God forgive me, it strangely excited me. When Mammy saw me she screamed; "You're fighting again! Was it the Tunneys or the Swords? I'll swing for them flamers for injuring you like this! Where are you cut?"

"I helped Josie and Mike Giblin kill a pig. They are giving me the bladder for a football and a bit of pork for you." Mammy let out a few more choice words again, but relented when she heard about the bit of pork. She scrubbed me clean; we had no running water in our house. There was a pump, two houses up, on the corner, which did our street. So we always had to have two full buckets in the house and the basin, where we washed – no bath.

It was a terrifying experience – I'd never seen a pig being killed before, or stabbed and never really knew how a pig got to be hanging up there, in the butcher's shop. But I never did it again. A day or two after, the Giblins arrived with a piece of pork and a bladder. They blew the bladder up as well. So we were away to Healy's field. That was where we always played. The bladder was not shaped like a football; it was like a blown-up kidney shape, so when it hopped in front of you, it was like a rugby ball and could fly in any direction. The word went round like wildfire: "The Dunleavys are in Healy's field with a great big pig's bladder!"

Before long, there were two teams of us, lining up to oppose each other. Again, we would play until it was dark and you could not see the 'ball'. I remember Eddie Tunney from Barrack Street getting a full wallop of the bladder in the face. His face was full of slime and there was a smell off him, worse than a pig! But we all smelled the same, because we were all handling it and rolling it in our ganseys – our jumpers. So we definitely wouldn't have bacon, on nights like that!

Talking about Eddie Tunney, myself and him were walking down the backway behind our street. Eddie lived about eight doors down from us. He came from a very big family: six or seven sisters and four brothers. Their dad was a big strong labouring man, who'd done several shifts back and forwards to England. His mother was a very friendly woman; again, she'd been to America in her young life and would tell us about the big houses on Long Island, and about the people she worked for, who were mostly Jews. Eddie was the second son, and the same age as myself. We'd see each other every single day.

We knew everyone in the town; but all the Barrack Street lads played together, and we'd all head for the Ball Alley, the old Town Hall and the Sandpit. But this particular day, Eddie and myself were heading down the backway, looking for anything we could pick up like: the odd porter bottle, which we'd get a penny for, or jam jars: we'd get a halfpenny for the pound jar and a penny for the two-pound jar. As the war was on, glass was particularly expensive; they had to recycle things. Because Pa was away and the war was on, at the time.

At the back, myself and Tunney, were running through the dumps. As we were coming past Mills' house, they had a corner house, fronting on to Barrack Street, but there was a little entry. So we were coming up the entry, and we saw a bowl on the windowsill. There was a sash window open from the bottom. We were too small to look into the bowl, but we could reach it and get our hands into it. It was full of some gooey, sticky stuff. We liked the smell and had a taste. It was d-e-l-i-c-i-o-u-s. Nobody saw us and we scoffed the lot! It was red jelly that was just setting. We started to lick our hands. When I came up, Mammy must have smelled it on me and seen it plastered across my face. So we explained about the bowl. But the Mills's never knew until years later. Mrs. Mills must have had a surprise at the time: "Where's me jelly? Maybe the cats had it!"

Well they could have had it, because she'd nothing covering the bowl. We were the cats Shirley! Years later, coming back from England, I met Mr. and Mrs. Mills and said: "Well, I've something to tell you. After all this time, the people who nicked your jelly were Eddie Tunny and myself!" We had a good laugh about it. That was the first time that I had ever tasted jelly. The Mills are dead and gone now. I still love jelly to this day. I absolutely love it! It was a big joke around Barrack Street, for years afterwards – The Jelly Thieves!

The three streets in Charlestown had backways. You could take a horse and cart of turf, or drive a car down them. The town was laid out very nicely – like the High Street in Solihull or the Dovehouse Parade, in the respect that it had a backway. A lot of towns didn't have backways: they all loaded from the front, so we were fortunate. The backways in the town are wide and they're all tarmac now; they're as good as some main roads behind the town.

We had a few chickens running round our backyard, at all times. They laid a few eggs, from time to time. We loved the eggs. Mammy would feel the chicken's bum, and say: "Oh, this chicken's ready to lay." She'd then keep that chicken in this particular stable that we had; because otherwise the chickens would roam into the next yard or garden, and someone else would have the eggs. She'd do this every other morning, keep them in for a few hours, and when we let them out, there'd be an egg or two there. You'd do the same with a duck or a goose.

But there'd be this lad in the town, called Sean Maloney. His family kept a few ducks – and a drake of course. So he got the drake and after trying it for a long time, he said: "No, no, this duck has no egg." When he let it down, his mum or dad said: "That's a drake!" So for a while afterwards, we called him 'Try the Drake Sean'! He was still known by that name, around the town, for a while after.

Although we kept chickens, we never seemed to have a lot of eggs or meat. Mammy would send us down the street, to the stall of Jim Webb, our butcher. Our order was always the same: a shilling's worth of boiling beef and a good marrowbone – the bigger the bone the better! And indeed, we often had to go back: "Mammy said this bone is too small." Well, if Jim Webb had no bones, (because there were more than us had a call on them), he would often throw in a few scraps of other meat. But as long as there were bones, there was plenty of soup and potatoes, so you were never so bad. It's amazing that a good marrowbone makes a terrific bit of soup. Mammy used to make great soup, with all the vegetables and so on.

We lived in the town, so we had to buy everything: milk, vegetables, butter, spuds, everything. We used to buy a pint of milk off Mrs. Morris Roe down the street. Mammy would send my older brother called Luke (Louie) down for the pint, in a can. When he got the milk, he would take a slug of it. Mammy would say: "Not enough to cover the bottom of the can!" Then she would see his milk tash and knew he had been at it. This was serious; the cane was introduced and he got walloped. But it never cured him. Whenever he was sent for the milk, he always had a milk tash and got the wallop! In our family, there's nearly always a Luke. It must have been a popular name with us. Louie obviously thought it was worth taking his punishment – as long as he got the milk! You couldn't buy it in bottles in those days. But halfway up the backway, he'd start to have a drink for himself.

I did not *dislike* school, but I wasn't very bright. I thought when I got big, I would go to England and become a boxer and make a lot of money. I remember listening to a broadcast, on the old battery radio wireless, the night Martin Thornton beat Paddy Sullivan of Cork, for the Heavyweight Championship of Ireland. We listened to the radio in Mrs. Salmon's shop, because we had no radio at the time.

Martin Thornton bought a hotel in Connemara with his winnings and I thought, 'That is the way to get Mammy and Pa a bit of comfort.' Pa was still in England. He would send £6 every week: not a fortune for a mother and nine kids, Then out of the blue, the money would not arrive on the day it should. Mammy would say: "Has the postman gone down?" He would come the far side of Barrack Street, go to a few houses down on the opposite side, and then turn and cross over and come down our side. Then we would see he had gone past. Oh God – we knew what that meant! The poor woman would have us at the door a full two hours and the post, long delivered. She'd be in bad form – which she was entitled to be.

It made life very difficult and sad for Mammy and me. I often wondered if the older kids were as affected as I was. But you got very bitter towards any kid that was well dressed, the clergy, the establishment, everybody. Mammy would send me down to Mary Tunney and I'd borrow £1 off her. Mary was equally as poor as we were. Isn't it funny how the poor borrow off the poor? I suppose it's not so embarrassing. Anyway, Mary Tunney used to borrow the pound off Mrs. McLoughlin: she had no children and her husband was a tailor, so she was well enough off. So she gave Mary Tunney the pound and she passed it on to my mum.

But the pound was always in transit. For some reason, she would never borrow directly off Mrs. McLoughlin, but would survive on that pound, for a whole week, until the money came from England again. Then we used to get bread – three loaves a day off Mary Carroll. So then of course, she couldn't pay Mary, and it would be: "Who's going to pay?" There were no phones, but when we didn't get the wire, there was usually a letter from Pa, within a day or two, explaining what had happened. That would be a Saturday, so nothing until Monday or Tuesday. Years later, I realised that he must have been working the weekend and had not had the time to get to the post office. Because the money would come the week after, we were in debt around the town. Then sometimes Pa would miss a full week, and we would get £12, or two weeks together.

This was bad enough, but then he would miss a week, and the week after, when we should get two weeks' money, we only got the £6. This was a time when Mammy got *really* down. But what could we do? Pa was not a drinking man and very occasionally had a pipe smoke. Maybe he *was* saving for coming home himself and – 'out of sight, out of mind' – this is what I'm surmising now. Maybe he was thinking, 'Well – they'll be OK. I'll pinch another week?'

But compared to men like Frank McCourt's dad, Mick was a kindly sort of man. I don't think I've ever seen him drunk. He'd have a few pints and he'd smoke a pipe occasionally, but if someone said to him: "That pipe's bad for the heart and lungs you know Mick," then he'd come off it for a year or two.

He never discussed the 'wire' problems with us, even when we were older. He may have spoken privately to Mammy about it – I don't know. We never spoke as to whether he was out of work himself. He worked as a ship's carpenter, but maybe there were voids, when there were no ships in dock, or work hadn't got under way? But I assumed that he always had work, because he was a good carpenter.

Women from the *Legion of Mary* used to come round to the house, in his absence. They wore big blue ribbons. It was a voluntary organization and there'd be half-a-dozen women in it. There was Mrs. Kilcoyne, Mrs. Howley and Mrs. Swords, Mick's wife, although Mrs. Swords was a very nice woman.

She was a schoolteacher. I've a bungalow now, next to her daughter, Bernie – a lovely lady who we mention elsewhere in the book. I have a picture of her brother, Kevin Swords, boxing my brother, Paddy.

The *Legion of Mary* were like social workers and I suppose they did a lot of good work. They used to come around on Saturday nights. The nine of us children would be waiting to wash our feet in the basin, when they'd arrive in. "How is your husband, Mrs. Dunleavy? When is he coming home? Does he send you money?" Mammy was a very private woman, and they'd be asking these questions in front of us children. She used to be absolutely *livid* – calling them allsorts under her breath. But she wouldn't say anything directly to them. It was when they were gone that she'd call them for everything. She didn't have the courage to stand up to them on her own, like. So I grew up, thinking they were a crowd of busybodies. Having said that Shirley, I'm sure that there were some that they would have helped, because a few of the husbands did flit off and never come back.

Mammy had to be resourceful, to cope as she did. They were very hard times. Nowadays, you'd be on the phone an hour after: "The postman's gone down!" Had he been doing it nowadays, given that he'd got the money, Pa could have sent it straight through, by text, if need be. The money's sent – it's finished – done!

Even in my time in England, if you go back fifty years. We all have houses now, but in those days you'd have maybe forty people in one house – all around the one radio every Sunday, coming up to the Ireland Final. There were no TVs to watch it on, and they'd come from all different parts. They were in digs themselves and had no access to a radio.

I used to see lads, coming into Charlestown, riding horses – just like John Wayne. They'd tie the horse there, do their business, then out again, on the horse. That was the way they travelled: no cars – just horses, donkeys or bicycles.

The other night, we were sitting in the *Riverside Restaurant*, in Charlestown, looking down the town. The whole place was lined with cars; you couldn't find a parking space anywhere. And to say: "I can remember when people used to tie horses up here." They'd say; "Are you daft Seamus? When was that?" But Charlestown remains exactly the same. Every shop front is the same, since the day I left. We've got a few modern restaurants, but the façade of our house remains the same. The house I was born in has been a restaurant for the past twelve years. It's called *The Cosy Bar*, and it has a particularly good chef. The *Riverside Restaurant* belongs to the O'Hara family, and is also a guesthouse. It used to be a shop, called *Mulrooney's*, with petrol pumps outside. There's a Chinese Restaurant there now, which used to be a dentist's. The shop frontages are almost all the same – the windows are the same. It's just the occupants and the trades carried out there, which are different.

By 2004, the population of Charlestown had increased to eight hundred. Located in the scenic heart of the county, it has been hosting visitors for almost a century. It's known as the International Gateway to the West of Ireland, and is easily accessible since the development of Knock International Airport. In the last few years there's been a terrific amount of business going on there, so they've all bought private houses. In our day they used to live over the shops, but that's changed. Although the shops all look the same, their owners are living just outside the town now. You'll have a trip there one day Shirley – and you'll see it all!

Sunday was the day that everyone dressed up in our town, to go to Mass, which was the custom in Catholic countries. But you'd see kids with new shoes on and you were very aware of it – they had new shoes and *you* didn't. Our pants would be sewn up and there'd be buttons missing here and there. We'd braces, but it was just like you'd see in *The Hillbillies* – two strips of cloth – whereas these other kids would have proper elastic braces. Those are the things that stick in your mind.

The kids would look at you and make remarks about you. You grow up and you leave home behind you, but that's the way it was. You don't know, at that stage, that things will be OK when you grow up; you don't have a crystal ball, so at the time it could be very depressing. I suppose it was the same in certain parts of England. But when we saw the odd fella coming home with a gabardine raincoat, we'd think: 'Oh we'll go to England and we'll be alright.'

Mammy was a jolly woman, but she was very embarrassed by her poverty, through the years. She was a short, stocky woman: very strong, in her hey-day apparently. But she just didn't want to go out, knowing that people would be better dressed than she was. She was very embarrassed meeting people. Maybe the confidence was knocked out of her – through the hard times? But before we came along, I think the shop was doing quite well. When she was growing up, the shop was thriving, but it declined, and was never any good, once her own kids came along. That's why her brothers and sister emigrated to America. I don't know much about her parents. There were certain people she knew, who'd been less well off than herself, but had since become more affluent.

Another source of income was that I became very good at catching rabbits. Every lad around the town used to buy what we call 'snares'. You'd have to see it done, to understand it. There were two pegs, as part of it. We knew exactly where to set the snares, in the fields around the town. When we caught a rabbit we'd sell it for 1/6d or 1/9d; for a very good rabbit you'd get two shillings. If you got one on a very wet day, so its fur was wet, all you'd get for the rabbit would be a shilling. We used to go to Mrs. Parsons, who lived down the town, her husband was a draper and they always bought a rabbit.

They had a housekeeper who used to tear the ear of the rabbit. If she couldn't tear it that told her it was old; if she could tear it easily, the rabbit was young. So we got 'wised up' to this you see? We'd knick the ear with a razorblade and fluff up the fur again. That was one of the scams – with the rabbits! There was another woman around the town, Mrs. Walsh, who bought blackberries from us. When they were ripe, we'd all be out there with tins, jars and saucepans – picking blackberries. That was another source of income for us. You'd be out all day picking blackberries and you might end up with a shilling!

Mrs. Walsh used to sell the blackberries: she'd send them away somewhere – and the same with the rabbits. I'm not sure where she sent the rabbits; whether because it was wartime, they were sent to feed the troops? Or maybe they were used for something else. We'd set the snares out in the fields. At the time, the fields were *teeming* with rabbits!

But you'd often set four or five snares and someone would pinch them on you – they'd be gone the morning after! There was a lot of that happened as well. Or someone would be out early before you, looking for snares, and would have the rabbits before you could get to them. There were night-catchers, with big spot-lamps to dazzle the rabbit. The way you catch a rabbit is you dazzle him. It's the pitch dark when you switch this lamp on; he stops and he's petrified – and that's when you kill him. So that's what we did. We used to eat rabbits a lot; they're very much like chicken; but I'd never clean a rabbit. Paddy, my older brother used to do that; I don't think me mother would gut a rabbit, but she would gut a chicken. Would you Shirley? (You can imagine the answer to that one, can't you?) God – you'd be a bad wife Shirley! I suppose if the hunger was on us, we'd eat the guts and all! But we've never been *that* hungry in life – unlike the Biafran people. But anyway, that was the rabbit and the blackberries.

The merchants of Charlestown, as in any small town, were all canny. But there was also a lot of generosity there. They knew that we were one of the families who didn't have much money. We used to go to the dancehall there; Andrew Walsh was the proprietor. He had twelve children; three of them started this dancehall, which became very successful. He was good-hearted, and he'd occasionally let you in for nothing: there was a lot of that. There's good and bad everywhere, of course.

We used to buy our flour off Luke O'Donnell, father of Jack O'Donnell, the chemist, who had Johnny Clark's handball medal. Luke was a very decent man. If we wanted a stone of flour, when the scales balanced, he always gave us an extra scoop of flour – enough to make an extra cake.

As I've mentioned, we've a pub called *The George*, up by the Bull Ring, in Birmingham. When I was up there one day, I saw Frank Finlan running after a woman, who was down on her luck, saying: "Would these be any good to you?" He had two or three handfuls of bruised apples, pears and so forth. He didn't need to do that, but he gave her the lot. It's a mark of the man himself. But that old spirit is in most people, isn't it?

There was a lot of that in Charlestown. If you were the last man in the *Eureka Cinema*, Luke Mulligan would say: "Get in there!" He knew we didn't have the shilling – and that we'd be running in the back door half the time anyway – down under the seats! I'd do the same myself if I had a cinema, and a few of the lads were gasping to get in; I'm sure I would. It's the same with the pub. If there was a fella there, gasping for a drink: "Give him one on the House!"

Drinking is another matter really, but the Pictures were different. We genuinely hadn't got the money, and we couldn't get a picture anywhere else. There was no television, so for us it was a great thing to get into the Pictures. Luke Mulligan had three sisters: they used to wear long, dangling earrings and turbans, which were very fashionable. Two of them, Marrion and Louisa, (who I'll tell you more about in the next chapter), smoked cigarettes out of cigarette holders, and smelled of powder and paint. They were quite sophisticated, with painted fingernails, and had big houses with tennis courts. That's *still* a grand lifestyle these days. But everything works out… at the tail end of the day.

Chapter Six

EUREKA

The main recreation in Charlestown all those years ago was the cinema; we had no wireless. The Picture House was just four houses away from the Dunleavy's home. In the summer evenings, with the bedroom windows wide open, you could hear the films playing quite clearly. Seamus was down there every weekend and sometimes midweek as well. The 'Eureka', as it was known, seemed to have been there forever. His love of old films remains with Seamus, to the present day.

The *Eureka Cinema* was owned by the Mulligan family – Luke, Joe and two of their sisters, Louisa and Marrion. The girls never married because there was no one in Charlestown supposedly good enough for them... or sufficiently wealthy. However, a third Mulligan sister, who *did* marry, was Mrs O'Rourke, who owned the Charlestown toyshop that I mentioned earlier.

There was another brother, Paddy, a solicitor, who had two cinemas in Ballina, a large town, twenty-five miles away. So the Mulligans were heavily into entertainment. The Mulligan sisters would have been very wealthy and maybe they left it too late in life, to get married? In my youth, I regarded them as elderly, although they wouldn't have been. From a young lad of twelve or fourteen's point of view, they seemed ancient, but I'm sure they were only somewhere between thirty or thirty-five at the time. They were very good-looking girls as well, but maybe there weren't enough bachelors around the town to suit them? Certainly not financially anyway – that's the way that we summed it up.

They used to go abroad, and they certainly went to America often enough. That's where they got their style from – they dressed up like film stars! The two spinster sisters always dressed up in lovely Crombie coats, turbans, and long earrings. When I say the word 'turban' Shirley, they weren't the workaday turbans, worn, for example, by Lancashire mill women; they were the glamorous types. But they lived a good life and they died in Charlestown, as spinsters... which was a pity.

Luke and his sisters knew all about travel. The Mulligans were also big shopkeepers, shipping agents, publicans and undertakers, as well as owning a lot of land around Charlestown. They had, according to my mother, the name of 'Landgrabbers'. They built a beautiful house – the best in Charlestown at the time – next door to our school. It was a lovely Art Deco design, with oval windows at the side. I would watch the builders through the school hedge. It was the most magnificent house I ever saw. It took two years to build and was built by famous builders, from Ballina.

Luke used to holiday in Florida. We did not know where it was, only that it was somewhere beautiful. Years later, the first time that I arrived in Florida, I could not but think of Luke Mulligan, who was there sixty years before me, when it was very civilised.

I remember going to Florida for the first time and being absolutely enthralled by it all. But it was more commercialised than in Luke's time, and more dangerous: you had to be alert to the likelihood of being robbed. We flew into Miami, which was rough enough. But sixty years before that, when Luke was there, they would have been the only people from our town who went there. So, eventually, we arrived in Florida at last – and we'd thought it was at the ends of the earth!

Mammy used to say: "Them two living like the Queens of England, and us living here, with all the young ones in tea chests!" There were always two or three tea chests in our kitchen. They were our playpens. But I pledged I would make things right for Mammy, when I became a champion boxer.

Although the two sisters never married, Luke did, and had a daughter, who now lives in Wales. Joe had a son who died. My brother, Mickey, (the goosekiller), eventually bought the Mulligan's house, and lived there for a while, having done well in England. It had been vacant for about twelve years before he bought it, but everything was still in perfect order. Oh Mam, would you be proud? A house you could never look at, owned by your own son! But by that time you were gone, although Pa wasn't.

This landgrabbing was the version I heard from Mammy, so that was a story we heard all our lives: a story, again, of poverty against riches, isn't it? Where the rich man is always the tyrant. The Mulligans owned very good shops in the town and they *did* give a lot of credit to the people from the country. The story was that if the country people ran up such a big debt that they couldn't pay it, then they took the land off them. Now whether or not that was true – I don't know.

Maybe one poor farmer had to sell his land – and that story escalated to momentous proportions? There's the alternative viewpoint that the Mulligans may have helped people, out, by rescuing them when they were in debt. I remember Joe Mulligan was an auctioneer. At one time the suspicion emerged that we might move to England to join Pa, so Joe came round, to see if we would sell our house. My mother took it in an *awful* way – she had no notion of going to England. "That land-grabbing so-and-so – trying to buy the house from under us!"

But back to the cinema. We were weaned on Buck Jones, Tom Mix, Johnny Mack Brown, Charles Starret, alias the Durango Kid. Tim McCoy; then Hopalong Cassidy, Gene Autry and Roy Rodgers – all cowboys. Bella Lugosi as Dracula – God, the heart would be crossways in us, after a night with Boris Karloff, Lon Chaney – and Bella – of course! We always used to call him 'Billy Legoosie!' – "Billy Legoosie's on tonight cove!" I saw Lon Chaney yesterday, on the television, in an old film. They used to call him 'The Man with a Thousand Faces'.

Then we had Sidney Toller as Charlie Chan – great! Boston Blackie and Peter Lorrie, Sydney Greenstreet, Jack Holt and Tom Conway, who was like *The Saint* of today, in a film called *The Falcon*. His brother, in real life, was George Sanders: two very handsome men. George did everything in his life, married very attractive women, but eventually he'd had enough of life. A very good speaker, like our friend, Chris Fairbank, whom I dropped out to the BBC, as we mentioned recently, in Pat Roach's third biography *Auf Wiedersehen Pat*.

George Sanders committed suicide at the age of sixty-two. There was also Jimmy Cagney, Humphrey Bogart and Pat O'Brien; Thomas Mitchell, Dennis Morgan, Willard Parker, Dennis Oakes and George Raft. Miriam Hopkins, Bette Davies, Joan Crawford, Jean Blondell, Alice Fay, King Kong – I knew them all – and all that came after them. *The Three Stooges*, George Kennedy, Lionel Athwell, Joe McDoakes and Ben Turpin; *Laurel and Hardy*.

Our cinema was just a long building with a line of wooden seats each side and a passage in between. There were backs on the seats. They were fairly comfortable – or I thought so. There was a balcony, where the 'Toffs' would go. It was a shilling to get in downstairs. Upstairs in the balcony would cost one shilling and fourpence (1/4d). For us kids to get in, we needed four pence each – and that took some getting! We would have to go around the backways and look for jam pots. You got a penny for an empty jam pot and two old pence for a 2lb jar. Also, if we found any porter bottles, we would get two pence.

The cinema was the biggest part of my young life; I knew all of the characters I mentioned there – vividly! We had a serial about *Flash Gordon*, which I've seen since on television. I understand that one of the chapters in Pat's new book, *Auf Wiedersehen Pat*, begins with a *Flash Gordon* game – young Ladywood children, playing in the snow, at night, with torches!

You imagined that you knew the characters – and that they knew you, (simply because you were watching them) …and, sadly, you'd never see the leading lady again – once the film was over! But the cinema was where we all met as young lads; we all congregated there.

The Mullaghanoe River still flows through our town. We used to trawl it, looking for stuff people that might have thrown away. Every bit of rubbish was thrown into it, and we often found stuff that we could use.

But we always seemed to cadge the *Eureka* four pence from somewhere. Sometimes we would get in when the first picture was over, but it did not matter; we would see the main picture. As we got a bit older, we realised that the back door of the cinema, which was also the Fire Escape, was sometimes left unlocked. So about eight to ten of us would rush in, through the doorway to the left of the screen. There were doorways to the right and left of the screen, and both had to be left open.

We'd be coming in either side of the screen. The cinema was pitch-black, except for the beam that showed the picture, so we were shadowy figures. We had to run down about six or seven steps, to get to ground level, scurry under the seats, then emerge somewhere in the middle of the cinema – or wherever. Of course, all the mates – 'coves' – in the cinema, knew what was happening, and made room for us, when we were under the seats. But I loved the cinema – and still do.

There was a boiler on a sidewall, in the middle of the cinema. If you were lucky enough to get one of the seats opposite the boiler, it was bliss! Heat on a cold winter's night… and the picture as well. But you had to be a fighter to get one. As we got bigger and stronger, and there were five of us brothers, so we all managed to get the good seats, by the boiler. The cinema people had bought the house next door, and removed all the walls, to make a place where all the boys and girls from the country could park their bikes.

Now the cinema had a lad called Johnny Clark, who used to park their bikes, take the lamps off, and keep them safe until the picture was over – the same barefooted 'Sparkety Clarkety' from Chapter Four. Johnny Clark got a shilling for this, and got to see the big picture, free, and half of the first picture as well. How I envied him! Well, Clark headed for England, and I got his job, parking the bikes – *and* the shilling. I was delighted. Mammy got the shilling and I got the free picture. I would be about thirteen or fourteen then. Getting that job was like winning the 'Pools'. I was guaranteed a picture every night, and the shilling as well. So you were 'Mr. Big'! Louisa Mulligan had seen me standing outside every night, and knew I had no money; so she thought, when Clark went off, that I'd be a good candidate. It was like getting a senior position over here, at a big firm.

The *Eureka* was where we all definitely learned 'the facts of life'! We always sat up at the front, near the screen, but the bigger lads and girls, all sat at the back. The seats sloped gradually up, so that they could see over your heads. That's where we'd see hands under girls' skirts and so on. It was sometimes difficult to follow the film, as we'd be turning round every five minutes. We'd go out to the toilet, at the back of the cinema. That's really where we'd see them groping and kissing. So we knew then – that that's the thing to do, with girls!

You were aware of it – like. You thought: 'That must be nice' – and the laughing and the giggling – and all of that. We never got to dance – because we were too young, so that's where it was all happening – at the cinema. You'd be going to the toilet, every five minutes. You can imagine a constant stream of young lads, walking up and down the aisles, while the film was on! But I'm sure the older girls and lads were too engrossed in what they were doing to notice. Great days! So that's where myself and all the young lads got our sex education from – the cinema in Charlestown!

My older brother, Paddy, got a job in a little mineral water factory, *P.J. Henry's*, just a short walk from our house. He was on thirty shillings a week, or in today's money, £1-50. This was a great help in the house. I used to hear Mammy talking to neighbours, telling them what a difference it made. We all had to do our bit in the house. When Paddy was working, one of the other boys had to get up, get the fire going, get the kettle boiled and make the tea. We sure had to look after the worker in the family!

We always lit the turf with a piece of bicycle tyre. We would cut about a foot off it. First, we would take the wire off each side of the tyre and cut it off, then score all the way around the tyre with a sharp knife, using about a foot of it, for every fire. The trouble was that the rubber emitted a horrible, thick black smoke, so the kettle would be absolutely black. If it touched anything, it would be destroyed. If we were not careful, we would get black hands and thumbprints, all over our kitchen – which was no doctor's surgery for cleanliness!

I was now in Senior Class, at school, around twelve years of age. I had not much interest in sport, but I was not a bad handballer, because, as you know, we were within earshot of the Ball Alley. So we spent all our spare time there. My brother Mickey was very good and would have gone on to represent Mayo, and possibly on to *All Ireland*. But England claimed him at a very young age, around seventeen or eighteen. Mickey was also a very good Gaelic Footballer, and again, would have made County Standard, but for the curse of immigration.

Although I was not much good at sport, I was *very* strong. Had there been a rugby team in our town, I might have been OK, but anyway, I wanted to be a boxer, and make all that money! Pa used to bring us small dumb-bells from England, and I trained a bit, from an early age. He also bought us a set of Chest Expanders. This was the first time we had seen them, and I was fascinated. I used them day and night – and practiced, practiced, practiced. I became very good with them, and of course, I was better with them than some grown men – who hadn't seen them either.

I was making my shoulders and upper body very strong, and rigged up a set of weights. I got an old, worn donkey cart axle; there were two worn wheels in our backyard; they fitted on the axle and – Bingo – I had a weight lifting set! A few years before, *Duffy's Circus* had come to our town. In those years, there was always a Strongman act. The Strongman at that time was called Timothy Geoghan (pronounced Gehagan) from the county of Leitrim. He called himself *Young Atlas*. I did not know him, or anything about him, but later in the book, I will reveal how I got to know him well, in future years.

There was a great circus picture done in different colours, with the artistes' names in different colours. Well, there was a drawing of Young Atlas, and two horses yoked each side of him – at arm's length. Then somebody beat the horses, so that they pulled in opposite directions. No matter how much they pulled, they could *not* pull Young Atlas apart. The horses were tied to his arms with a special harness. I was *completely* fascinated with this. We used to make a fist, put the knuckles together and get a lad each side, pulling; but they were not horses!

I remember going to school one particular morning, with a few school-friends. We had to pass the big circus tent. So we hopped into the field, known as the Fair Green, and had a look about. It was early, so there were not many circus people about. We wandered into one small tent and found a set of Atlas's weights. He also did a great weightlifting act and invited anybody in the audience to come into the circus ring, and have a go. I remember three or four young fellows trying, but no good. There was a young fellow called Lenihan, who got to his knees, but that was it. Well, now it was our turn, in the small-sized tent. Three or four of us could not even get the weight an inch off the ground. But I wanted to do it, and left with a feeling of elation. Although at about twelve or thirteen years of age, I had a long way to go!

School was not too bad, although I was not very bright. I got to Fifth Class, which seemed to be my limit then. The very clever boys got to Sixth or Seventh Class. Then we had an exam, which all of the Fifth Class took. It was called the Primary Certificate. You had to take it, and lo and behold, myself and Johnny Fitzpatrick were the only two, out of about twelve to fifteen, who failed, although we did not get the results for about three months.

I don't recall being disappointed at the time, because I was going to England and would be a champion boxer – get all that money for Mammy. I suppose if she had been interested in my academic qualifications, Mammy could have found out, a week after I did the exam. But with four older children and four younger and Pa away, totally short of money, she had other things on her mind. My failure mate, Johnny Fitzpatrick, took the exam next year and passed. So I drifted into the history of academic failures, of Lowpark National School, Charlestown. Still, I had my Chest Expanders and my homemade weight, and I was better than most of the boys at that.

You may recall that my oldest brother Paddy, was working in the mineral water factory, across the road from our house. So after a great bit of bowing and scraping, the second oldest, Louie, got a job there – again – at thirty shillings a week, so he was OK; a little bit of pocket money and the rest for Mammy. At this stage, my oldest sister, Mai had left school. Her best friend was Mauna Frain. Mauna's dad was a tailor and she worked with him, as an Improver; he also had a dressmaker. Mai decided she would like to be a dressmaker and got herself a little job there. I can't think whatever she got paid, or whether we had to pay George Frain, the tailor, to teach her, but I did not notice anything different in our household finances.

A year or two passed, and all of a sudden, my sister Mai decided it was time to bale out – and head for England. She would be about eighteen at the time. Everybody seemed to be heading for England; there was no way of making a living at home. Pa sent her the fare, although it didn't arrive on time.

Mai managed to get to Liverpool, where Pa met her. Mammy, meanwhile, was very lonely. So were we all. We had got used to Pa being away, but when my oldest sister left, it upset us all. I could hear Mammy crying many and many a night and her saying: "The best one is gone!" and "Everything would be alright, if Mai was here." A short while later Paddy, who was the first of the brothers to get a job, headed for England, to Liverpool as well – to Pa – another sad and lonely time. The family was splitting up. Then another short time passed, and Louie was away. So two brothers and one sister had now departed for England.

Chapter Seven

LEAVING FOR LIVERPOOL

The oldest brother, Paddy, a strong, young, handy lad, was the second of Seamus'
siblings to leave for Liverpool, when work dried up in Ireland. That was during the
war – which is exactly what happened in 'Angela's Ashes'. Many Irishmen went over
to England to work then, because jobs were so scarce in Ireland. When their father,
Michael, worked as a ship's carpenter, in Liverpool Docks, ships would frequently sail
into port, for repairs. Michael rented a house for nine shillings a week. Mai, the eldest
sister, and the first of the children to come over, was the head of the family; then Paddy
came afterwards. Like their father, he was a carpenter so the two of them started
working together. They all went to Liverpool eventually – all of the children.

At the time of writing, Seamus is seventy-one; his brother Mickey is seventy-
three; Tom would be seventy-four and Louie seventy-six. Paddy (now deceased) was
a good six years older than Seamus, who was the strongest built of the family.
Although Mickey had been a wrestler too, the last time Seamus went home, Mickey's
weight had increased to fifteen stone, but when they were younger he was a stone-
and-a-half lighter.

Returning to our story, Seamus began to attend local dances. There were two
dancehalls in Charlestown: the Town Hall and a private dancehall, owned by a man
named Andrew Walsh. This small, shed-like hall, was the main dancehall in the
town, when Seamus was growing up. But it became outmoded, so Andrew and his
family built a new one, with a maple-sprung floor and a balcony, where you could go
up and watch the dancing below. It was very modern and also, for the older people
and courting couples, there was a grand dining room. Seamus loved the dances – a
few local girls taught him the basic steps.

The charge was about three shillings, (25p in new money) so I could not
afford to go every week. But Andrew Walsh was very good: as often as not,
he would give us the wink and let us in for nothing. There was a huge
window in the dining room and if you were eating with your girlfriend, you
could look out at the dancers; we could see who had a girl in for a meal (2/6d
or 25p). But I was *light* years away from that and I really envied those diners:
lots of lads who had been away in England or America and were cutting a

dash. Boy, if you took a girl for a meal, you just *had* to marry her! They used to have lettuce and ham – a kind of cold buffet.

Well, the dancing was still very ropy. We used to have a dance called the *Paul Jones*, where you left your girl, and the men walked clockwise and the girls anti-clockwise, and when the music stopped, whichever girl was opposite you, you had to dance with her. But you never knew when this dance would occur; you asked somebody you knew very well then went maybe once around the floor, but the MC would suddenly change the dance. You could not leave the floor, so you were caught! You would be so embarrassed when you landed up with some older, well done-up girl. I remember, they smelled so well – lots of powder and perfume. Then, as the dance ended, you saw the couples pair off and I wished I was a bit older: 'sexual awareness', it is called!

The dancers all followed big show-bands. In my youth it was Hugh Toorish, Brose Walsh (pronounced 'Bros'), Mick Delahunty, *Melody Aces*, Bert Flynn, Stephen Garvey, Jack Ruane, Mick Mulligan and Willie Cafferkey; Sonny Blake and Mike Towey's band. I myself have always been a bit musical and could always knock out a tune or a march on a tin whistle. Mammy could play the melodeon a small bit, so I suppose the music might have been in me. The dancers followed the big bands, rather than the venues, because the bands themselves were the draw.

There was a mechanic working in old town, called Johnny Duffy. He was a great fiddle player, and his brother Paddy had a clarinet. When Paddy went off to America, Johnny lent me the clarinet for a while – I was 'over the moon'! Now there was a little street called Boar Street, given that name because an old man who lived there kept a boar to service the sows. Boar Street wasn't its official name of course: it was really the Ballyglass Road. Well, another of its residents was a Mr. Giblin, a music teacher. So I had a few lessons with him – no charge.

Sonny Blake, who was a good accordion player, used to visit us nearly every night. He and I played together a bit. He was playing with a little band and said I could sit in with them. He had an old saxophone, which he acquired somewhere, over the years, and I started to blow that for a while. Well, I became a fixture in the band, but all I could play really were a few tunes. There were four of us in the band: a fiddle player (Billy Cafferey), a drummer, Sonny Blake on the accordion and Jimmy-Joe Mulligan on the trumpet. Now if I started the dance on my sax, the accordion and the fiddle could follow and it was OK. But the trumpet player could not play. We were all in different keys – and that is how bad we were! If the trumpet started, I could not play, but the accordion and fiddle could.

So if Jimmy-Joe started off, I had to sit out… it was hilarious really! It was supposed to be a four-man band, but in fact it was only a three-man band, because the trumpet and sax player could never play together. The other two could follow either of us, but Jimmy and I would be in different keys!

I well remember one night in Cluan na Cool, in County Sligo, the three boys went for a tea break, so I was left on my own. I had just started playing when they gave me a signal that they were going. They were usually back before the tune was over. You played three tunes – and I was on my last tune. Everyone got up for the Olde Tyme Waltz. It was the easiest dance you could ever learn. The floor was packed and I was the sole musician, apart from the drummer, who was keeping the rhythm going.

But the boys had not come back! Although it was a tea break, Sonny Blake and Bill Cafferey were from poteen country (pronounced 'pocheen' – 200% proof!) and always had a drop with them, for the break. I played the last tune – *Danny Boy*. If I stopped, and they had not come back, I would have to start up again with a quickstep – and I could not play quicksteps! Well, I played the same tune over and over again. The dancers were sweating buckets, but I still played on. I was getting some dirty looks, I can tell you!

After what seemed like an eternity, they appeared back again. It was better to see them than the Apparition at Knock! When they took the stage, I nearly collapsed. The boys had had a drop and they were in great form – well they would be, wouldn't they? They played to their hearts content and the patrons seemed to have a great night as well. I was paid a pound a night, and I felt like a millionaire. We would play two or three times a month. I loved the spins in the car, going to and from the dances.

They were marvellous days Shirley, I was young and free and getting this pound. I loved music. I was improving as well, and was eventually able to play quicksteps. One night, the big drum, which should have been fixed onto something on the stage, started to move, a little at a time, with the drummer shuffling his seat forwards, each time that it did so. We hadn't realized how close to the edge it now was. Then all of a sudden, it fell of the stage, and rolled onto the dance floor! You had to regulate the drum and apologise to people, so it was a bit like a comedy floorshow too! Of course, you'd have an eye for all the young girls. Being in the band gave you a lot of 'kudos' anyway, and there would also be people there who I knew.

The dancers had a habit of handing you a slip of paper, requesting new tunes that you'd barely heard of! They'd expect you to play it, like a top class band. You'd have to say, "Well, you know, there's such a back-log of requests" – (perhaps they'd have asked you for *Mumbo Italiana*, or something like that)

Charlestown tradesmen from the past: third from the left are Uncle Tom, Uncle Jim and my father, Mick Dunleavy. The rest are unknown to me.

Brian Taylor, pictured here with his trophy cups, used to live in Barrack Street, and was a Champion Runner. He died recently, in Birmingham, aged ninety-one. The little boy on the windowsill is Mickey Vesey, who now lives in Salisbury.

The man himself, around six years of age. My sister, Kathleen, is in the background.

The Tunneys: L-R: Tommy and Maura Tunney, (now both deceased). Eddie, the Jelly Thief, and neighbour Johnny Clark - 'Sparkety Clarkety'.

Johnny Fitzpatrick's dad, Jim (Terry), the main town blacksmith, c. 1946. The locals would congregate at his forge, to watch him shoeing, and casting wheels.

Myself and brother Mickey, seated in a Charlestown backway, with our dog, Spot.

The Dunleavys, in ascending order of age: L-R: Monica, the youngest, Kathleen, Angela, myself - in boxing pose. Mickey is missing; Tom, Louie, Paddy (deceased) and Mai, the oldest of the children.

Charlestown Football Team: Back Row, L-R: Eddie Kilroy (deceased); W. Regan (deceased); P Beirne (deceased); Paric Carney; McDermot; S. Fleming; B. Caffery. Front Row: V. Blythe; M. Vesey; S. Honan (deceased); E. Walsh; J. Cassidy (Bishop); S. Beirne (deceased); S. Walsh (deceased) and E. O'Hara.

L-R: Louie and Paddy

Two old Charlestown warriors: Dennis Molloy, farmer, and Pat Horkan, postman.

L-R: Seamus Beirne, my brother, Louie, and Paddy Cassidy (deceased).

At the back of our house, myself, with the trumpet; Dad, with Monica in front; Mammy; Angela and Kathleen - happy days!

Myself, from the left, Mickey, Monica. Mary Kate (Mammy) and Kathleen - note our posh house!

Angela and Mammy.

Make-shift band: L-R: Mickey, on fiddle, with a broom handle for a bow. Tom and Louie, both on accordion, and me on sax.

Far-off days: L-R: Brother, Tom, Sean Foley and brother, Mickey. Tarpey Field in background, which Louie bought, and later built on.

Four Charlestown coves, at Howley's Corner. L-R: My brother, Tom Dunleavy, James Jordan, Gerald Healy and Johnny Fitzpatrick, the blacksmith's son.

Peter Murray and my brother, Tom, with Peter's two boys, Jerry and Pat. Jerry is our Sinn Fein councillor. Picture taken outside Murray's pub, which is still going strong!

My brother, Louie, with his old Hillman, and Barrack Street man, Sean Foley.

Murphy's Garage, Charlestown. L-R: Sean Sullivan, John Mahon, Paddy O'Donnell, 'Franie' Murphy. James Jordan, Frank Connington. Martin Murphy (garage owner) and a young, barefooted Mahon boy.

Early days in Liverpool, at 12 Hemer Terrace, Bootle. Pictured with me in the back yard are my older brother, Luke (Louie) and Mai, the oldest of all the Dunleavy children.

Seamus' wife, Mary, with Travellers, in Charlestown.

Seamus meets the
'King of the Travellers',
Charlie Ward.

Seamus, with a group of Travelling People, who lived
around Charlestown.

Seamus revisits the Charlestown Ball Alley of his youth. The young players are
Brian Colleran, his brother, Lukie, and some Maloney lads. The 'S' in the bottom
right-hand corner marks the beginning of Seamus' name, which he inscribed on the
wall, years before, below his drawing of a boxer.

The Travellers were in Charlestown around 1960/61, when the various photos were taken with Mary and Seamus. Charlie Ward is on the far left.

Seamus with Garda, Sean Riley (deceased).

Mary and Seamus with relations, Kate Dunleavy and her daughter-in-law, outside Kate's comfortable farmhouse in Glann, Kilkelly. The turf shed to their right contains their fuel supply for the year.

Charlestown - from a different angle! Seamus, c. 1961

Pictured in front of the old town hall, Charlestown, on the back row, from left to right: John Fitzpatrick, Eddie Tunney and Mickey Dunleavy. Kneeling, on the front row: Peter Duffy (deceased), Padaher Frain and John Mahon.

"Please let me go to the toilet girls!" Seamus, with his sisters, Angela and Monica.

Seventeen-year-old Mary, outside the Pontoon Ballroom, with Seamus, who, at twenty-six, was nine years older than her.

The first photo ever, of Seamus and Mary, taken at the Shamrock Club in Birmingham.

Seamus with Paddy Faul, from Tubbercurry, who first introduced Seamus to Mary, at the Shamrock.

Mary and Seamus at the dancehall, when they were still single.

Engagement photograph, July 1961.

Mary's twin sisters, Monica and Carmel.

Mary Kate Dunleavy was laid to rest, on 4 July 1959 in the Family Plot at Carrycastle.

*Wedding Group Photo of the
Dunleavys: Seamus' father, Michael,
is the one with the electric hair!
Back row L-R: Brothers, Paddy
(deceased), Tommy and Mickey.
Front row: Sisters, Kathleen,
Monica, Mai and daughter
Joanne, myself and Angela.*

*Mary and Seamus' wedding,
on 16 April 1963.*

*Mickey's wife, Margaret, who became a
famous dance teacher, with their son,
'Puggy', outside the Dunleavy's Barrack
Street shop.*

*Early picture of Mary, and daughter,
Tracey, c. February 1964.*

Putting a wrestling hold on neighbour, Tom McDonnell, in Barrack Street, Charlestown.

Holidays abroad: Mary and daughter, Tracey.

The Dunleavys in Galway: L-R: brother, Tom, Uncle Jim - hotel owner, Seamus and Jim's son, Eugene.

Jim Irwin, Mick Dunleavy and Johnny Brehany, in Barrack Street.

Seamus with Mary Tunney, mother of Eddie, his fellow Jelly Thief!

Chief Shamrock doorman, Joe Enright, flanked by a very youthful Seamus and his brother Mickey.

English Heavyweight Champion, Billy Joyce, about to do battle with Seamus, in Malvern. The referee is Billy Riley.

Seamus - in all his glory!

Old opponents, Joe Kovacs -'The Butcher of Budapest', and Seamus.

Seamus, flanked by fellow wrestlers John Lees, to his left, and Eric Taylor, on the right.

Joe Keegan - about to hit the deck!

Two sets of brothers in a Tag Match. Mickey and Seamus are momentarily 'floored' by the Cadman Brothers.

L-R: Mickey, Jack Atherton and Seamus, at the end of a match.

✳ **PROGRAMME** ✳

10 x 5 Minute Rounds HEAVYWEIGHT CONTEST
2 submissions, 2 falls or 1 knock-out to decide.

SEAMUS DUNLEAVY v. BILL HOWES

(Charlestown and Birmingham) Irish Heavyweight   Contender for British Mid Heavyweight title.
Has fought some of Europe's best.

8 x 5 Minute Rounds

MIKE DUNLEAVY	**TIGER RYAN**
(CHARLESTOWN)	(TIPPERARY)
	Irish official Welterweight Champion,
versus	versus
BRIAN BURKE	**KEITH WILLIAMSON**
(NEWTON)	(BOLTON)
Northern Area Middleweight Champion.	Rough and tough.

8 x 5 Minute Rounds

Referee—ERNIE HOBBS	M.C.—PATSY DUNNE.
(Specially appointed by the Wrestling Board of Control)	Official Timekeeper—SEAN WALSHE.

All for Dad: *Bill Riley and Jack Atherton staged a special Charlestown wrestling tournament, on the Dunleavy Brothers' behalf, as their father, Mick, had never seen them in a live wrestling match before.*

Picture taken in Charlestown, one Sunday after mass. Back row, from L-R: J. McIntyre, somebody, Tom Brennan, M. Horkan, Mrs. Doherty. Middle row: two people not recognised, Pakie Joe Brennan, Patsy Dunne. The seven young lads are not known to myself.

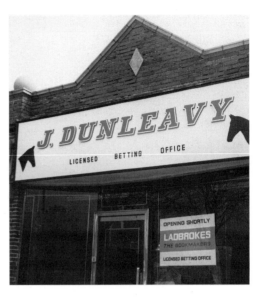

Seamus with a fellow Charlestown man, before the start of St Patrick's Day celebrations in Birmingham.

One of Seamus' three former betting shops.

Seamus' brother, Paddy Dunleavy, in Aden, second from the right.

– "but if you're back here in three weeks' time, we'll play it for you then!" That would give you time to practice it. I could read a bit of music then, so I used to send away for the sheet music and after three or four hours, I could play it. But those were happy days – and paid for as well. It was absolutely great fun, because some tunes you'd get off very well, and you'd start together and finish together, so that gave you a great sense of achievement.

Tom, the middle brother of five, was now getting ready for England. Meanwhile, Pa had decided that he himself would live at home; there was great joy when he decided to do so. We had a yard at the back of the house, so where most people have gardens, *we* had a big shed: a workshop, open on two sides. He started to make horse and donkey carts and to do general building work around the town. It was a bit strange at first, having him at home; there was a bit more discipline and we had to work harder. But of course, nobody had any money, so financially our lot did not improve much. Brother Tom had left for England, but came back after a few months. Pa was scraping a living, but my two brothers, Tom and Mickey, became very good tradesmen – they really could turn their hand to anything. However, *my* interests lay elsewhere.

I always dreamed of England and the riches and the nice clothes. You would see them coming home with their gabardine coats, gloves, cigarette lighters and cigarette cases. I was useless as a carpenter, could not plaster so good, and knew nothing about plumbing. It was all weight lifting and chest expanders. Pa continued to say: "What will you do when you go to England Seamus?" But I knew I would be a great boxer and make lots of money.

I was now fifteen or sixteen and getting very itchy feet. Tom and Mickey seemed happy enough at home, but we were getting nowhere and I wanted to get away. So at just seventeen, I went up to Mike Doherty in Chapel Street and got my passport photograph taken. Funnily enough, I had my passport for years after, but eventually lost it. I wore an open-necked shirt, and a jacket, which we had bought second-hand, at Sonny Whittington's second-hand clothes shop. The 'V' in my cotton pullover was stretched so much that it was nearly down to my navel, so Mammy sewed it nearly all the way up. You could see it very clearly in the passport photograph. How I would love to see my old passport now… I must say a prayer to Saint Anthony!

I remember getting my passport together. When Mammy saw it she said: "Seamus, are you really serious?" I said: "Mom, I am going." I was leapfrogging Mickey, who was older than me, and Tom, who had already been away, but come back.

So, in 1952, I went down Barrack Street, to the Square, and got on the Dublin bus, with my cardboard suitcase, and £6 in my pocket. As the bus came up Barrack Street and passed my own house, where Mammy gave me life, seventeen years before, she waved me off. I cannot remember Pa actually being there, although he probably was, because the rest of the family was present.

The big adventure had started. Ironically, who was on the bus that morning, but Jimmy-Joe Mulligan, the trumpet player from the old band! He was going to Wigan, where one of his brothers was sick. He had a flute with him, so we would have a bit of music on the boat. I did not know anybody else on the bus, and, to begin with, I was not sitting with Jimmy-Joe; but further up towards Dublin, when a few got off, we were able to sit together.

As the bus left Charlestown, I began reflecting on my life there. I had never had a new suit in my life and never owned an overcoat. Fifth Class in school, no trade, but very strong and fit. I weighed about twelve-and-a-half stone, so I would be a Middle or Light-Heavyweight boxer.

We arrived in Dublin about four o'clock in the afternoon. First time I had been to a city and it was drummed into me to watch my money and not talk to anybody. I was bad enough, but Jimmy-Joe, who was thirty-five years old, was terrified! Dublin at that time had about half a million people and Charlestown only three to four hundred. First time for me to see a double-decker bus… and hear the strange accents.

Well, it was like the blind leading the blind. Jimmy-Joe had never been to England either, so we were both frightened and confused. We eventually got to the docks, and there was the boat to England. A mixture of sadness and delight engulfed me, for this was not the boat I had heard so much about, the famous *Princess Maud*. Whoever Maud was, she must have been somebody Royal. According to Shirley, Princess Maud of Wales was one of Queen Victoria's granddaughters. I had heard about *Princess Maud*, all my life, from the immigrants around Charlestown – the rough conditions, seasickness, fights, dancing on deck, hopelessness – most leaving with nothing but the fare – to the farmlands of Lincolnshire.

As a youngster I'd imagined the *Maud* almost as a rowing boat, rather than the big ship that she was. After the original *Mutiny on the Bounty*, starring Charles Laughton, I then imagined her as a sailing ship, commanded by the cruel Captain Bligh!

When Martin Higgins, a friend of Mammy's, was due to return to Ireland, via Holyhead, he'd say it was "great to see the old girl." But when he had to make the return journey back to England, it was: "I hate the sight of that f*** *Princess Maud*!"

However, the vessel that awaited me was a passenger and freight-carrying ship, which, as far as I can recall, belonged to the *B & I Line*, as I was bound for the Liverpool Docks, not Holyhead, in North Wales. So, my voyage on the *Princess Maud* would have to wait, until another time, although I was to travel on her several times in the future.

When we were growing up, we became very familiar with towns like Skipton, Boston, Sleaford, Spalding, Lincoln and the flat, flat lands of Norfolk, through the accounts of those who returned. The indescribable fens of East Anglia – the fen fields as flat as a pancake – and as far as the eye could see. It was wet, boggy land, but great for sugar beet. The stories of lads around Charlestown, picking the beet! A beet in each hand – knock the two together, to knock the soil off, then top-and-tail, with a machete-like knife, and into a rope basket, called a creel. When that was full, you threw the containers into a trailer, pulled by a moving tractor. If the weather was bad and wet and you had pulled two beets, one in each hand, you had about six-stone in your hands. Do that all day, and you would *definitely* sleep at night!

It was no First Class accommodation either. When they were finished, they would sleep in the farmer's barn. They were given a bundle of straw and that was their bed. Anybody that pulled one beet, and left the other hand free, would be run off the fields! You could not let the tractor and trailer get ahead. But I was not going to the farming. I was going to Liverpool and would be a great boxing champion!

We were at home last year, and went into this pub, in Charlestown, which was very close to where I was born. The pub of course had changed hands since my time and had new owners. There was just me and Mary and the lady behind the bar. We got chatting and I said: "You don't know me, but I lived just up the road." (Fifty years had leapt since that time, of course). "But the first person who walks in the pub will know me." The door opened and this fella came in. He spoke to her but he didn't know me. She said: "Now, he's not from this town." But the second man that came in was Tommy Haran, from Tavneena. "Jesus Tommy – how are you?" "How are you Seamus?" We got talking about England. I said, "I was in Stamford Lincolnshire the other day," (which I was). He said: "I used to do Stamford, I can tell you the name of the farm." And we got talking Shirley, he told me the name of the farm that he used to go to, every year – him and two or three lads from Charlestown, and two or three lads from Achill Island.

He is the same age as myself. I hadn't seen Tommy for years and years and years. I said: "Tommy, what was it like?" "Well," he said, "we'd arrive at the farm in Lincolnshire," and he described what I've told you about 'as far as the eye could see.' "We'd sleep on the straw bales and we had a blanket. The farmer really wasn't bad to us. We'd go to the local shop in the village and get all our stuff and pay every week." I said: "Could you sleep Tommy?" He said," I used to sleep like a log. Now, I've a good bed and I can't sleep." He's over seventy, but he'd have been so worn out in those days, that he'd go straight to sleep. He said: "The farmer used to like to see a whole gang of workers and if he saw them going to Mass, he'd say to himself: 'Those lads are alright.' " If you'd any religion you wouldn't be a hobo. But Tommy said that some of the lads would let the side down. "We'd pay the shop every week, for the food we had, but the last week, one or two of the lads would skip off, and wouldn't pay." The farmer would pick up the bill in those cases – it wouldn't be a lot. But that was his experience of farming in England. He did that for ten years, then went into building, in Dublin.

There was a father, mother and three or four sons from Charlestown, called the Durkin family. They had a mule, which was a cross between a mare and a donkey. There's also a 'jennet', which is the other way round: the product of a horse having sex with a female donkey. So this family had a mule with a cart. They liked a drop of beer and before going into the pub, they always tied the mule and cart somewhere. They might end up at a different pub, eventually and have to collect the mule and cart in Barrack Street. But they were working in Lincoln or Spalding. This time they came out of the pub and Mrs. Durkin said to Michael: "I don't know where we've tied the mule!" Of course, the mule and cart were back in Ireland, but she was a bit tipsy: "Where for the life of me have we tied the mule?!"

So we got out tickets and we were on the boat. Now, when I returned home again, although I could not talk about the *Princess Maud*, (that would come later when I made the Holyhead crossing), like all the great working men who left Charlestown, I was on board ship. I was their equal – a man. The boat was packed. The few seats that were available were taken, so we had to sit on the suitcases. The leaving of Dublin was sad. I could see the lights for a long time, as we set sail. Then, when we were a few hours out, somebody started to play a melodeon and somebody else sang a lonesome song:

> *Good-bye Johnnie dear,*
> *When you are far away*
> *Don't forget your mother,*
> *Far across the sea.*
> *Write a letter now and then and*
> *Send her all you can*
> *And don't forget, where'ere you roam*
> *That you are an Irishman*

Chapter Eight

BIRKENHEAD SUNSETS

The voyage was a particularly poignant one, as Seamus was leaving home for the very first time. Jimmy-Joe Mulligan was simply going over to visit friends. But for Seamus, although the adventure had certainly started, it was also a bit intimidating… there was no way of telling what awaited him, at the end of the line. But that night, people were dancing and enjoying themselves. All the passengers got involved, and the 'craic' was great.

My eyes were welling up with tears when Jimmy-Joe, who was going to Wigan, opened his case and got his wooden flute out and joined up with the accordion, and a few dancers started to waltz on deck. Some of the older people had a few drinks and there was a good session going presently. Nearly everybody was on top deck and the craic was good. Although it's spelt 'craic', it's pronounced 'crack', which is becoming an accepted word in the English language now. You know, a lot of people will say: "The craic was great." That means: "The fun was great." If we had a good session here Shirley, laughing, talking and joking, and perhaps a few drinks, we'd say, "It was great craic," – absolutely! It means that everybody enjoyed themselves. It's almost been assimilated into the English language now – I hear a lot of English people coming out with it – great excitement – great fun! We say if someone's had a party: "What was the craic like?" You've got to be careful, of course, because 'crack' can actually mean cocaine too. So you could be asking: "What were the drugs like!" I was talking to Jim Noone, Mary's cousin, in America recently, about that. He said: "It means heavy 'coke' over here!"

As the night wore on, we drifted away, one by one, and somebody sang that very lonesome song – *Goodbye Johnnie Dear*, which drew our previous chapter to its close. That was the very first time I went over, but I made the trip several times afterwards: every time I went over, there would always be a 'session' on the top, with music and singing, especially Ceilidh music; there'd be two or three people playing instruments. It was often very informal. Irish music is often called a Session, and that's what we had on the trips over.

After a few hours out, it became very cold. Most of the older men had tried to have a sleep and eventually the musicians called it a night. Jimmy-Joe and myself tried to settle for the night; he had a heavy overcoat but I had none. I must have nodded off a time or two. A woman beside me became violently seasick, then all of a sudden, every other person seemed to be sick also. It was like the 'Domino Effect'! I went off to the toilets and the floor was covered with in vomit. That was enough for me – I vomited my guts up! I was never so sick in my life!

We docked in Liverpool at about 6.00am in the morning and had to queue for a long time, to get off; I was tired and sick – and glad we were in. When I got off, I said goodbye to Jimmy-Joe as he was off to Wigan. His brother was meeting him and picked him up right away. My brother-in-law, Sean McConnell, was supposed to meet me, so I waited for half an hour, but no sight of him. An hour passed and still no sight of Sean. They had no phone, and anyway, I had never used a phone in my life, so I was completely lost in the middle of the docks in Liverpool. The only address I had was number 12, Hemer Terrace. I now know it was 12 Hemer Terrace, Bootle, but I did not have Bootle on the address. So in the middle of the city, naturally, nobody knew where Hemer Terrace was. All I knew was that it was in Liverpool! I moved away from the pier head, started walking and eventually reached the city centre.

I remember the huge tall buildings, and everything. But for the life of me, I cannot understand how I managed to find 12 Hemer Terrace, Bootle, because it was four or five miles away from the city centre, so nobody knew. I saw the famous Liver Birds building with what looked like swans on top. I recall a terrific amount of people – all hustling and bustling about – which added to my confusion, as I was used to a terribly small town.

Eventually, I asked yet another person for directions to Hemer Terrace. He took me to a bus stop. I got on and paid. The conductor thought he knew which direction I should be going in, but when the bus had gone one stop, and stopped, I thought I had to get off. So I attempted to get off the bus, but the bus conductor told me to sit down and wait. Everybody I spoke to called me "Pat" or "Paddy". Although I was put off the bus and given some directions, when the bus pulled away I was lost in minutes. Every street looked exactly the same – rows and rows of redbrick houses. I'd left the boat at 6.00am and it was now 12 o'clock midday. That had been six hours ago and I *still* did not know where I was.

To make matters worse, just at that point my suitcase handle broke! The old case was just cardboard anyway, so now it was up on my shoulder. My brother Tom had told me that when I got to 12 Hemer Terrace, it had a yellow door, so that was the only information that I had. I must have looked at every yellow and off-yellow door in Liverpool. It is crazy, because now I know that I should have asked the police. I am sure that nowadays, with my limited address, they would have found out where it was, or where it was supposed to be, by using the *A to Z*.

I had a lot of trouble with the Liverpool accent. It was the first time I had heard it and I really could not make 'head or tail' of it, nor them of me. To this day, I will never know how I found that yellow door! But I eventually found myself walking across a huge cleared bombsite. In the distance, I could see a row of houses, stretching out, like a long ribbon. Somebody must have pointed me in the right direction. As I approached, I could indeed see that one of the doors was painted marigold yellow, and before I reached it, (I was a good way off, with my suitcase on my shoulder), the door opened and somebody looked towards me, in the distance. As we both walked towards each other, the person started to run and shout: "Seamus!" It was my sister Mai, and I was found… or I had found them!

She threw her arms around me and I cannot tell you how I felt! Tears and hugs and joy. She took me and my battered case into the house. The time was either ten or fifteen minutes to three, in the afternoon. So I got off the boat at 6.00am and reached number 12 Hemer Terrace Bootle at ten to three in the afternoon. I had taken me nine hours to find them!

I remember it vividly – the door opening and Mai coming across the bombsite; the feeling of euphoria was tremendous. To be totally lost was very strange: we weren't in the jungle or anything, we were in a city – but it was desperate! Everything was the same: the buses were all the same colour, people coming and going; rows of identical houses.

Mai's husband Sean had slept a bit late and by the time he had reached the boat, I was gone. There was also a bit of confusion, as Sean reckoned it was the day *after* that I was expected! But nevertheless, I was safe. When I left Charlestown, there were no numbers on the houses: everyone knew everyone else, you see? I said: "How can you tell the difference between the houses?" But they did it by numbers.

As you know, I had a passport at the time Shirley, to get into England; you don't have it now, but in those days you did. I'll tell you a funny story about my dad. I was born on 28 November 1934, so that was shown on the passport. But Pa said that I wouldn't get a man's wages because I'd be too young. That wasn't true really, because you were never to show your passport. So he got a piece of white bread, erased the 'four' and put down 'two'. Of course, the ink spread, because a blind man could see that it was a sort of a forgery! It was an official document and really, I suppose, if I'd had to show it I could have been in a bit of trouble.

I never had to show it, but for a substantial part of my life I had to pretend that I was born in 1932, whereas in fact I was born in 1934. The lie kept alive all through the years, until I was sixty-three and my pension was due in two years' time. My accountant said: "Seamus, you have to go right, and tell them your proper age." So we didn't take the pension until two years after, when I was legitimately sixty-five. Although it was offered to me when I was sixty-three, I declined it.

My sister Mai had taken over the old post-war house from Pa, who used to share it with an old Galway man named Mick Madden. Pa, of course, had gone home, so my sister Mai took over. Mick Madden still lived there. It was rented from somebody who I never saw. Mai paid the rent. It was eleven shillings per week (60p today). Mick Madden gave her four shillings. He lived upstairs and would come downstairs to share our kitchen.

But back to me arriving. My sister Mai put on a great fry-up. It was the first time I had baked beans and I thought they were beautiful, if that is the right word to describe beans!

We always believed that there was no food in England, because everybody who came home would always say it was great to get a bit of proper food. So I did not know what to expect.

Mai had a coal fire – I had never seen one before. But it made a lovely fire – a lot warmer than the turf or peat at home. She always used sterilised milk and I really hated that. I never got used to it and still hate it. Mai said she never saw anyone eat so much, but I was starved after walking all day. I loved English bread as well – I will never forget *Mother's Pride* bread: it was sliced nice and thin and I loved it.

I should have slept well that night, after all the walking, but Mai's house was right in the middle of the docks. Liverpool was a thriving port at the time, so the ships' horns would be sounding off all through the night. We were right in the docks, so it was *really* loud. I swear that the walls of the house used to vibrate! So as tired as I was, I could not sleep. You would just be nodding off, when another ship blew her siren. The following morning, I asked them about the ships' horns. Sean and Mai said: "What ships?" They were so used to it, it did not bother them at all.

They took me to town – to the centre of Liverpool – and this was the first time that I had seen an English double-decker bus, as opposed to a Dublin one. So they took me upstairs and that was an experience! I had come from a small town, but this was something extraordinary. I was amazed when we got back on the bus, that they knew when to get off! Then on the way back, getting off again and coming home, every street seemed to be exactly the same.

They had gas lighting in their house and a gas cooker. I was very wary of the gas cooker, because I had heard tales of them blowing up. You'd always to let it run a few seconds before putting a match to it. That part of it terrified me. We were not too far after the war, those years, so there were likely to have been some damaged gas mains remaining, in many cities.

I cannot remember if we had a bathroom or not. With the gas mantle lighting, all the rooms in the house were always in semi-darkness. So it was a sort of Sherlock Holmes-type atmosphere… rather spooky, with shadows on the wall. When you come from a background of superstition and ghosts and everything, you'd always be watching the shadows. Like horror films where shadows fell across people's faces! Mai used to put the coal under the stairs. It was pitch-black down there, because there was no lighting. So as I would be scooping it up, I always imagined a rat being scooped up into the bucket as well. But there *were* no rats.

Mai kept me and did not charge me anything for food. After about a week Sean, Mai's husband, got me a job with him. It was in a place called Kirby. We had to catch a bus and a tram. I had awful trouble finding my way back to Hemer Terrace. Again, the houses being all the same, it was: "Oh my God!" But Sean was with me.

I was a general labourer and found the work very hard. We were building a factory and the firm I worked for was *Jones's*. I would be very tired at night and remember being very hungry. My appetite seemed to have increased. I used to *devour* the dinner in the evening. Mai reckoned she never saw a person eat like me. I was young and still growing. Also the work was regimented: you'd start off at eight o'clock in the morning and might still be working at 6pm. I'd be very tired, because at seventeen, I wasn't yet a man. I was working beside men who were much older than me. I was just a kid.

At that stage there was no time or energy for anything like body-building. Even my son, Russell, who was a very good amateur wrestler and is now a carpenter, gets very tired. He said that if he'd been training in Russia or America, he could have been training full time, and maybe have eventually become an Olympic Champion. But in England, they don't have that system. My other son, Shamus, is a very big lad, but he's very 'laid back', so he didn't become a wrestler.

We lived close to the shore of the River Mersey in Bootle and I liked that a lot. I would go out to the sand dunes at Crosby most evenings. I was very lonely and missed home a lot – and my brothers. I used to shed many a tear. I had made no friends yet. The shore was quite deserted; you wouldn't see a dozen people out there. You'd be looking across to Birkenhead (as opposed to Liverpool), as you watched the sunsets; the River Mersey flows out to the sea from there. I enjoyed watching the different boats sail by. I knew all of the docks in Liverpool, and could name them all, right into the pier head. You would hear them say, "Such-a-ship is in," – the *Empress of Scotland*, the *Empress of Canada*. They were big boats and very well known.

As I walked along the sands at Bootle, I'd daydream about how I was going to be famous one day, by becoming a famous boxer, and make Mammy and Pa very comfortable. I was very lonesome for the first year or two in England. I had no friends at the time – no mates – and I'd think about the 'Old Country', and about other lads who'd left Ireland, mostly for London – and what *they* might be doing. I missed the rest of my family and the fact that, had I been in Charlestown, I'd have been able to go home of a night time and have tea. But I was writing regularly to my parents, so at least I had the comfort of letters going back and forth between us.

The first pay packet I got was about £6-00. I used to send £2-00 home to Mammy, and started to pay Mai £1-00 a week for my board. For the first time ever, I had money in my pocket. I felt like a king! When I had enough saved up I bought my first suit from a tailor's shop called *Roberts and Bromley Outfitters*, in the city centre, on London Road: a beautiful blue striped suit and a polar-neck jumper. I thought and felt like a film star. There was a picture out at that time called *The Al Jolson Story*, starring Larry Parkes. He wore a suit and a polo-neck jumper, on the film poster, so I thought to myself: 'I'm like Larry Parkes!'

My older brother Louie had been working up in Scotland and came down to Liverpool, so things got better. We would go to the cinema a lot. My job became less of a problem, as I got used to the work, although if Sean was not there, I could not find my way home; it was so different to Charlestown. But eventually, I kept my eyes open and could get the 24 bus to town and come back by myself. Getting to work was still difficult. I had to catch a bus, get off at the stop after the biscuit factory and then get a tram. But as time went by, I conquered that as well. There was a big pub where the East Lancs Road crossed; the tram stopped there and I'd then walk to the bus. Once or twice I panicked because I'd gone past the pub, on the bus. To this day, I'm useless. If I'm driving a car, I might go off the road two or three times, before I find the right route. Mary is brilliant at finding her way to places, but I'm hopeless at remembering landmarks and other details.

Sean had by that time finished his job and I was making my own way there. I still remember a lot of the faces that I worked with. As it is now over fifty years since I worked there, I suppose most of the older ones are dead. I remember a fella named Matt Riley from outside Castlebar – a village called Borradrumough. He was an older man – a charge-hand. I heard him say one day: "That's a lovely bit of concrete!" But looking back he was right: there's good and bad concrete. He worked all his life with it.

Then there was a lad, about six foot three, called 'Lofty'. 'Daft-as-a-brush'; he despaired sometimes – about himself! Although he was only thirteen stone, he'd say: "Ah – I'd have been a good Heavyweight, if I'd been trained!" He had a very good mate named Geoff. In those days if you were short, you were 'Shorty'; if you were tall you were 'Lofty'. I can still see all the faces on that very first job. There was another lad called Eric.

In those days, the canteen conversation was all about football – Liverpool and Everton – but I didn't know a *thing* about football. "What about the game last night then Pat?" (Liverpudlian accent). So as far as the other labourers were concerned I'd never lived at all – because I knew nothing about football! Our football teams back home were Sligo, Mayo, Roscommon and Galway – Gaelic Football, which was different altogether. Also, I seemed to be the only Irish lad on the job – which would have been totally unusual.

But maybe if I'd investigated further? Come to think of it, there *was* one young lad who was a brickie's apprentice – 'Sully' (which would *have* to be Sullivan). He was certainly Irish, because I remember, one St. Patrick's Day, he wore a shamrock. There was a big division on the job, between bricklayers and labourers, which has stuck with me ever since. The bricklayers were paid better, for a start. I put one of my sons into bricklaying – which is the worst trade in the whole of England – because you work for a week, until the job is finished, and then you move somewhere else. What a trade to go into Shirley – I must have been mad!

After being in England for about six months, I discovered a club called *Duffy's Boxing Club*, in an area called Litherland. It was a very good club – semi-pro. They had a few area champions and they trained amateurs as well. The boxers trained three nights and the other three nights there was wrestling training, in the same building – that was called *The Pegasus Wrestling Club*. Well, I joined and started training. My brother Mickey, who was next to me in the family, but older, had come across to Liverpool, and joined the club too.

After getting fit, with skipping, running and bag-punching, we started to spar with the rest of the club. Remember, I was going to be a boxing champion and make all this money! But alas, it was going to be a wee bit more difficult than I had thought. I was built very short and strong, but it meant I was always sparring with boys who were six to nine inches taller, with longer arms. There was always a 'straight-left' stuck in my face. When I got closer in, I always had the inclination to pick the lad up and throw him to the ground … but you can't do that!

My brother Mickey was doing a lot better, so after a few months I went to the club on the wrestling night and they invited me to have a go. So I started the amateur wrestling. Now this was a lot better. I could use my strength to greater advantage. My physique was much more suited to wrestling than to boxing, so I switched to the *Pegasus Club*. My job in Kirby was finished and I was laid off.

The next job I got was at a place called Netherton, a suburb of Liverpool. They were building a jet factory, and the work was easier. I was going to make a lot of money, win big fights, and look after me parents very well. The main contractor was William Moss. I was behind a big concrete mixer: myself and another man filled the hopper with two barrows of sand, two batches of stony pebbles and two bags of cement. We would be at that all day when the concreting was being done. A bit different to today, when you get your lorries of *Readimix*. There was a canteen on this job. You would buy tickets for your main course and sweet. I remember often eating three dinners and three sweets – I could not get enough! When I finished work in the evening I was always in the gym now.

It turned out that the other three nights at the club were for wrestling, so I went to the Amateur Wrestling. There I found that I could use my strength the way I wanted. I stuck at the Amateur Wrestling for a few years. After about eight or nine months, the club entered me for the *Northern Counties Championship*, which was held in Bark Street Bolton, Lancashire. My trainer was Gerry Grant, a Liverpool man.

I won the first couple of matches and wrestled through to the finals. Then I met the bold Bert Owen, who was the reigning *Northern Counties Champion*. He beat me after about eight minutes, which was not so bad. The trainer was very pleased because the new area champions and their runners-up automatically qualified for the *All England* Championships, which were due to be held three or four months later, at the *Empress Hall* in London. Also, all the Commonwealth countries would be sending their champions too, so it was a big event. But I'll come back to that.

On the run-up to the *All England Championships*, the *Bootle Times* sent a reporter round to the house and they did a little piece about my wrestling. You can imagine my joy and surprise when I got the *Bootle Times* and there was a story about me... and a picture! Well, now I thought I was famous. To top it all the General Foreman on the job pulled me up one day afterwards and wished me well for the championships. Well, for the GF to speak to you was really something! The first thing I did was to send the paper to my parents. They were delighted. So... the trainer and myself set off for London.

Chapter Nine

THE EMPRESS

The Empress Hall was huge. When Seamus and his trainer, Gerry Grant, arrived, the best amateur wrestlers from all over England and the Commonwealth were assembled there. There seemed to be hundreds of them. Seamus was wrestling Middleweight (twelve-and-a-half stones). The wrestling weights are heavier than in boxing. Middleweight in boxing would be eleven-and-a-half stone.

Ken Richmond, the man who strikes the gong, at the start of the J. Arthur Rank pictures, was there. He was the Heavyweight Champion nine times in succession – a wrestling legend in his own lifetime. He had also competed in the Olympics and had won a silver medal – beaten for gold by a Russian. I was fascinated by it all.

Ken, who was a Canadian by birth, took on challengers for the title every year. He was a natural, well-built man; we all had weightlifters bodies, but he had the *natural* build for it. He also played walk-on parts in British films; a terrific looking man and that day, he won the championship, while I was there, in *minutes*. He was a big, 17-stone fit man and a great athlete.

To start off, we all had to march around the arena with our name on a badge, to the tune of *The Gladiators*. It was very moving. Also, the greatest of all wrestling heroes was introduced to the ring – the Great George Hackenschmidt, the famous Russian champion. George was a very old man when I met him, but he was one of the 'Greats'. In his time, he drew up to 100,000 people, with matches with Frank Gotch, you know, of the Great Americas. Coincidentally, Shirley discovered, on an international website the other day that a match was being held in Frank Gotch's memory.

When I was growing up in Ireland, Tom Henry, an old stonemason, used to sing a song about George Hackenschmidt. I can only remember a little of it, but it went something like this:

> *When Hackenschmidt wrestled with me*
> *He'd a hand like the branch of a tree*

He threw me so high
That I reached the sky
And he mixed up my dinner and tea.

That's all I can remember, but it was great to meet him. You grew up hearing the songs about him, then all of a sudden, there he was – in front of you! He was a squat man, but very broad – he weighed about 200lbs in his heyday.

Like myself, former wrestler Bill (aka Wayne) Bridges also recalls meeting George at a wrestling championship in London, in the early 1960s. In Bill's case the venue was Manor Place Baths, where Bill was competing in the *British Championships*. Despite his age, George, who was known as 'The Russian Lion', was more than happy to go on the mat with Bill, Jimmy Brown and at least one other young wrestler.

Bill recalls: "George was immaculately dressed in a suit and waistcoat. He was wearing a 'Rollaway Hat', which was a Trilby, with a rolled-up brim. He took the hat off, put it on a chair, kicked his shoes off and removed his jacket and waistcoat. Then, with his braces dangling, he was ready for action. He even advised me about how I should have tackled a certain move, to beat my opponent, after I had just lost!"

According to Bill, George is buried in Thornton Heath, near Dulwich. He was born Georges Karl Hackenschmidt, in 1878, at Dorpat, in the province of Estonia, and was of Swedish descent.

So, the wrestling for the *All England Championships* started. The draw was made and the first bout I had was against a fellow called Wilson from York, who I beat. One fall. Later in the day I wrestled Lowery who was the Australian champion. Beat him also. One fall. Then my old foe for the third match, Bert Owen from Bolton, who had beaten me in the *Northern Counties*. Well, this time I got the better of him and won on points! Then the prelims were over and I went out, and we had something to eat.

My trainer said I was on course, so now the evening part arrived, the place is full and Ken Richmond had pinned everybody he met! My next match was against Harry Kendal, a deaf mute, who has been champion of England twice. We wrestled for about five minutes, and I was doing alright, but he got a fall in the ninth minute and became champion again, for the third time. So my aspirations were over for that year. As the years went by, I was to meet Harry Kendal again, but that was a long way off yet.

Gerry Grant said: "Next year you'll definitely have a chance of winning." But I never competed the following year. I went home to Ireland for a few months.

Meanwhile, I started to go dancing in Liverpool. I'd found an Irish Dancehall called *The Shamrock* in Lime Street, in the centre of Liverpool, where I went most Saturday nights. It was OK, but I never met anyone that I went out with there. Later on, we started to go to *Saint James* or *Saint Jimmy's*, as it was called. It was a Catholic club or dance, run by a big Cork priest called Father O'Sullivan. This was very near where I lived, so we could walk there – no bus. I loved *Saint Jimmy's*, and got to know some lovely girls; several of the lads boxed a bit, so we had a lot in common. I'll be telling you more about all of that, in Chapter Eleven.

Christmas was now approaching. Mickey, Paddy, Louie and myself were all going home. Tom had stayed at home, after returning from England. But first we had to get the 'gear', as they say in Liverpool! I had bought a gabardine overcoat – the first one I ever owned – a scarf, and a pair of leather gloves. That was the way you were supposed to come home, after being in England for a while. I think I had about £80 or £90 saved and don't forget – I sent home money every week, to keep the home fires burning.

We all arrived in Dublin, and had a meal at the *Green Rooster*, a café-cum-restaurant. We felt like kings! We had the gear on – the coats – and money in the pocket. Then we got the bus, to take us down to Mayo, which was about a four-hour journey. You broke at Longford, which was the halfway point of the journey. We had an hour's break there to go to the toilets, have a snack and whatever. Then the rest of the journey took you to the hometown.

When we arrived in Charlestown, there was great excitement. Everybody shook your hand when you came home. The Christmas dances at home were marvellous… and the stories around the fire, in the kitchen. Some said I had got bigger – put weight on – and so forth. My Uncle Jim was there too. He reckoned he was a great wrestler in his youth – a 'hand under and a hand over' wrestling version. Well, the week, or ten days at Christmas went quickly, and I was back in Liverpool again.

The jet factory was nearing the end as well, so my brother Paddy, who was a skilled carpenter, said I should go to his job and ask for a job as a chippy's labourer. This job was over the water – a Liverpool expression for across the Mersey. It was a place called Eastham, where Sir Alfred McAlpine was building a new dock…

Chapter Ten

CYCLING UNDER THE MERSEY

Seamus' brother, Paddy, was already employed on the job, as a skilled carpenter, building Sir Alfred McAlpine's new dock. The two brothers travelled across to Eastham. Seamus can still recall the journey vividly – they had to take two trains and a bus, to reach their destination. Paddy instructed him to ask for a man called Tom Baylis, the Foreman Carpenter, on arrival. Tom had fifteen to twenty charge-hands underneath him, looking after around a hundred carpenters and labourers.

I asked Paddy how I would know Tom. He said: "Well, he'll be wearing a new donkey jacket and a flat cap." So I asked several people: "Are you Mr. Tom Baylis?" Eventually one of them said: "I am." Tom spoke with a Devonshire accent. He said: "What do you do?" I said: "I'm a chippy's labourer." Paddy had explained that every two carpenters had a labourer to help them. He said: "Fine – when can you start?" I said: "Whenever." He said: "Come here at eight o'clock tomorrow morning and bring your Employment Card with you."

So I started there the morning after, and I was put with two carpenters. One of them was a Welshman, called Bill, but known to everyone as Taffy – they were always called Taffy – and the other one was an Englishman called Ronnie. He was a Liverpudlian. So I worked with them and I didn't find the work very hard. It was a lot easier than the pick and shovel labouring. It was like a step up, actually. I had to carry their tools from our shanty to the place of work; that could be a quarter of a mile away. So I helped them during the day and fetched the tea and sandwiches.

Taffy was very friendly. He had left Wales, and his family was in Birkenhead. At the tail end of the day we'd be filling huge sections with concrete; there was a *huge* amount of concrete to be poured. Sometimes you'd get overtime. If you worked with the carpenters and they wanted to finish a section, you'd be working until seven and eight o'clock at night. I thought the money was great – and I was very happy there.

It was an enormous project, with hundreds of men working on it. I was delighted to be employed there. It was also better money than the jobs I had before. If you worked Sunday, you got 'double time', but not if you had a day off in the week. They had stopped people having a weekday off, then coming in on Sunday and getting paid double time; the firm had 'cottoned-on' to the fact that the fellas were coming in on Sunday, then taking the Monday off. So they changed the system: if you had a day off in the week, they wouldn't let you come in on the Sunday.

I remember one incident. I needed a weekday off, for a legitimate reason, but that would have meant that I couldn't come in on the Sunday. It was a very tight Union – you know what Liverpool is, or *was*, for Unions. The main Shop Steward was a Dublin fella, called Ernie Hogan. Ernie was *ferocious*! Everything had to be spot-on. If there was a drop of rain, they had to provide you with oilskins, and all that. Someone suggested (it may have been my brother, Paddy), "Ask Ernie – explain that you have to go to the dentist"... or something along those lines. I wasn't malingering – I was just doing something that I had to do. So I said to Ernie: "I have to have a day off, so I can't come in Sunday." He said: "Of course you're coming in Sunday!" He was the complete ruler of the job. He was on that job, from start to finish, but he was unemployable afterwards, because he had given the firm such a terrible time: every *single* thing, he was onto them – and he had absolute power! Because it was all unionised. He left when the job finished – he *had* to go then.

For anything at all, there was a meeting in the hut: "Down tools lads – come on!" There was a grievance and we'd *got* to sort it out. He could eclipse the foreman; anytime he wanted to – over-rule him; because they wanted the job done, the firm had to tolerate him. But I came in that Sunday and explained that I had to do something, so he sorted that out for me.

There was also a canteen on site, serving very good grub, so I was not hungry, for a change! I used to love two or three fried egg sandwiches. You'd have a break at ten o'clock in the morning, then the main dinnertime. You went along to the canteen and it was like a Self-service. You bought the tickets, which you then exchanged for a meal. It was a great way of socialising with some of the other workmen, and you could relax for a while. You'd sit with whoever you were working with.

I was helping Taffy and Ronnie to lift stuff and put it in place. "Seamus I want a piece of 6 by 4 for this." You got to know all the various sizes of timber. They had a joiner's shop on the job, so if either of them wanted a special piece of timber cut, they'd say: "Seamus, go up to the shop and get me a piece and cut that edge off; I want a piece 6 foot tall." They made that for you at the Joiner's Shop. I did hardly any sawing or woodwork at all myself, although I had served my time in Ireland as a carpenter, with Pa, and later on I worked as a chippy. But at that time, the Union was so strong that the job would stop if you tried to deviate from your appointed job.

There were different gangs, including gangs of Irish lads, doing heavy digging – all the big machines were driven by them too. I'd say that the job consisted of eighty per cent Irish and twenty per cent English.

It was a long time ago, and I hadn't seen any of them since. There was one lad, Tommy Quinn, who I sold my bike to, because he was living in Ellesmere Port and could ride to the job more easily. It was only twenty to twenty-five minutes each way for him. I used to see a lot of lads from the job, in the Irish club, the *Shamrock*, at the weekends. I'd know them from there. To get there each day, we would go to the overhead railway train from Seaforth where we lived, to the Pier Head. Then we'd take a train that went under the River Mersey and came out in Birkenhead, followed by a bus from Birkenhead to Hooten. Eastham was about a quarter of a mile walk from there.

Sometimes we'd work until seven in the evening, which made it a long day. There were great gangs of big heavy Irishmen, from different parts of the country, but I did not mix with them much, because I was with the carpenters, and we were on different sections. All the big machines, the 54 RB and the drag lines: there were as many Irish on that as anybody else.

The 54 RBs were far bigger than today's JCBs. They were the biggest digging machines that were made, at that time. They had a banksman on them: his job was to go around oiling all the holes and nipples on the machines, to keep them going. I thought many a time: 'I'd love to be a banksman.' It was a *great* job – they had no boss, like. And eventually they ended up driving the machines, because in the evening the driver would say to them: "Do you want to throw the bucket out?" Next thing the young lad would learn to drag it in, and gradually, he ended up driving. At that time, if you could get a job driving one of the machines, you'd be like a king! I never got the banksman's job, but I would love to have had it. The Kilgallen lads that used to fight in the *Shamrock* … they were all great drivers. I was very wary of them, but I got to know them very well, during my time in Liverpool, and they were sound.

The Dragline was another digging machine. The JCB has one arm down and it's rigid all the time. But the draglines are on chains and they drag the bucket in; not as economical as JCBs, because the buckets they were pulling in would be rickety, you see? They were great machines, but I don't see them nowadays at all. Later, the Germans invented one called a Pochlaine: they became a great machine; the *Hymac* was another. They both came in later. It's like the contrast between your old laptop computer and your new notebook. The technology improves!

There were three of us working on that job at the new dock. My brother, Louie had come down from Scotland, and of course Paddy was working there too, so it was great, because there were three of us brothers working on the same site. We could meet each other in the breaks, as they were the same time for everyone. If you worked until 7pm that would be overtime. The normal finishing time was around 6pm. But carpenters and labourers might keep on working, to finish a section.

My working gear was Wellingtons, turned down, and a donkey jacket. Nowadays, on the building sites, everyone changes – they take their gear off in the hut, before they come home. But in those days, you came home as you were. For some reason or other, I always seemed to have leaky Wellingtons. My feet were constantly wet. I must have worn the Wellingtons until there was a hole in the sole. You were in concrete all the time and you were slipping on the stuff. They made a 'key' in the big bay. It was like a trench, so that when the next bay went on, they'd key in together. The key was always full of water, so I'd be squelching about, in my leaking Wellingtons. Why I never invested in a new pair, I'll never know! I should have ended up with very bad feet, but I didn't – they're perfect. It didn't do me any harm.

Meanwhile, summer was coming on and I decided that I could save myself a bit of money if I bought a bicycle. I saved for a few weeks and bought a brand new racing bicycle. It cost me £19... so I was ready for the big cycle. It was a racer bike, with low handlebars. I had not done much cycling at home and certainly not on a bike like this!

So I set off from Seaforth. I was on my own again by this time, as Paddy had left his job and Louie had gone to a job in Scotland. Most of the streets were cobbled and crisscrossed with tram-tracks. When I reached the Pier Head, I had to cycle into the Mersey Tunnel. The way it was constructed, it was three miles in distance: one mile-and-a-half downhill, and one-and-a-half uphill. Well, by the time I got out of the tunnel, I knew that cycling certainly was *not* a good idea! After the tunnel came another five or six miles through Rock Ferry, New Ferry, Port Sunlight, where they made Sunlight Soap. Then into Bromborough, then Hooten, and finally Eastham. By the time I got to work, about an hour late, I could hardly walk!

I'd never ridden a racing bike, with low handlebars and all that – you know how you're cycling down low with them? When we saw the racing bikes back home in Ireland, we used to call the people who were riding them 'hikers', because we thought they were going on holiday somewhere. But I thought they'd be ideal for speed... I got that bit right!

Although it had several gears on it, I wouldn't have had time to change them. I never knew how to use them anyway – to be truthful! So it was a brand new bicycle, but cycling was just something that I was never very good at.

The mile-and-a-half uphill was absolute murder! When you got to Liverpool, as I said earlier on, it was all cobblestones and tram-tracks, and eventually you'd slide into a tram-track. But you'd soon be scurrying out of it, because you couldn't keep the bike absolutely rigid all the time. I thought that it would be quicker and that I'd save a bit of money. But it went disastrously wrong!

By the time I got home, I was well and truly flithered. I stuck at the cycling for about three days, but it was hard labour, and I soon packed it in. I sold the bike later to the lad I mentioned earlier, from down Roosky, four miles below Charlestown. He worked on the job, but lived in Ellesmere Port, which was a lot nearer to the job, and no Mersey Tunnel in between. I got £12 for the bike. This was my first lesson in financial commerce – and it was a bit painful! The lad I sold the bike to was called Tommy Quinn.

Tommy was a blond, handsome lad. I didn't know him at home, although Roosky was only a few miles from Charlestown. We were near enough the one age, but everyone I knew, he also knew them. So I left the job and I hadn't seen Tommy for years and years, but then I met him here recently, in Birmingham. I can't remember exactly whether it was at a church or at a Social Club, but we had a good laugh about the old days. I think he may have been a banksman; he was certainly all dressed up on the job – as opposed to me. We weren't together, but we'd see each other at break-time. It was a very big site. So I hope Tommy's alive and well – I'm sure he is now – and in Birmingham. We've ended up in the same area of the country again!

I worked on, all through that summer. Sometimes we would leave the job early. You would have to get someone to shout your number through the timekeeper's window, and we would be over the fields and away, a couple of hours early. But the timekeeper copped on to us and waited in the field we used to cross, and we would be docked the time. If you were caught two or three times, you were sacked. When work on the dock finished, a lot of us finished working in that area.

What we'd do, we'd get together and decide to leave a bit early. The charge-hand who was over us was a man named Arthur Jones. He was 'sound-as-a-bell'. If things were going well he'd say: "D'you want to have an early night

Seamus?" The lads would say: "Oh, alright Arthur." "Ah – you can bugger off now," he'd say. It might be half four, but he was in charge. The foreman might have been going down to Devon for the weekend or something. So we'd all scamper off across the fields but we'd have to get someone to shout our name in – mine might be number six. The timekeeper sat in the hut and he'd put 'Number six – Dunleavy', so that he'd know the time.

You were all supposed to leave at six o'clock. We'd have someone else run past his hut and shout: "Number six – Dunleavy!" Half the time he wouldn't lift his head up, because he'd have a hundred men coming past him. But someone tipped him off that we were all going off across the fields and that the numbers were being shouted in. We used to do it in the factories as well, you see? Someone else would clock you out – you'd give him your ticket. But anyway, several times Shirley, he ambushed us! He knew the fields we were going across and all of a sudden he'd come on us, and he'd say: "Dunleavy, and such-a-one and such-a-one – you're all caught!" And we'd say: "The timekeeper caught us last night!" Three times and you were off the site. But I was never caught three times – although I schemed *more* than three times. But you were young, and you didn't care. To get away early seemed to be like half winning the Pools! "I'm away! I should be working, but I can go home on the train!" You'd get a great sense of freedom from doing it... like a stolen kiss!

Eventually the job was finished and we moved on. A lot of people you would meet on the job would say: "If I were a young, strong fellow like you, I would leave Liverpool and head for London or Birmingham. There is nothing in Liverpool." There was one fella in particular, called Felix, from Dublin, he said: "Jeesus – what are you doing here in Liverpool? There's no work at all!" Felix was twenty years older than me. He said: "You're wasting your time. Get down to Birmingham. There's hundreds of factories, doing *all* sort of jobs!" Actually, it was Felix who inspired me to move down here – to get out of Liverpool.

But before that, Christmas arrived, so once again I was heading home for Charlestown. It was great to be home. I was getting a bit of sense now and dispensed with the gloves and scarves and very rarely wore the coat. Fashions must have changed. But you'd stick out like a sore thumb, with all that gear on! If you were a smoker, you just *had* to have a big silver cigarette case; you'd open it with one hand – (I don't think I've see any about for years now), and of course, the cigarette lighter was a must too. I didn't smoke, so I didn't have a cigarette case – but I'd have loved one.

Now, I must have given most of my money to Mammy and Pa, because I was broke again. I remember I pawned my suit in Liverpool once. It was a new suit, but all I could get for it was thirty shillings. I can still see the pawnbroker: "Thirty bob Pat," he said – so I took it. I remember the shop was in Strand Road. There was myself and about eight or nine pregnant women, all in financial trouble – desperate times! I cannot remember redeeming it, but I suppose I must have, because I couldn't go to the dances without a suit.

A time or two when we went home for the holidays, a man called Tom Egan used to come to our house. Tom wore a hat, with the rim turned up all around. Himself and my dad might be having a Guinness or two. Tom would look at me and say to my dad, Mick, "That son of your would make a great Garda (policeman)." And Pa would say: "Well, indeed he would." Now you had to be at least five foot ten inches tall, to get into the Gards, and I was barely five foot nine; Mickey was only five foot eight. Tom Egan reckoned I was six foot or over. Himself and Pa might have been a *little* inebriated at the time! So we would be bundled across to the Garda barracks and I was measured – at five foot nine. Then back across the street to our house. The sergeant said that we weren't tall enough. But Tom Egan would say to Pa that that would not matter, because he reckoned I would never leave the depot. I would be training the recruits – and anyway – I was six foot! Now this was the Guinness talking.

Then they came up with the idea that you are taller when you get out of bed in the morning. So, up in the morning and straight across to the barracks… no good. This happened about four times, until I told Pa and Tom Egan that I had no intention of joining the Gardi – and anyway – I would not pass the exam in a month of Sundays, even if I had been the right height. But I am sure that the sergeant was happy when he heard that we had departed for England again!

Well, another Charlestown holiday was over and I was back in Liverpool. The holidays seemed to fly by. You were home and then it was all over and you were back in England again. But it was great to see all of the school pals. Most of the Charlestown gang seemed to be in London, so I was thinking of moving there. I can't remember exactly what happened to put me off the idea. But eventually, once the events of our next chapter unfolded, I was to leave Liverpool and head for Birmingham.

Chapter Eleven

CAROL IN LITHERLAND

It was like a Wild West saloon. When they came in, everyone thought: "Oh my God?" A sort of murmur went around the dancers, as if to say: "What-the-hell's going to happen?" Seamus knew them, so he was OK, but you can imagine this tremor going round: "Oh no – here they are again!"

I mentioned, in Chapter Nine, that I'd started to go dancing in Liverpool at the *Shamrock,* but eventually found that I preferred the more local dances at *Saint Jimmy's.*

The *Shamrock,* you may recall, was in Lime Street, right in the centre of Liverpool. There were three or four storeys to the building, with the *Shamrock* right at the top. They'd begin the evening with an Olde Tyme Waltz, followed by Ceilidh music, which was purely Irish music; so there was no quickstep, or anything like that. It was always full up, and there were lots and lots of fights!

I never got involved in the fights myself, but some of the lads would come in a bit drunk – and there'd be this-and-that-and-the-other! Arguments about bits of jobs that should have gone to various people and about those who didn't pull their weight. There were four brothers from Mayo called the Kilgallen brothers, who used to go into the club together and liked a drop of drink. Richard and Pakie Kilgallen were twins – I mentioned in the previous chapter, that they were worked on the new dock, as bulldozer drivers. They were very blond-haired, handsome lads, but they were devils for fighting Shirley! They were from outside Castlebar, County Mayo, and I knew them well, so I was safe. But there'd be a fight, almost every night.

Having said that, I used to have some nice dances there. But I never met any particular girls there or took anyone home from there. The girls there were probably a bit older than me, because I was very young at the time: seventeen or eighteen; some of the girls would have been ten years or so older than me, so I might have been a bit intimidated by older women in those days! I went every week for a year or two and then I started to drift into the English dances.

As I explained, *Saint James* or *Saint Jimmy's*, was a Catholic club or dance, run by a big Cork priest called Father O'Sullivan. It was in Bootle, close to where I lived, so I could walk there. I got to know some lovely girls, and started to walk one or two of them home. Lots of the lads boxed a bit, so *we* had something in common too.

I remember I was going with a little girl there called Kathleen Henderson – a very nice blonde girl – very friendly. You'd take a girl home and do a bit of snogging outside her door. It was totally simple, but very enjoyable; no going to bed with them, or anything like that.

Then there was a girl called Anne Steadman. Anne was a tall girl. I got friendly with her, and again, you'd go home. All of the dances would end between half past ten to eleven o'clock. So you'd be out to her door, and in the summer, there'd be another couple, five or six doors up, in the doorway. That was the way it was done in those times. There was no such thing as pulling their skirts up or anything like that. Well, I never did it. Maybe I was a bit slow! I'd go to the pictures with Kathleen Henderson, a few nights, and I'd go out with Anne too.

Margaret Ellaway's brother, Billy, was a boxer; he fought Pat Macateer, for the Middleweight Championship of England. I went out with Margaret a few times. I had quite a few girlfriends, around that time. They were more around my age, and I had more in common with them. I had some lovely times at *Saint Jimmy's*.

My brother, Mickey, started to go to *Saint Jimmy's* too, because he was in England by then. He courted Sheila O'Connell for quite a while. Her family was also into boxing; her brother, Jimmy, was an Area Lightweight Boxing Champion. So we were in with a nice crowd then, and we started to feel more at home. We could actually walk to the dance there too, whereas with the *Shamrock*, you had to get a bus into Town. As my girlfriends lived locally, I could walk them home; they'd live maybe five or six streets away.

There was a dancehall called *Litherland Town Hall*. Now this was a bit up-market from the church halls. The crowd was older, and a lot more sophisticated, and I began to go every Saturday night. It was there that I met a lovely, brown-eyed girl called Carol-Ann Lyon. We got on great and I started to look forward to Saturday nights with great excitement. Carol-Ann had straight hair, as black as a crow's wing, which was of average length – just below her ears. She was around five feet four – about the same height as Mary; a well-built girl, with dark-brown eyes. I think she told me, as we became friendly, that she was sixteen or seventeen, but it turned out, after a while, that she was only fifteen, so she was actually younger that I had realized!

It was her first dance there and she had come with her elder sister, whose name was Olive Lyon. Then her brother, Brian, began to come to the dances too. Anyway, I started to dance with Carol, and we became very friendly. There was a break in the dance, after a couple of hours, when everybody would go upstairs to the tea-bar. I would take Carol up there, for tea, so it was all very nice and civilized. Then we began to go out together. We went to the cinema two or three times a week – it was great! We met every Sunday on the Crosby Dunes, and strolled along the shores of the Mersey –the same beach that I told you about before, where I enjoyed solitary walks. Carol-Ann and myself spent our time there, larking about.

I wonder, on reflection, if she had some sort of job, or maybe she was still at school? At the time I'd have been nineteen, and as she was fifteen, she may have been thinking: 'Well, he won't want to go out with me if he knows that I'm a schoolgirl.' That's probably why she kept quiet about her age, at first. She used to meet me in Bootle, when I finished work. We would sort of 'bump into' each other, although, looking back on it, she'd actually be waiting to see me. But it was great to be seeing her, all of a sudden, like that. I'm certain I was only nineteen, because it was around the time that I had my photo in the *Bootle Times*, because of the wrestling. She either rang me or wrote to me, to say: "I've seen your photo in the *Bootle Times* Jimmy. It's fantastic!" It was something great, like, to be going out with a lad, then all of a sudden, his picture's in the paper.

She called me Jimmy because that's the name I went under in Liverpool. Billy Riley always used to call me Jimmy too. In fact, my name was James, but in Ireland I was always Seamus. It was James on my passport and everything. If, for example, someone named Sean came to England, he might be called John while he was here, but the minute he returned to Ireland he'd be Sean.

Carol-Ann told me that one of her grandparents was Spanish, and that's where she got the brownness from. She was a lot browner than me – the Spanish look, and a good eight-and-a-half to nine stone, although she was short.

I remember one night I took her home to her house, and she invited me in. I was absolutely terrified that her mum would come and ask me what I was doing there! She made me a cup of tea. I thought: 'God, this is marvellous.'

Then we'd meet and go to the cinema. I used to love the cinema, from my days back in Charlestown. Carol-Ann enjoyed it too. There was a great big seat in the *Regal*, in Litherland, where you could sit together, so we'd head for the back seat. It was lovely – we had a great time! And again, I used to meet her of a Sunday. She lived in Thornton and I lived in Seaforth; the next district to us was Crosby and then there was Thornton. She'd come in on the bus and get off at the bus stop just outside the *Regent Cinema* in Crosby. I'd travel there by bus too. It seems funny, because I've become so used to driving everywhere. How could you be getting buses? Why hadn't I a car? But in those days, of course, we didn't.

She was a quiet girl. We'd walk along kicking leaves together, in the autumn, and all that. Looking in shops together. Liverpool was great for Funfairs, so we'd go to those a lot. We'd spend hours on the Waltzers… her and me… going round and round and round! I still like the funfairs today. That's where we spent most of our time.

I was going out with her for several months. I liked her a lot – it was me first romance. Then all of a sudden, Pa was building a house back home, and he wanted me and my brother Mickey back home – to help him with it. Pa was a small builder, as you'll know by now. In our time, he built a house each for Johnny Scally, James Carty, Jim Lundy and one for Johnny Cook. It would take about eighteen months to build each one. He'd be doing it slowly, and cycling to the job. There'd usually be about three of us working together – Pa, my brother Tom and Louie. Paddy never did, because he was in England the whole time. Then when Mickey and I came back, Pa would have help from us too. He never made any money on it at all. By the time they were finished, he'd have drawn all the money out, in bits and bits, but it was just the way he made his living. We had a shop, although it was absolutely useless. He made enough to live on, but there was no real profit. Later, when finances improved, we helped him to smarten up the shop front.

They were all bungalows; he never built a two-storey house. He was a very good tradesman. He put on what they called a 'Hip Roof'. He'd strike it out on the grass, mark it out from a steel square, cut all the timbers, and then we'd nail them. He was a carpenter, of course. That was his trade. He served his time as a cabinetmaker. The builders over there, like my dad, did floor-laying, plastering, slating – the whole lot. Over in England, you specialise – if you're a slater, you're a slater. Windows and floors are a different area altogether; plasterers are completely different, and so on.

If I had to categorize myself as having one particular area of building expertise, it would be carpentry, like Pa. But I actually did all sorts of things over here in England, as you'll discover in later chapters – a 'Man for All

Seasons'. But you do in your life, don't you? Especially when you go to a different country. Many of you reading this book may have been born in Britain, but we came here. Although we speak English, the same as you, there's a big culture difference – especially when you're a young lad – and I'm talking well over fifty years ago. Nowadays, when people leave Ireland, they're often highly educated: very few of them earn their living by labouring, as we did.

So we had to be very adaptable to the situation we found ourselves in, and take whatever work was available. Nowadays, everyone is watching television, at home, and they know everything about England. The Match of the Day, for example, is as popular over in Ireland as it is here. But we were going into an almost entirely unknown situation, for which we weren't prepared. It was a different country: everything – the food, the transport, the houses and the humour. Over in Charlestown you could stop and chat to anybody and they'd all be very sociable. Over here, the English *tend* to be more reserved, as a race, so you have to remind yourself to act accordingly. To this very day, if I see a few kids in front of me, and want to ruffle their hair in a friendly way, or something like that, Mary will say: "Don't do that!" But it was the way we were brought up. You'd never pass anyone without greeting them, over in Ireland.

The pubs were different as well. In Ireland they'd be small, pokey places, each with their own Snug. But when I was in Liverpool, going up Strand Row, all the pubs would be open and there'd be people drinking outside. You'd never have that in Ireland – they all drink inside. I never saw chips until I came to England! You'd get them in newspaper. I'd think: 'This is great' – three penny pieces for a bag of chips – and later four pence. I love chips – I love potatoes. You'd get them anywhere – up and down the street – a chip shop here, a chip shop there.

We were brought up to think that the grub was very bad in England. The people who came back said: "Thank God we're back, and can get a bit of proper food!" So you thought there was no food at all in England! It was the rude awakening, because it was after the war when I came across, so the shops were full of food. I had a Ration Book; they were still in use in England, during the early 1950s, when I first arrived.

Carol-Ann and I had a lot of fun together. It was a light-hearted relationship that we had. Very few of those places where we spent our time exist today – it's funny, isn't it? After a few months at home, helping Pa, we came back to Birmingham, rather than Liverpool – different faces and different places. So my first romance was over.

I loved the *Top Twenty* on the radio. You'd have *Shrimp Boats Are Coming*, and Lita Rosa. Guy Mitchell with *She Wears Red Feathers and a Hooli-hooli Skirt. How Much Is That Doggy in the Window?* and *When You Hear Big Ben You're Home Again*, and Nat King Cole, they were great – absolutely! It would be such-a-one has gone up three places and so forth. Eddie Calvert with *Oh My Papa*, on the trumpet.

Then there were the big Bands: Joe Loss and Billy Cotton – "Wakey-wakey!" I *loved* the music. And Wilfred Pickles was on the radio – "Give them the money Mabel!" By then I was getting into the way of life, getting used to the Liverpudlian accents, and becoming a bit more like a Lancashire man.

Chapter Twelve

INNOCENTS ABROAD

Moving to Birmingham proved to be a wise decision, as work was easier to find there in the late 1950s, than it was in the North. Seamus and his brother, Mickey, found lodgings in Perry Barr, Balsall Heath and then Saltley. They worked on Hams Hall Power Station, for a while. Then Seamus moved on, to a job in the old Singer Factory, Small Heath.

I went to the Labour Exchange, in a place called Coleshill: that was another area in Birmingham. From there, they directed me to Hams Hall, where I found the Foreman, and got the job. When all that was done I had to find digs, so I moved to Wenman Street, in Balsall Heath. The landlady, Mrs. Grant, was a lovely woman. She was from Newcastle and was married to a Brummie named Bob, who was a thorough gentleman. I had no money to pay her in advance, but I had a job to go to, so she took a chance with me. Again, I had great trouble with the Birmingham accents. I had got used to the Liverpool twang, but this was completely different. As she was a Geordie, I never understood one word that Mrs. Grant said, but she fed me well, and gave me a spam sandwich to take to work, as well.

Bob was a very small, quietish, Birmingham man. He worked in a factory, as a toolmaker or a tool-setter. He was supposed to be doing an overtime shift, but there was nobody about. So he asked if we'd like to see where he worked. That was the first time I was ever in a factory. He showed me all of his tools – the jig et cetera, but it was all Greek to me! I was in my twenties, and Bob and his wife would have been about forty; which seemed old to us at the time. But they were a very sociable couple. He worked there all his life and probably stayed there until he retired.

There were about six or seven of us – all Irish. I was in a room with two brothers from Belfast – great lads. By this time I was working as a carpenter. My brother Louie was with me, and he was not a bad chippy. We stayed in the digs in Balsall Heath for about three months, then moved to Perry Barr,

Our landlady in Perry Barr was Mrs. Ham. She had a very big house, along the main Birchfield Road. We had full board, but her food was absolutely *desperate*. She'd give you a little sandwich in the morning, and that was absolutely desperate as well – we wouldn't take a bite out of it! She had a little girl working for her and every Friday evening, as soon as we got in through the door, she'd say: "Have you got the money for Mrs Ham?" So you'd shell out the money, there and then, like. She made sure that she got paid. I'm sure a few of the lads must have done a runner, or something.

At that time I'd bought a saxophone, and I managed to practise a bit. After we left, she said: "I'm glad he's left – and taken his bugle with him!" But it's a wonder she didn't chuck me out straight away! I've still got a saxophone upstairs now. I play it for enjoyment, rather than for any practical reason, as I've not been in a band since the early days. My brother Louie was a good accordion player. You'll find a photo in the book, of a group of us playing together, with all the instruments.

But we didn't wait in Perry Barr long and soon moved to Havelock Road, Saltley. We had a room where we kept ourselves. There was a kitchen, where we cooked, which we shared with fifteen others, and there was a penny gas meter; so you never knew who was using whose gas – plenty of trouble there as well!

They were a great bunch of lads living there and we got to know them very well. There were four lads from Clare and four from County Galway Then there was a fellow from the Aran Islands, called Peter Flaherty, and a few more. Peter spoke mostly in Gaelic and didn't understand much English, but we became very good friends. He would go to the Pictures a lot, at the *Rock Picture House*, up Alum Rock. There was also a lad called Martin O'Donnell.

The Clare boys were Mick Heatherman, Paul Murray, Pat Quelly and Tom Collins. Martin O'Donnell is dead now, but he was a real character. He was marvellous with words and speech and everything, and a great reader. He used to read all of James Joyce's books. He was in court for something once and he told the magistrate that he wasn't very good at English. The magistrate said: "But my God! You've got a *stranglehold* on the English Language!" He was terrific – very eloquent.

The landlord of the house, Danny Lane, was from Limerick and he had a live-in girlfriend. As they were not married we thought that she was the most scarlet of all women. We just could not get over the fact that a couple could sleep together, but not be married. We were like the innocents abroad! If we met her on the stairs, we'd be embarrassed.

There were special work buses laid on, at work, to take us into Birmingham city, but as I lived in Saltley, I had no need to go to the city centre. There was a small shop directly opposite us, so we could buy all our food there. We would have the big fry-up every night. It was the handiest to cook and it was a good meal. I would cook bacon, egg and beans and a raw onion, and a bit of sweet cake or apple pie afterwards. I still like the same fry-up to this day, but the Continental and the Chinese were a long way off. Having the shop there was absolutely marvellous for us. I seemed to be in Saltley a long time, and I enjoyed it very much there. I used to walk from there, into the *Shamrock Club*, as well. When I left the Hams Hall job, I was still living in Saltley.

Hams Hall was a big power station. There were huge cooling towers, such as you see throughout the country. I started there with a firm called *Stavertons*. They were from down Devon way. I worked for them for a couple of weeks. My brother, Louie, was with me. Then we left *Stavertons* and got a job with a French firm, named *Kier's*, who are still in business now. They were building the cooling towers; to get on the cooling towers was very good money.

It was repetitive work. I was a carpenter at the time, although I was a bad one. But you didn't have to do much carpentry, because it was shuttering all the way round. You went up in a lift, every time. All you had to do was put the shutters up, board them together, and go round in a ring. We built a ring of the tower every day, to contain the concrete, inside and outside. We fixed the shutters and bolted them into the ring. Then we made it secure and the concrete gang poured it in. A day or two after it had set, you'd go up again.

It was hard work, because the shutters were so heavy, but that suited me because I was very strong and had good arms and shoulders. And I really enjoyed it. We were going up all the time, so by the time we got to the top, by building a ring every day, we were 350 foot high. This was the best job I'd ever had. We used to get a wage then and a bonus, the harder we worked – and Height Money as well: the higher you went, the more money you got; definitely not a job for anyone with vertigo! However, we were well scaffolded all round. So although we were very high up, it didn't make that much difference.

On either ring or lift there were about twelve carpenters, eight to ten concrete men and about ten to twelve specialist scaffolders. There are certain carpenters who work on heavy concrete work, all the time, as opposed to house carpenters, who hang doors and windows, and so forth. But it was a very good muscle-building job.

The concrete was mixed on the ground and would come up on a hoist. For us to get up or down, to the toilet, we would have to climb down twenty or thirty ladders and back up again. So you would not have to be bad after the drink, or you would be worn out, going up and down to the toilets! Some of the lads would put soap on the ladders too, so that they were slippery! Of course, we all pissed from the top. If you saw anyone underneath that was the big craic – a few of us all pissing together and the fellow or fellows underneath getting a good soaking. But then – I was often caught myself!

So that was life on the buildings. We mostly worked the seven days. I well remember I spent my twenty-first birthday, on the cooling tower that we were working on. No such thing as a day off, or any sort of celebration. We were getting near the top of the tower. For the first two hundred feet the tower sloped inwards; for the last one hundred feet it would slope like an upside-down police cone. There was a gang on the outside as well. The inside was reinforced with steel bars, about an inch in diameter. They were put in every two or three lifts and tied onto the existing steel that was already concreted in.

Well, they were put in place on day, but not tied and there was a young Mayo man, called Tom Hennigan, from a place that was on the border with Galway. I knew the Hennigans well. Tom had a brother there and a cousin. He was working on the outside, just where it was splaying out. He hooked his safety harness onto one of the vertical bars and leant backwards. Don't forget, the tower is now leaning outwards. Well, the steel bars had not been tied to the existing ones. He was catapulted over the scaffolding, fell over two hundred and fifty feet, and was killed instantly! I was up there at the time, working on a different tower, so I didn't see him fall.

It was the first time I was close to someone who had died or been killed, and it shook me quite a bit. Where he fell and hit the tower, you could see the track – all the way down. Whether his family got compensation I don't know. I'm not sure who was at fault. Although we were obviously aware of the dangers of the job, we were all shocked about it – especially as we knew the lad. You never thought, in those times, of the desperation the news would bring at home... and it was coming up towards Christmas.

Louie had already left the job and I was thinking of home and of Christmas. From the top and near the top I could see the spire of Coleshill Church...through the fog, on a bright winter's morning. It was lovely... like a Christmas Card.

I had about £400 saved, so I jacked the job in, about ten days before Christmas, and headed for Liverpool. It was dusk as the train passed through Crewe. The houses were beneath me, in a hollow. It was frosty and I had £400 in my pocket. I used to save in the Post Office, and I drew the lot out. I was so happy and secure and *massively* rich.

That train journey was the best of my life. Even the Trans-Siberian journey could not compete with it! I was so happy and secure... and rich. Never had money in my life, then all of a sudden I'd got £400. The journey was lovely and warm, and I'd be arriving home like a king, because I had all this money in my pocket.

I met Louie in Liverpool. There was plenty of home cooking from Mai. I stayed there for about a week and then headed for home. Mammy and Pa knew that I had saved the £400 and were delighted I was going home. All those years ago, all the boys and girls that had left with me – and during the years before – they would all be home. Great stories: how we had done; what town we were in. Had we met any nice girls? The craic used to be mighty! Had you done the 'bold thing' with any girl? And of course, with everyone being less than truthful about that, you would not want to be left out – so of course you had!

Over the next few years, I wrestled up and down the country, in practically every town and village in England. I'd meet loads of people who'd left Charlestown; they would knock on my dressing room door to say hello. They'd seen my name on the bill and they knew what I was doing.

There were a lot who never made it home – fell in with bad crowds and drink. There was a lad who lived next door to me in Charlestown, Jimmy Blake. He left, and we have never seen him from that day... and that is well over fifty years ago. Just as one of my uncles who emigrated to America had disappeared, Mammy's brother, so Jimmy appeared to completely vanish from the face of the earth too! As far as we know, he set out for England, as he had relations in Buxton, in Derbyshire... but he never turned up.

It was a strange story. He was born out of wedlock. His Dad was a man called Pat Blake. Pat got this girl into trouble, which, in those days, was an execution job – he'd nearly be hanged for it. The boy that was born was Jimmy Blake. Pat went off to America afterwards – in shame, and everything. He never returned for years and years. I remember him coming back and meeting Jimmy Blake – I don't think they'd met before, in their lifetime.

Jimmy lived with his grandmother, Beesy, as a boy, and she was a character. She kept chickens, and so did we. One of her favourite tricks was to pinch the odd one from us. But whenever she did, she'd shout to Mammy, from over the garden wall between us: "Mary Kate, is there one of my chickens in your yard? One of mine is missing." So she covered her tracks, but we would see feathers flying over the wall, for a few hours after! I don't know whether Mammy was afraid of her or not, but she never challenged Beesy. Beesy is now long gone and Jimmy Blake never appeared – even when she died. We don't know to this day whether he was shot, kidnapped, or perhaps committed suicide... or whether he's alive and well.

Having said that, there's another lad who I was at school with, Johnny Fitzpatrick – I know his house in London; we've included his photograph in the book. He left Charlestown and he never *ever* went back for a holiday. He was the lad who failed the Primary Certificate with me, but took it the year afterwards and got it. I met him several times in London, over the years, and from time to time I would say: "Johnny wouldn't you like to have a ramble down Barrack Street, where we both lived?" He'd reply: "I'm definitely going next year." But it's been five years since I last saw him and he's still not been back. He was a popular lad at home; he had brothers who made it home – but that's fifty years now, since he was there – and never been back! His Dad was a blacksmith. And he's only an hour's journey away. There is a picture of the blacksmith in this book.

Well, the dances were great when you were twenty-one... and so the Christmas holidays came to an end. But just before I left, to go back to England, Pa called me to one side. He was building a house, about four miles outside Charlestown, in a place called Cluan Ravar, for a man called Johnny Cook. Pa was supplying everything and had it up to roof level, but he was broke. He could not afford to buy the roof, and he was banjaxed. So he put the tap on me. The roof would cost about £400 and my money would be safe as houses, when the house was finished. My poor old dad was a great builder, on the practical side, but not so good on the financial aspects. So, sadly, I parted with my £400. I *did* get the money back... although it was thirty years later, when Pa died! He left a little bit of money and it was all shared out. Although he had a hard struggle in life and never made much money, we were never hungry.

So my euphoria was short-lived. I found myself back in England – minus my money – and was getting absolutely nowhere. I thought to myself: 'I'll never have £400 again, in my life.' But you couldn't let your dad down. He was struggling and we were all family. So I jacked in the building and got a job on the Coventry Road, in Small Heath, at the old Singer Motor Factory. This was the first time that I'd worked inside, but it was winter, so I was glad of it.

My job was to get any small wheels that had cogs on them and to dip them in a vat of hot wax, which coated them; so if they knocked together, they would not be damaged. I had a corner of my own, with a partition around it, on a floor in the factory. The wax came in blocks and when I needed some, Les Oliver, the foreman, would give me a ticket to go to the storeroom and collect them. You'd melt the blocks in a vat. But no one ever bothered me at all. Whether the job I was doing meant nothing to the factory – I don't know.

There was a basement in the factory. I made up a set of weights and used to spend most of the time training. The parts I was putting in had to be de-greased first of all, in another vat, so I went down to the basement to do that. There was terrible vapour came out of it. There were two Welshmen working down there and they said: "If I were you young fella I wouldn't go near that vat. I'd be away from here!" I should have worn a mask for protection but I had nothing at all. You had to get the parts absolutely clean. The fumes were deadly, if you looked in the vat for too long!

Then I'd take the parts back to the vat upstairs and coat them in wax. As they were car parts they had to be spot-on. But there were half-hundredweight weights down in the basement, and that's what I was doing – weightlifting – building my body up. It was absolutely *great* for me. I loved that job. The money was useless, but at least I was inside. I was working there when we heard that eight members of the Manchester United Football team had been killed, in an air crash at Munich, Germany, on 6 February 1958. They had been returning from a European Cup Tie, in Belgrade,

I must have worked in the factory for about nine months. But 1958 became a very important landmark for me, because it was the last time I ever worked in a job, for a boss, in England. I was offered promotion as a charge-hand, over a group of four men: a daft Brummie, an Hungarian, an Indian and a Polish dispossessed person – what a gang – I declined the offer!

So I left the Singer Factory, to begin a different way of life as a wrestler, combined with working on the door at the *Shamrock*, for ten years. I never stuck a job long, for some reason or other. Once we started wrestling and we'd bought the first house, because Mickey was with me then, we made a good living from wrestling, and the houses were a bonus, after that. Yet, you hear of people who've worked for the same firm for forty years. And you think: 'How could they do that?' But there you are. That was the changing point. I was on my way...

Chapter Thirteen

WARS OF THE ROSES

In Pat Roach's Auf Wiedersehen Pat, the final biography in the Pat Roach Trilogy, Pete Roberts describes Seamus' phenomenal strength, and the way in which both Seamus and his brother Mick played a vital part, in coaching Pat and himself, when they were first learning the art of wrestling, at Severn Street Amateur Club, in Birmingham City Centre.

There was a move called the 'Hook In'. Once they got that hold on you, that 'Nelson', you were well-and-truly beaten – you couldn't move: it was like 'Check-mate'. Someone made the mistake of trying this grip on Seamus. But all of a sudden, he stood up, with a wrestler on his back! They said: "We have never seen that happen before!" The word went round: "Seamus Dunleavy got up with the Hook on."... "No – he didn't!"

They took him up to a bombsite one day, to wrestle an opponent from Bradford. He was a coalminer, and there was a bet on, of between seventy to a hundred pounds. The miner said: "Is that the strong Irish fella who gets up, with the Hook on?" They said: "Yes." He replied: "Bloody hell – you should have told us!" Seamus beat his opponent that day and made a few pounds out of it into the bargain, for himself and his friends.

We kept going until we got a Submission; it wasn't a fall – you kept going until your opponent had had enough. It was *totally* different from normal wrestling. You couldn't use it in a 'Pro' game. I enjoyed it and we had some good times.

My sister Mai was still in Liverpool, so I arranged to stay with her. I planned to come down on Monday and go back on Fridays. That way, I could still do the Friday and Saturday nights and Sunday afternoons. When I went down to Wigan, I had already left Liverpool, although my sister still lived there and retained the same rented house. So I was in Birmingham now. At this time I started going to an Irish Dancehall in Hurst Street, in the City Centre. The *Shamrock*, as it was called, was the only big Irish dancehall in Birmingham. It shared the same name as the club I used to go to in Liverpool.

There was a dance, from three in the afternoon until six o'clock, and on a Sunday night as well. So the money from that would keep me in food and pay for my room. I wasn't playing in a group, as I used to do in Ireland. I was working on the door. That came about because I was still very interested in wrestling and wanted to turn pro, but didn't know how to go about it. Now the owner was a powerfully-built man called Matt Byrne, from Kerry, who used to say that he was an ex pro-wrestler. The Sunday afternoon dance was very popular, because we were all in digs and you had to be out of digs or in the pub, so I was always in the *Shamrock*.

One Sunday I approached Matt and showed him the write-up and my photo, in the paper. I asked him how I could get started in the pro game. He was very interested in helping me, but first he asked if I would be interested in a job in his dancehall, as he put it. The idea was that if there was any trouble with his customers, I would be on hand to separate them. He said there was very little trouble anyway. So I took the job.

There was a brute of a man from Limerick, called Joe Enright, a Kerry man called Patsy Flahive and Sean Ruane from Foxford, in County Mayo – a townie of my own. The *Shamrock* was the first Irish ballroom in Birmingham. Before that, there were church halls and a few Irish Socials, but the Byrne brothers spotted the opening and took a lease on a ballroom – a fine big dancehall. It could have held about a thousand, or even twelve to fifteen hundred, but on busy nights we often had two thousand in the place! It used to be packed. And, as it turned out, there was plenty of trouble as well!

I used to do the dancehalls Friday, Saturday and Sunday afternoon. I'd return to Liverpool on the Monday morning, and spend Monday to Friday in the Gym. I'd come home on Friday evening, from Wigan to Birmingham; do a Friday night shift at the dancehall, Saturday night, Sunday afternoon and evening at the *Shamrock*. Those wages kept me going admirably: I wasn't smoking or drinking at the time. Even if I came in a bit late, of a Friday, they knew where I was, so they were good to me that way. The *Shamrock* dancehall owner, Matt Byrne, was married to Jane, Billy Riley's daughter, so they all knew where I was.

As Matt was a Kerry man, we both spoke the same language – we were *very* friendly. I was rather like Billy Riley's second son. He had only one son, Ernie, and I spoke with an Irish accent, his son-in-law was an Irishman, his dad was an Irishman – a grand fella, so I was sort of one of the 'fair-haired lads', so-to-speak: he taught me everything. He wanted me to be a brilliant wrestler. So that's how I did my training.

Having jacked in my job (which I'll tell you about in the next chapter) Matt Byrne, the dancehall owner made it OK that I could train there. I was on my way! So one cold Sunday evening, I arrived in Wigan. I had been in Wigan before, when I was a lad in Liverpool, just having heard that it was a good gym and having worked out there a bit. But then I was away for years, like – they didn't remember me, or anything. But this was an official time when I was coming in. They knew I was coming down to train, because Matt Byrne had told them.

The gym was located by Central Park, which was the Wigan Rugby League Ground. So when I asked for the Central Park, everyone thought I was a new Wigan Rugby League man. I was carrying a sports bag and asked three or four people for directions to the Rugby Club. They said: "Are you coming to play for us?" But I explained why I was going there. I'm talking with a Northern accent now! You began to speak with a Northern accent when you were training up there – "Ay-up! Right-oh!"

It was straight up, past the Central Rugby ground. *Riley's Gym* was only a very small shack. I got there about six o'clock in the evening, but it was closed. What I did not realise was that the pro boys were wrestling all over the country in the evenings, and trained in the mornings. So I headed back to Liverpool on the bus and into Hemer Terrace; although it had definitely been arranged with them beforehand, that I was coming down.

Mai was glad to see me, and put me up again. Up early Monday, I got the early bus into town to Lime Street, and then a bus to Wigan, which took an hour. Inside the gym, there was a mat on the floor, as big as the usual standard ring; well padded; a punch-bag, various weights, a shower, a toilet, and two benches to seat about fifteen to twenty people. Also, a trapeze or chinny bar, plus a rope attached to the ceiling for rope climbing – something I could never do.

On that Monday morning, there were about eight to ten pro-wrestlers there. Billy Riley, the gym owner and trainer, welcomed me, and we all had a try against each other. All the greats were there: Ernie Riley – Light Heavyweight Champion of England, who was Billy's son. Jack Dempsey, Welterweight Champion of England, and Melvyn Riss – Lightweight Champion of England. In Wigan cant you'd say: "I'm going for a Melvyn Riss!" It wasn't Cockney Lingo, but Wigan Lingo – like Cockney Rhyming Slang.

Brian Burke was there too; Frank Sullivan; Gerry Hogan; Jimmy Hart – all the top class wrestlers and contenders for various titles. I felt a very small fish indeed. But I'd come to learn…Oh – and I forgot to mention the great

British Champion Heavyweight, Billy Joyce, and young Bill Robinson. I trained all during the day and I fell in with their particular style of wrestling – but it was very hard. Submission Wrestling was always against the joints, so you had to submit.

Billy Joyce was a legend, at the time. He'd be about fifteen stone, but he hadn't a muscle in his body; he was absolutely straight up and down, and he was soft-looking to feel; no muscles at all – and he was pushing on, at the time. He looked like a farmer or a fisherman, but he was absolutely dynamite! You couldn't get near him. His technique was *perfect*. He'd have you off-balance and you could never touch him. He was absolutely brilliant! I never realised how good he was, at the time, because you assume that unless a wrestler has big muscles... His technique was so good that you were always off balance: he was a great mover; always one step ahead of his opponent.

He'd shift you into a position so that you couldn't move, or you couldn't use your strength, and he was always against your joints as well. There were no rounds; you wrestled until you 'knocked': until you gave in and you knocked the mat, to show that you'd had enough – you were beaten. They always said that if you got behind someone, he'd very rarely get away from you. Now Billy Joyce would *always* be behind you – you never saw him!

Billy Robinson, on the other hand, was a young Manchester lad who came along, and *he* was very good. He was a big, well-built, muscular man, but he could never beat Billy Joyce! Billy Robinson's in Japan, coaching – he's an old man now. He'd always say: "Billy Joyce was the man – he used to be all over me!" But they were the men, Shirley.

Young Billy Robinson and myself used to train together. Billy Joyce didn't come to the gym that much, because he knew everything, and no one could teach him a thing. He'd ramble up for a chat and then he'd slip off. But Billy Robinson was there... and he was absolutely as hard as iron.

Former Cruiserweight Wrestling champion, Weightlifting Expert and entrepreneur, Ray Robinson, from Scunthorpe, was quite often asked if he was related to Billy. In fact, he wasn't, although he explains that Jackie Robinson, a retired wrestler, now living in Morecambe, is a cousin of Billy's. My co-writer, Shirley, recently discovered, in conversation with Ray, that my brother Mickey and myself were a particular source of inspiration to him, during his sports career, which he began as a schoolboy boxer.

As a schoolboy, Ray would pick up the *TV Times*, to find out who was wrestling that week. His other heroes, in those early days, were his namesake, Billy Robinson and Albert 'Roccy' Wall. Billy Howes was also a great favourite of his. While watching us, Ray would dream that some day he might become a wrestler too.

They really trained us hard at *Riley's Gym*. We would start about eleven o'clock in the morning, then all the lads would be away around one or two o'clock in the afternoon… I would stay a lot longer. I used to practise how to fall, for *hours* on end. It was a long and painful job, but eventually I could land any way and break my fall, with feet and hands. I was becoming very fit and strong. Then, learning to roll up, you would have to be thrown, and you would roll up, and be on your feet. I became very good at that as well.

A 'drop-kick' is where you run at the punch-bag and use your two feet. There was a man drawn on the bag and you could aim for his stomach – (or his belly or his guts). I'd hit it straight off. Then the trainer might say: "Right Seamus – go for his face or his chin." And I could go for his chin and over his head if he wanted; I could do that *naturally*.

Then they used to hike the punch-bag up, so that the bottom of it was about six-foot from the floor, but strangely, I could drop-kick it, the first time I tried it. I could also hit it at nearly seven-foot. You got so used to it that you could catch a man on the chin – no bother at all. My brother, Mickey, would come afterwards, to the gym. He was very good and very technical, but he could never hit the punch-bag, above the bottom line of your stomach, no matter how hard he tried; it was just the difference between the two of us. I could do it the first day I went in, but he never got above the solar plexus. There's only an inch difference between us in height, but it's just something that people can either do, or they can't. It's just like you can write; it's just something that you can do. Mickey became a very good wrestler, but he couldn't drop-kick like I could.

I was there a few months and discovered that there were a few pro-wrestlers I could handle very easily. Then every Sunday I was back in Brum. I would be in the *Indoor Stadium* on the Pershore Road, which was situated on a corner. As you come back into town, there's an old pub called the *Earl Gray* on the corner – it's closed down now. The *Indoor Stadium* was on the left-hand side, but it's been demolished; there's a police station there now, in its place.

So I realised that I could beat a lot of those who were there. The other wrestlers in the gym all said I was ready, but before I made my debut, Billy Riley put me on Matt Moran's booth; three wrestlers and three boxers 'on top' and £5 for anybody who could last three rounds.

The first night was in Farnworth, just outside Bolton. It was the first time I was in a ring that was smaller than the mat that we had trained on – which

I found very awkward. I had no contest on the first night, but the second night I had two challengers from the crowd, although they didn't last the three rounds. The booth owner was very happy and so was I. I also saw some very good scraps with the boxers. At the end of the night the boss, Matt Moran, would ask for 'nobbins'. This was where the crowd would throw money into the ring, if they felt that they'd had good value. We always got the grub money from that and the travelling expenses.

The booth was a very serious business. In the gym you knew all the wrestlers, but this time it was all strangers and I tended to forget a lot of what I had learned. Also, you could get a fellow two or three stones heavier than yourself. I used to catch the side of my foot when I fell, which was very painful. But I stuck it out, and corrected most of my faults, by the time the booth had left Lancashire. Matt Moran wanted me to travel with the booth down to the West Country. But I had bigger things in mind.

It was a very good booth, and Matt Moran was a great character. He was a real Lancashire man, with the gab on him, and great spiel. There were three boxers and three wrestlers and he'd give the spiel about each one of us; the boxers followed by the wrestlers. He'd come to me and he'd say: "This is Seamus Dunleavy. I was down in the West of Ireland one day – a very rural area – and I saw this lad ploughing a field. It was Seamus. I said: 'Which is the way to Dublin?' Seamus picked the plough up and said: 'That way!'"

One night he caught a girl, climbing in over the top. It was a place as high as this ceiling, and completely enclosed. So he was looking up her dress as he said: "I'll give you twenty-four hours to get down Madam!" Actually, these are the characters whose stories should have been kept and recorded – but sadly, they're gone now.

There wasn't much money to be made on the booths, but I did it for the experience. Matt would maybe give me a few quid for the night, and a share of the nobbins. I think the entrance fee was a shilling, or two. But the people who ran the booths always made money. If the takings weren't good, they'd pay you accordingly. The boxing and wrestling were always good theatre, because everybody wanted to see what would happen; a few lads drunk and a few lads fancying their chances. If I saw a booth advertised now Shirley, I'd be down there straight away!

In *If –The Pat Roach* Story, Ronnie Taylor said that although Pat always put on a good show, if he had an opponent who wasn't up to much, he's go out of his way to ease off and make his opponent look good. My approach was different – I'd get stuck in, because you'd be that nervous that things could go wrong for you, like. But there was an unwritten rule, that all good boxers and wrestlers wouldn't humiliate their opponents. You might not get professional opponents, but you'd get plenty of good 'piano-movers', and this-and-that. Archie Moore said that once; he'd won about eighty fights on the run. They'd say: "Well Archie, you've fought a piano mover here and he was a big lad of eighteen stone, but he couldn't fight." But Archie said: "Well, I still had to *beat* him!" And Archie was right. They can come up, and they can be useless, but you still have to beat them.

We had drunken opponents – many a time. The booth would be there for weeks – for three or four months, so you'd have to fight a *lot* of people. Some nights, nobody would come. So it would just be a shorter session, but normally you were in action. I wouldn't do it again, if I was wrestling; it was too dodgy and you might get a fella who would rip your eye out, or something – a total eedjut! We never got anyone who was totally sadistic, but you never knew who was coming up. You'd look at the size of them and how they were built.

One night, at Derby, Jack Atherton said to me: "Seamus, there's a fella here who reckons that wrestling isn't what it's supposed to be; that's it's mostly a 'put-up job' – that you all know each other." So Jack said: "When the show's over, I want you to wrestle him." I thought: 'Thanks Jack!' So I'm there – I've got me boots on – I'd wrestled earlier. Jack could be very serious at times; he said: "Don't change Seamus." So this big fella came into the dressing room. He was a foot taller than me and I thought: 'Oh God!' He was badly built, but very tall.

The fella started to put his boots on, but when I looked closely, his hands were absolutely shaking! He was terrified, but he'd gone so far that he couldn't back down. So I beat him in about two minutes – he was absolutely useless – but what a relief! A big, tall, gangling lad – never been in a ring in his life – but somebody must have put him up to it. Once he'd made that accusation, Jack pulled him in and said: "Right, we'll put you on with someone." So that was the only time I was ever challenged in that way, but he was absolutely terrified. If I'm a bit nervous, and I'm doing six or seven nights a week, then this fella's *got* to be.

Going through the rounds, the day after the match, Billy Riley said: "How did you get on Jimmy?" I said: "Alright, but I was tired – and had three or four rounds." But he'd say: "When you're tired, the other fella's tired as well." You'd never think of that. There's two men, and if you're tired, so is he. He stuck those things in our heads and I always say to my own lads: "Whatever you do, if you're working if you're tired, well the man opposite you has just lifted the same stuff – and he's tired too."

That applies across the board, in life, no matter what you're involved in. If you're nervous about doing something, the others involved in that situation probably are too. Everyone's the same – and if I could put this into my kid's heads, that everyone is the same; everyone has their fears. Muhammed Ali was *always* nervous, before going into the ring, but we all felt the same – because we were in somebody else's hands. There's not much difference in us all Shirley… we just *think* there is. Take Philip Green, for example, who owns all of *British Home Stores*. You think: 'Well, how can I speak to that man?' But he's still the very same man that he always was – just as I am.

Pat Roach and I became really good friends, but when you first met him, with the sheer size of him you thought: 'Oh my God!' But in reality, he was one of the kindest of people you could wish to meet. Outward appearances are often deceptive. You couldn't get a more humane, down-to-earth person. I was at Pat's scrap yard the one day, and this fella came in. He said: "Are you from *Auf Wiedersehen Pet*?" Pat said: "I am – yes." The fella was unable to speak for seconds, like. "Bloody Hell!" he eventually said. But Pat was just the same as ever.

People will say to me: "God Seamus, you've done well for yourself!" And I say: "Look, I'm the exact same man who left the town fifty years ago." I didn't get any more formal education, although I learned from the University of Life, I suppose. You put your foot one way, and you sink. You go in another direction and you find 'terra firma' – solid ground. That's all there is to life, isn't it? A bit of luck on the way – you meet the right person – as I did in Mary.

It's amazing the part that luck can play in a person's life: you can choose one direction or the other; even within the space of a few minutes. I was driving into town the other day and I saw the police calling people over to one side, so that they could check various things. I had my old banger with me, but I was alright. I was only going three stops further, but I thought to myself: 'When I come back out I'll take another road on the way back.' But I forgot – and came back up the very same road! Three or four people were flashing their lights at me, to warn me that the police were up ahead. Wouldn't you believe it? They pulled me over, together with five or six other cars. The officer said: "Do you know why I've pulled you over?" I said: "No." He said: "You weren't wearing your seatbelt sir." Wasn't I delighted? Usually it's "Have you got your driving license on you?" "Let's look at your tyres." I knew they were there Shirley, and yet I forgot – so that was a bit of bad luck. But you don't know where your luck comes in.

Bobo Matu was on Matt Moran's booth at the time. He had a walk-on part recently in *Coronation Street* – I saw him a few weeks ago on that. Bobo was a hard wrestler. He was a big star at the time, but as the years went by, he never made it in the wrestling.

Getting back to those early days, having served my apprenticeship, Billy Riley got me a fight in Colne, a small town on the Lancashire-Yorkshire border, for *R & A Promotions*.

I remember getting to Colne early that day and all round the town the wrestling posters were up. It was *marvellous* to see my name on the bills and people paying to see me. As the evening drew near, I went into a café for a glass of milk and the café owner had a wrestling poster up on the wall inside. We got chatting and he asked me if I was going to the wrestling. I told him who I was and he ended up asking me to sign an autograph for himself and his family. So I was feeling very important. Then, as I left the café, I suddenly got really nervous... what was a lad from Charlestown doing here?

Colne is a real Lancashire town – houses all in square blocks. We were wrestling in an old theatre, with a very hard ring in it. It was a small crowd as well. As I arrived, the people were starting to queue. Boy – the nerves were bad now! As I sat in the dressing room I used to look out at the crowd. The ring was on the stage, so the people were very close to it. There were seats on the stage as well, so you could nearly touch the people from the ring, which made my nerves even worse. The top of the bill was:

Farmer John Allen versus Dave Armstrong
Halifax   **Newcastle**

I was pitted against a fellow called Alec Bray, who was in fact a Wiganer, but never came to our gym. So I hadn't met him before. He was about thirty-five to thirty-eight years old. I was twenty-four and in good shape.

The first match that evening was Joe Critchley, versus somebody else. Joe Critchley came in afterwards and said: "Poxy crowd," meaning a small crowd. I must have been on second, so I had to get my boots on then. It was a hard ring, and I remember seizing up and forgetting all the things I'd learned. But nevertheless, I won by two falls to nil. Afterwards, I did not remember much of the contest! The old nerves were very bad. But I started my career with a win!!

It was a *Riley and Atherton* Promotion, so Billy Riley was connected with it. Billy was probably refereeing that night too, but Jack Atherton gave the word back that I'd performed alright. *R & A Promotions* was *Riley and Atherton Promotions*. I used to work for Jack, all around the country, throughout my career. Jack kept me on, all the time. But I was glad to get my bag and away, for that very first match.

I continued training in the gym, five days a week, and did the dancehall job at the weekend. I was really going – I'd made my debut – and won. The promoter fixed me up with another fight, in Neath, just outside Swansea, in Wales. This was against a wrestler called Monty Swan, from Ellesmere Port. Another win! Monty was a good bit lighter than me and I handled him easily. I was between thirteen-and-a-half and fourteen stone.'

I got to know Monty well, as the years went by, but I beat him easily in that match. Again, Neath was like wrestling in a different country: you were in Wales. But the crowd were very enthusiastic and I actually enjoyed the match, and did a whole lot better than I had previously. You'd get good crowds and bad crowds. We'd go to Dudley, for instance, and again, it was a ring on a stage. They were a hard crowd to please, as were the Scottish, who would want to see plenty of blood – and people getting carried out of the ring! The Welsh were very good – they'd appreciate every move; that's what you'd call a good crowd. But you'd get some, in Yorkshire, for example, who were as hard as hard. You can imagine, like – (Yorkshire accent): "Knock his bloody head off!" They wanted you to be carried out on stretchers.

You may recall from one of our opening chapters, that Mammy had a cousin called Johnny Gallagher – a very generous man – who would visit the Dunleavy household about three times a year, always with a present of milk and a delicious cake, baked specially for us by his wife, Delia. Well, I was wrestling one particular night in Sheffield and things were going rather badly for me. Suddenly, I heard a shout from the crowd: "You could do with a slice of Delia Gallagher's cake now Seamus!" It was Gerald Gallagher, Johnny's son, in the audience. He lived in Sheffield for many years. We met afterwards and had great craic.

Submission Wrestling was never used in traditional wrestling. It would only be used in self-defence normally. All of the holds were totally illegal, so you couldn't use it in a pro-match. It was very serious; it was really for outside, in the street. That's why the Wigan wrestlers could always look after themselves.

Wrestling originated in the North. There were two main schools. The biggest school was Wigan – and Bradford after that. All the Yorkshire lads wrestled in Bradford and the Lancashire lads in Wigan. I think the first wrestling began in Cumberland, in Northumberland, and was 'catch-as-catch-can'. They wrestled from the waist up.

Ray Robinson is into Strength Wrestling, which probably comes from Westmorland and Northumberland. They only wrestle from the waist up, so their legs are never used at all. In Submission Wrestling, on the other hand, your opponent would try to beat you, with no holds barred. There was a body called the *Wrestling Alliance*. They all joined up together and we used to wrestle under the Lord Mountevans rules, otherwise you'd have had broken limbs every night of the week. So it was nothing against the joint or the throat and no punching.

Submission Wrestling was the most dangerous kind of wrestling, but if you were in competition, you couldn't do it then. I didn't mind being involved in the most dangerous kind, because I was young and strong then. But if someone jumped the ring and said that wrestling wasn't all that it was supposed to be, then you'd go back to that. That's why Jack picked me for the challenge, on that particular night, because he knew that I'd put the challenger out of action.

Being a Submission Wrestler meant that you could take on anyone. Pete Roberts would tell you that – they used to call us 'Shooters'; that's how he describes me in *Auf Wiedersehen Pat*. But I suppose if I'd lived in London, I wouldn't have been doing that style of wrestling at all. Pete Roberts never learned it, although he'd have a few moves, but I can't say that he was as good as me, although he was very skilled. Pete would tell you himself. It's like someone saying: "They're all gangsters, but *that* one there's a Mafia man!" There's a difference.

So we were the 'Shooters' – all the Wigan men; Billy Robinson, Billy Joyce. I've seen Pallo say: "Oh God – I'm wrestling Jack Dempsey!" Dempsey wasn't very attractive to watch – but he was the man! So wrestlers from the South weren't too keen to take on Northern wrestlers, because they'd be all the 'hard cases'!

Around this time, in my early twenties, after wrestling in England for a while and building up my strength to a considerable degree, there was a special feat that I used to do, on my return visits to Charlestown. In Dad's back yard in Barrack Street, there was an enormous anvil, weighing three-and-a-half hundredweight. It rested on a huge slice of a tree trunk, and was two-foot six inches high, from the top of the block. I used to knock it off the block, then lifting it up from the ground, I would put it back, on top of the tree trunk. I've never seen anyone else do that… in my time!

Chapter Fourteen

SPARKHILL LANDLORDS

Seamus and Michael were now in living in digs in Park Road, Sparkhill, after moving from Saltley. Joe Enright, their landlord, happened to be a Bouncer on the door at the Shamrock. Hearing that Joe had a house to let, Mickey and Seamus decided to rent it off him. One Sunday morning, the brothers were chatting with Mick O'Reilly, from Cavan. They normally dropped the 'O' from his surname and just called him Mick Reilly. A few other mates were also there, in Sparkhill Park, which was directly opposite their new lodgings. Mick commented: "You're paying rent up there. What you should do is buy a house for yourself." The idea had never occurred to Seamus, but Mick assured them that it was definitely the thing to do. He already had a house himself, which he filled with a crowd of lodgers, enabling him to pay his mortgage and make money as well, into the bargain. So he talked the Dunleavys into it. They put all their savings, £500 each, and took out a mortgage for £750.

Mickey was a lighter wrestler than Seamus, but as he progressed, he became very skilful. By this stage, Seamus had been taken over by 'Dale Martin Promotions', who covered the whole of the South of England, including the whole of London. They were the biggest promoters in England, and booked him for nearly five or six nights a week, injuries permitting.

My brother, Mickey, was on the Northern Circuit. Now and again we would be on the same Bill, which was great, because we could go together. He was a handsome boy and a great favourite with the ladies – (take note Margaret!). We used to go by train, to all the bouts. We palled with all the Irish lads around Sparkhill; because of being on the door of the Dancehall and also because of the wrestling, we were well known.

We bought our first house in Wilton Road, Sparkhill, taking in Irish immigrant tenants.

The house cost £1750 and was a freehold terrace, with five bedrooms and a big attic. I remember the first coal fire that we put down, and then sat in front of it. Fancy owning a house in England! I remember saying to Mickey: "Have we done the right thing? I'm broke again." He said: "Yes, but we have a house – and half of it is yours."

We got the beds in and a bit of furniture. Then a few of my mates came to live with us. In no time at all there were thirteen or fourteen people living with us. We used to charge about a pound a week and we all cooked in a communal kitchen. I was in the attic, with three other boys. We collected between £50 and £60 a month; our mortgage was £10 a month. So we were on another adventure.

We knew all the lads who stayed with us, so we used to have great fun. We continued like this, wrestling during the week. Having so many lads in the house meant that there was very little individual space. There was one room downstairs: three lads had their beds in it. The next room, on the first floor, slept two. So that was five lads. It was always cramped, but with young single lads, all they wanted was their bed, and their jacket hanging up somewhere. So they weren't too bothered and there was a kitchen for the grub. In the summer they were always out in the park, in the Dancehall, or in the Picture-house. They only needed somewhere to sleep.

The first three lads, downstairs, were Sean Hanrahan, Tom Broderick and the third one I can't remember. One of them was a bus driver and the other was a bus conductor; Sean worked in a factory. Upstairs, there was Martin Coleman. Martin was a bus driver and there was another lad in that room with him. The funny thing was, if one of them left, out of one room, we would put a stranger in with them. You would never do that now, if you were running a guesthouse or hotel. But in those days, when somebody left, a complete stranger might suddenly arrive, to share the room with you!

That's the way it was, but we were all Irish lads. Tony Flaherty was in the attic with me; he was a factory man. Don O'Donnell was in there too, together with Mick Kane. Don and Mick Kane were both on the buildings; mostly in construction. There was a 'mish-mash' throughout the whole house, but everyone was working.

The first rule was that there was no drinking at all, in the house. And there were no women ever came in. "Can I bring my girlfriend back?" "What!" Because we'd be afraid of the priest coming along and saying: "What sort of a house have you got here?" The religious aspect was very serious with us. When we were growing up, we were more afraid of the priest than the Garda, or police, because of their look: they could put a pair of horns on you! Yet nowadays we've discovered that some of the priests were naughty boys themselves, although there are many more good priests than misguided ones. But there you are…. It's strange… the effect they had on us.

That was the first house. We had plans to eventually rent out more houses, so we couldn't afford to have a bad reputation. I'm not sure how long we had that house, but it was very good – we were always full up there. I used to climb up to the attic, after returning late from a night's wrestling. I'd check that all the lads were in when I got back, and then when I got up in the morning, they'd all be gone.

We never cleaned up. We'd just throw a few milk bottles out and this-and-that. Sweep up, maybe every six weeks; shoeboxes and cellophane packets from shirts. We'd have four of five binfuls of stuff. And that was it. I can't remember us ever changing sheets at all. We'd go for months before any of the lads would say: "Have you got a set of sheets?" They'd just take their clothes off, and knock any dust that there was, out of the bed. We had a bathroom there, but for some reason or another, no one ever used it. We used to go to the Public Baths.

We continued like this, wrestling during the week. By this time I'd left Wigan and also my brother had too. We always seemed to have the house filled, which was great. So after a few months, Mickey decided we should try and get another house, which we did, in the next road to where we had the first one. Again, we put a small deposit down and applied for a mortgage; the same procedure. We filled it up with lads. Mickey, being the M.C. in the only big Irish Dancehall in Birmingham, had access to a pool of young Irish boys coming into the town, so he filled our other houses as well. Things were looking up for us.

At the dancehalls, years ago, there'd be a Master of Ceremonies, who called out every dance. He'd go on the stage and say; "Take your partners for the next dance", and he'd announce what it was. You don't see it now. Mickey was a handsome lad, with a dickey-bow. Of course, he was popular with all the lads, so, all of a sudden, he'd pick the men to come and live with him and rent each house. It was great craic and that's what we did. We had different bands of mates: me on the door, with a different section of mates, and him, with another section of mates. He had enough to move on to the next road, with another section of mates, but the houses were still owned between us.

But now, the travelling was getting harder, with all the trains. I must have waited on every train platform, in the whole of England! Just an example: I could be in Derby on Monday; York on Tuesday; London on Wednesday; Brighton on Thursday; Barnsley on Friday; Liverpool on Saturday… and very often, Sunday as well…somewhere.

I got a lift home one night, from a venue, with a very good performer, Tony Vallon. He said: "Why don't you buy a car?" I said: "Tony, I've only been in this game a year and it might all be finished. I might get no fights, or get injured." He laughed and said: "Well, I've been in this game ten years, and as long as there is wrestling in England or Europe, you will be a big part of it." Well, that settled it. I spotted a second-hand Volkswagen, in Cricklewood, London, for £350 and I bought it on the 17 March. It was nearly new and I had not much idea how to drive it. My brother, Mickey, was already a driver, so he drove her up, from London to Birmingham.

Our second house was at 53 Fulham Road; the next one to Wilton Road, where I lived. We followed the same procedure again. There were five big bedrooms, a front room and an attic, but this time we decided to put water into every room, so that you could have a drink and a wash, or urinate – down the sink. We put a cooker in every room, so that they were self-contained. In the old days, when I was living in Saltley, or elsewhere, you had a big community kitchen. Seven or eight lads would use it, and some people would be a bit embarrassed, cooking; you'd stack the grub in the kitchen. But this time, everyone had their own little mini-kitchen. We were very successful at that. Some lads would come and say: "Oh God – that's great! Water in the room and your own kitchen; you don't have to share with anyone," so that was a great improvement upon the kind of bed-sitters that I'd been going into. Word got around that if you got a bed-sit with the Dunleavys you'd have your privacy. It would be you and your mate – or whatever. After a further six months with the second house, we continued on in the same vein, gradually buying more houses.

We continued to coach Pat Roach, Pete Roberts, Gordon Corbett, and other lads at Severn Street. They'd do a sort of trade-off with us; Pete with the locks, as he was a carpenter, and Gordon Corbett with saucepans and kettles, as he worked at *Bulpitt's*. We needed locks, nails and hinges, although many of the places we bought wouldn't have them, as they had all been family houses. So we were always looking for locks and handles. Gordon had all the kettles we wanted, and saucepans.

Pat Roach arrived one day, with a bacon-slicer. While they were wrestling, me and Mickey nicked the bacon-slicer, took it out to the car and hid it. Pat said: "I had a bacon slicer when I came in." Rather like that song: "I had a hat when I came in, I put in the rack," et cetera. Years after, it was a big craic with us. He'd say: "What did you do with that bacon slicer?" "Never saw it Pat!" We must have thought it would be handy for meat in sandwiches – or something.

The third house was in Wilton Road. They were all around Sparkhill. When I married Mary we had seven or eight houses. We lived in Weatheroak Road when we got married, by which time it had become a thriving business.

Mary and I lived on our own, for a little while, in Weatheroak Road, but I'll tell you more about that in a later chapter.

I first met Pat Roach at Handsworth Gym, on the Soho Road. That was before I started training wrestlers at *Severn Street Amateur Club*. Gordon Corbett used to come with me. He was the mainstay for getting me out there. Pat and myself became mates. He was bloody huge, wasn't he? I mentioned a hold, in an earlier chapter, called a 'Figure Four', when you hooked a man and you could turn, and lift him up on your shoulder. But not Pat Roach – none of us could shift him!

There were a few of us there when I tried it: Mickey, myself, and I think it was Pete Roberts; maybe Gordon Corbett too – and a few others. I was used to the Figure Four, but I couldn't budge Pat. His arms, his legs and his chinbone were long, and I just couldn't get a hold on him. So I always said if I wrestled Pat Roach, I'd do my best to see that he never got the Figure Four on me!

He was always quietish. In our game at the dancehalls, you'd get involved in a lot of fights. But I never heard of Pat being involved in any fights, except a bit of business.

This applied with the Fewtrells' clubs too. We all knew, around town, who the troublemakers were, but Pat was never mentioned in that vein. You could go anywhere and there might be various bullies. You'd want a squad of lads with you, to see that they didn't get out of hand, or to stop them at the door. But I never heard Pat's name linked with *anything* like that, although he'd got the size and weight, if he'd wanted to.

Mickey was the first person to show Pat how to do the 'Roll-up'. With experience Pat became a very flexible wrestler, tackling moves such as the Snowball, and so on. I used to see him in the clubs. We'd always sit together. I was well known at the time, to the wrestling, and so was he. We'd talk about anything and everything.

I had an *Equity* card at one time, because we wrestled a few times in *Raymond's Revue Bar*, in London, which was half Strip Club, plus Revue and Burlesque. To work there, we had to have *Equity* cards *en bloc*, so that any wrestler who wrestled there would have an *Equity* card; it was one of the regulations that *Equity* laid down. It was relatively easy to get the cards in those days. I stopped wrestling around 1970, when I was thirty-five and just did the odd match.

World of Sport used to be a televised Saturday afternoon show. I was on several times and despite being very excited, I was always a bit nervous going along. Because the cameras would be honed on you and the cameraman would zoom right into you. It was very strange, but you had not to look at the camera; you had to pretend that it wasn't there. I sometimes see, and you probably do too, the odd person appearing on TV, who's looking at the camera. But it was great. You'd start in the afternoon, then when you were finished, you had your money – and you were famous, weren't you? "I saw you on the telly today," and this-that-and-the-other.

I appeared from time to time, on *World of Sport*, over a four of five-year period. So I suppose you might say that those four or five years were my heyday. I was on with Tibor Savacs once, the Hungarian champion; he was a very good wrestler. I wrestled Clayton Thompson on the telly and Jimmy Dula – a big coloured lad from some part of Africa. Lots and lots of Heavyweights, although I was actually a Light Heavyweight myself. Mickey was the Middleweight. But I was only fourteen-and-a-half stone, wrestling fellas who'd weigh seventeen-and-a-half stone and upwards.

So that made it very difficult for me – always fighting people heavier than myself, but I was very fit and very agile and could do nip-ups and handsprings. I won at least seventy-five per cent of my fights. I've got the ratings somewhere. I was rated fifth or sixth in Europe, at one period. It was published in the wrestling magazines. I was always number two or three in England, and usually part of a Tag Team. I tagged with a fella called Jimmy Ryan, 'Tiger Ryan' – when Mickey was off, or sick, or getting married or something. But usually it was always me and Mickey... and we were rated as one of the best Tag Teams in the country.

People sometimes say that wrestling was fixed, but you'd never get a match if you knew who was going to win. You see, I always say, Mickey and I were the only Irish wrestlers in Birmingham. If it was fixed like that, there are a lot bigger, better-looking Irish fellas than me about, who'd say: "Well, we'll have a bit of this." There was always showmanship in wrestling Shirley, as you well know, but how would you fix a match? They rang me up this one time, when I had already retired, asking me to go down to the *Embassy*, to wrestle a Hungarian there. How could you fix a match with a man who couldn't speak English...and go into an intricate fall, or something? But everyone has their opinions... and that's the story that goes round.

Ray Robinson says that there are two kinds of wrestlers: the Performers – like Big Daddy – and then the more serious, authentic kind, who have so many moves that it's difficult to know who is going to win. Big Daddy was absolutely useless, and how he got to where he was I'll never know. It was a family business with the three brothers, wrestling, refereeing and promoting.

As far as the serious side of wrestling, which I was in, if you lost twenty matches on the run, they'd stop booking you. Having said that, showmanship abounded, but there was also a lot of hard work involved. The biggest clown of all was Les Kellett, but he was one of the hardest men in the game. He was as hard as iron. You had to hit Kellett with an axe, to stop him! But he'd roll around the ring and laugh and joke. He used to hit you with a hand that was like a claw. He was a farmer, and he had rough hands on him. You'd watch him then all of a sudden he'd catch you. He appeared to be the biggest clown in wrestling, but in fact, was one of the hardest men in the game.

I was wrestling on the Isle of Man once, and I'd a car parked in Liverpool. Kellett was on the same Bill, on the Isle of Man, so on the way back I said: "I'm going home to Birmingham." Kellett said: "Ah, I'm fighting in Birmingham tonight." So I gave him a lift back. It was a rainy day. A stone hit the windscreen, during the journey, and it broke. We had to put newspapers across our chests, because it started raining. When we got to Birmingham I dropped Les off at the venue and I went home, because I could walk to the *Embassy* from my home in Sparkhill.

When I got there, I was wrestling Kellett, but neither of us knew beforehand. So although we'd travelled back together, when we started wrestling it was as if I'd never met him before in my life! He did everything he could possibly do, the claw hand across your face, and so on. I'd decided: 'He'll never catch me with that tonight!' But the next thing I knew – Bang! The claw was there, right in your face. But that was Kellett.

He lived *totally* on his own, then married this lady, late in life. She'd been married before and she was from Cavan, where Mick O'Reilly was from. So it was the first time he'd got close to anyone. Being as she was Cavan and we were Irish, he sort of took a bit of a shine to us. Having said that, you had to watch him in the ring – but at least he'd talk to you: "How you doing there Seamus?" I'd say: "Well, not too bad." In the ring, as far as the audience was concerned, he was a funny man.

But in Brixton, late at night, if you were with a group of mates, you'd see Kellett, walking the streets on his own, with his bag. You never saw anyone with him. They said, allegedly, that he used to dabble in witchcraft and all that. He'd a son called Chris, who's alive and well. Chris was a very good amateur wrestler, as a matter of fact.

Today's wrestlers are very fit, strong men. Although there's a lot of showmanship and gymnastics in it, they're very fit, strong men; fine, physical specimens. There's no one with big bellies nowadays. And they do very dangerous stuff. I wouldn't like to be the recipient of it. I'd say that it's a lot more dangerous. But that was my time in it – and I enjoyed it.

Chapter Fifteen

MARY GRIFFIN

This chapter is mainly about Mary Griffin, as she was known for the first eighteen years of her life. Mary and Seamus have been married for forty-three years, at the time of going to print. We'll also take time out, to reflect on the changing fortunes of other family members, whom you've met in earlier chapters.

Life is full of co-incidences, is it not? For example, on holiday last year, having crossed the Atlantic to Cape Cod, my husband and I were relaxing on a bench alongside the ocean, waiting for friends who were to join us shortly, at a nearby restaurant. It was at that point we chanced to meet Oliver Muldoon, formerly of Lenaboy Gardens, Salthill, Galway, who was strolling with his American wife Susan on the prom at Falmouth Heights. It was a tremendous surprise to discover that, although not having ever met Seamus, Oliver had known Seamus' Uncle Jim, and his family, as he explains in the following account:

The Dunleavy Family had come to Galway in the early 1950s and started a guest-house. By the time we moved into the house just across the road, in 1960, (only months, so I'm told, after Seamus first met Mary Griffin), Jim's guesthouse had become a small hotel, known as the Sacre Coeur, and would soon have a bar license.

In time, we got to know most of the family: as a boy I served Mass for Father Louie Dunleavy, Seamus' cousin, when he came home in summer to escape the Florida heat. Later I sang in the University College, Galway choir, with Frank Dunleavy, another of Jim's sons. It was clear that they were all exceptionally clever people. I believe Frank took a first-class honours degree in Latin and Greek, before qualifying as a doctor.

In those early years, the hotel structure was being expanded, supervised hands-on by Jim Dunleavy, usually clad in his boilersuit. Jim was very modest about who he was, and must have taken great amusement from the many hotel guests and visitors who thought he was just one of the workmen on the job. The story went the rounds at the time that Agnes Dunleavy one day upbraided Jim and his crew for less-than-stellar progress in finishing up construction before the summer season. She ended by observing resignedly that "Well, I suppose Rome wasn't built in a day." Jim is reputed to have retorted "Sure, that's because you weren't the ganger, Agnes!"

Before they had a bar he'd sometimes call me over, when I was hanging around, and have me go get cigarettes for him from 'The Bal', the nearest pub. We thought nothing of that in those days. Imagine the fuss today, at coaxing a minor to buy tobacco products, in licensed premises, no less!

My father was a keen dogman whose pointer bitch had won the coveted Best of Show at Crufts Dog Show in 1956. He found that he could augment his dogs' daily diet with leftovers from Jim Dunleavy's hotel, thus enabling him to say that his animals were the best fed in town…the only ones eating hotel food. Every evening, one of Jim's kitchen staff would come to our back gate, with a bucket of slop for the dogs – a win-win situation for both sides.

Indeed, the Dunleavy's food hospitality became famous all over the West of Ireland. Eventually, hardly a weekday went by (excepting Lent) that didn't have either a wedding reception or organizational function at the hotel. When the time came for me to organize a college dress-dance, I naturally turned to Seamus' cousin, Sean Dunleavy (who had taken over the management of the hotel from his father) and his staff.

It was during a wedding reception, in 1968, that there was a knock on our front door, enquiring if I could play the piano, at the Sacre Coeur. My skills were very minimal, but enough to have me invited to join 'The Usual Trio', until someone better came along. But by playing with Ronnie Bourke and Gerry Macken, veterans of the big band era-Des Fretwell Orchestra, I learned way more than a succession of frustrated music teachers ever managed to convey.

Now that the hotel is no more, I no longer have an anchor whenever I visit my old neighbourhood. I'll miss it greatly and the friendliness for which it came to stand.

Oliver Muldoon,
Cape Cod,
U.S.A. February
2006

There were a few girls, from time to time, but one Saint Patrick's Night, a lad called Paddy Faul, came in with his wife and a young girl of about fourteen or fifteen. Paddy used to be the Chief Spokesman for TOAC (all the black taxis in Birmingham). He was from Tubbercurry – my next town at home in Ireland, seven miles from Charlestown. In time to come, if Ed Doolan, the radio broadcaster, wanted information about the black taxis, he'd say: "Get Paddy Faul."

Paddy was one of the first people I met, from near home, when I got a job on the door of the *Shamrock Club*. It got round like, where I was from. Paddy said: "What part of Mayo are you from?" I said: "Charlestown." He said: "Oh, I'm from Tubbercurry – the next town!" There's a picture of him in the book, taken on the actual night I met him. The word 'tuber' is Gaelic for 'water well'.

We got very friendly, me and Paddy. He'd come in every week. Paddy was married and he had a room, you'd call it a flat now, which he rented in one of Mick Reilly's houses. He had a little girl called Frances. But both parents worked. Paddy was on the buses at the time and Mary was a bus conductress. They used to leave the little girl with Mary's mother, Mai.

Mary was just coming up to fourteen, when Paddy and Mary brought her to the Saint Patrick's Night Dance, in Hurst Street, at the *Shamrock Club*. Mrs Griffin, Mary's mother said: "She'll be going with them, so she'll be fine." On the way in, I had a big craic with Paddy. He introduced me to Mary: "This is Mary Griffin. Her mum looks after our little girl." They went into the dance. There were two floors: an upstairs, where you could do all the modern ballroom dances, like waltzes, foxtrots and quicksteps; downstairs was all Ceilidh music – totally.

Saint Patrick's Night at the dancehall was absolutely *thronged* – you couldn't move! Somebody asked Mary up to dance. When the dance was over she could not find Paddy Faul. This sounds funny, but imagine two very big dancehalls, jam-packed with people; there must have been three thousand there, all jammed together. It was her very first dance, so she was certainly 'going in at the deep end'!

There were four or five of us on the door, all linking hands to try to keep the crowd out. Then at one stage the dancehall owner Matt Byrne said: "Let so many of them in lads, even without paying." It was that packed. Mary and Paddy left after a while, because they were on early duty. They said: "Mary's upstairs. We don't know where, but we've got to go. You live in Sparkhill. Will you look after her?" I said: "Certainly, no problem at all." Mary came up to me afterwards and explained to me, tearfully, that she couldn't find Paddy and Mary. What could she do? So I said: "OK. I live in Wilton Road; you live at the bottom of the road, in Stoney Lane. I'll take you out and drop you back at your own house." Which I did – and that was the start of everything.

She absolutely *loved* dancing and began to come back regularly with Paddy and Mary to the *Shamrock*, for quite some time. Then they took in a lodger at Mary's house, called Mary Theresa McHale, a first cousin of her mother's, from Fisherhill. She'd be ten years older than Mary. She was a dancer, so she used to enjoy going to the dances and Mary started to go with her. So we got to know each other and began our courtship, which is still going strong to this very day. It's her 61st birthday, as I'm speaking these words!

Paddy and Mary Faul eventually went back to Tubbercurry and they have a lovely house there. They bought the one next door too and put the two together. They're living there now, as happy as Larry. Mary was doing a paper round at the time I met her. She was still at school, and was doing the paper round part-time. The family were extremely poor; her father was dead and her mum was having to support eight children. Mary was the eldest.

She went to Bishop Challoner Secondary Modern School, and became Head Girl at that school. She did her paper round every morning, before school started. My sisters lived in one of the roads that she had to pass, and Mary was very embarrassed if she saw them; she'd jump across the hedge – or do various other things to avoid seeing them; because they were much older than her, and here was the paper girl, going out with their brother!

There was an Irish dancehall called *The Harp*, owned by the same man who owned the *Shamrock* in town, Matt Byrne; we were part of the same organisation. Mary started to go there on a Tuesday; it was over by 11.00pm, and she would walk home.

The Harp was directly opposite the Ice Rink, known as the *Embassy*, on Walford Road, Sparkhill, the wrestling venue that I described in the previous chapter.

I picked up a bit of courage and asked her out to the Pictures – the *Carlton Cinema*, which was just a short walk for the both of us. The first picture that we saw there was *Splendour in the Grass*, starring Warren Beatty and Natalie Wood. A good love story – I think she enjoyed it. It was in the great days of Hollywood. Warren was a very handsome lad at the time. He's probably still alive now and going strong. It became one of Natalie Wood's most famous films. She married Robert Wagner, but tragically, died from drowning in 1981, when they were on their boat; no one knows to this day whether it was an accident, suicide, or foul play. It remains a mystery.

Mary and myself had two tubs of ice-cream and she licked the lid – she was very young and innocent; but very nice. I was away quite often and used to be out of town a lot, so I would only see her now and again. I went home one year, during the summer. I was a bit of a star now, at home. I used to send the odd wrestling bill home and everybody was amazed. Dad would put the bill in the window and there would be great wonder.

Well, Sunday night came and down we went to the *Central Ballroom* in Charlestown – Walsh's Hall. Great meeting everyone again and then, low and behold, who was there but Mary Griffin!! She was with a carload of people from Fisherhill, close to Pontoon, near Castlebar. I was glad to see her and her me, I think. So I said I would drive her home.

It was all arranged and believe it or not, I took her to supper. This was the ultimate for me. Sitting behind the big window, having supper: a plate of ham and salad; tea and bread… and looking out at the dancers. God, I felt posh – and all the mates passing by the window, giving me the thumbs up! Supper over, we left the hall. Mary told her friends that she was being taken home by somebody.

Now I had hired a car, out in Dublin, although I was no great driver. I'd left my car in the Square in Charlestown, just beside the dancehall. But when we got in the car, it would not start. I had left the lights on, for the duration of the dance, so Mary had to go back to the dancehall, tell her mates what had happened, and rather sheepishly ask if she could go home with them. One of the boys in the car, Tony Dempsey, really fancied her and thought that she was going with him; but her mates took her home.

I had arranged to see her the following evening, in Pontoon. So I set off, the evening after; a beautiful evening. She set off on her aunt's bike to meet me, but whatever happened, we both missed each other! The thing was I'd never been to Pontoon before, although it's only fifteen miles away. I must have spent an hour, going up and down, looking for her, and she'd gone there as well.

Now it's an awful experience, when you're really looking forward to meeting someone, and then, for whatever reason, they don't show up… the disappointment. You're looking forward to it. I'd driven there and was getting to be a better driver, a real 'Jack-the-Lad'. So I'm picking up this lovely girl…. But she's not there. When I saw her afterwards in Birmingham, we were both saying: "Well I was there!" We both thought that we'd been 'stood up'. But she didn't know the country either; it was her first time there. We didn't know any of the local landmarks, but there's only one road going through Pontoon, and we just never met. And really, it's a big area; you'll see it some time. You could be down there; she could be up here. We could have said, had we known the place better, "I'll see you outside *Healy's Hotel*." We go to the hotel now and we know the area much better. There are two fisherman's hotels there – absolutely lovely.

I did not know the name of her village, so I could not contact her. I knew that her mother was from Castlebar and her father was from a place about three miles from Charlestown; but he died when she was only ten years old. She and all her brothers and sisters were born in England. Mary had five sisters and two brothers.

With our families coming from the same area, Mary and myself are both familiar with the story of a great local character, Bab McHale. She ran a pub in Breaffey, just outside Castlebar, for donkey's years. It's still in the family, although she's dead and gone, but it's leased out. Bab always kept open, all through the night, although she should have been closed by half past ten. You could go in, any old hour of the morning, and there'd be a drink there for you. The Gards would leave her alone for a while, but then they'd be obliged to raid her, at odd times, otherwise there'd be people complaining about it. When she was well into her seventies, Bab was summoned to court for license infringement. She was thumbing a lift, and told the motorist who offered her one: "I'm off to the courthouse, in Castlebar."

Mary continues: "The man who gave her a lift didn't let on that he was going to the courthouse too. So they're going along in the car and she's telling this fella her story, about how she was finding it hard to make a living – feeling very sorry for herself – that she was a poor old lady and they should leave her alone… but she could put it on a bit! Her daughter was well up in the Gards, at the time, but she lived in Bandon, down in Cork. And lo and behold, when Bab went into the court, wasn't your man the judge? But he let her off and the case was dismissed. She was *such* a character – such a laugh! She loved a drop of gin, every night. Her theory was that if you acted soft, people would take pity on you. So she always 'played daft'. She was a striking-looking woman in her day, but she was very up front as well. If anything was wrong she believed in having it out in the open – the way things are; just be natural. But she played it soft, and got away with it – several times."

There's another story about a time when she was in hospital, and they put a woman in the bed next to her, whom Bab didn't like being so close to. So she called the doctor over; the woman would have about fifteen visitors and they'd all sit on Bab's bed. Bab said to the doctor: "I'm a woman that catches infection very easily. I wonder – could you shift me away from those people?" It was only a lie that she made up, but she got away with it!

Back in England, I saw Mary coming from work one evening and we had a chat. I thought she had not turned up for our date in Ireland, and she thought I hadn't, but we were glad to see each other again. She had now got her first job, in an office. She would be about sixteen years old and I would be about twenty-five. So we arranged to meet for the Pictures. She was waiting at the glass shop, on the corner of Stoney Lane and Fulham Road. When I arrived, I was driving my new car. Mary was delighted and thrilled.

I started to drive to my wrestling matches and every Saturday she would come with me. Lovely long spins, all over England. They were marvellous times. We were becoming very close. Every Saturday, without fail, she'd get all dolled up and everything and we'd head out. It could be Norwich, Blackpool, and Liverpool – whatever. We'd have a lovely long drive and a meal. We used to stop at a restaurant in Salisbury, regularly. I could still go there, to this day. We'd have Chinese chicken and chips, followed by pineapple with ice-cream. We'd always have the same meal, but it was absolutely lovely. You'd have money in your pocket and you'd the girl you loved. It was great... marvellous times. Mary was totally innocent – and 'untouched by hand' – you could say!

A very romantic situation, especially when you compare it to life in the 21st Century. It would be much more difficult now, to find someone as innocent – although not so unusual in those days. There are so many single person households these days, and a divorce rate currently around 50%. So unless you kidnapped someone at an early age, and protected her, while she was growing up... Nowadays, people practically jump on each other; but in those days, you didn't do that. But when I look back on it, it was far better.

I was now a Top of the Bill man, and would always be on third. So we would be back on the road, around ten o'clock. Then we would stop for something to eat, at a café, or Chinese Restaurant. We got to know the roads well, and we knew where all the good transport cafes were. Great times. That was the way life went.

I always sent money home every week, to my parents. My three younger sisters were in England, by this time; all three came to Birmingham. My oldest sister, Mai, who I first stayed with in Liverpool, all those years ago, came to Birmingham too, with her husband, Sean, and family. So I'd started something! Mai and Sean bought a house along the Warwick Road, in Sparkhill. Then after a while they moved up to Phipson Road in the same area. They had a family of six children and they're all up and away now. She and Sean eventually decided to go home to Charlestown. But sadly, Sean had a very bad stroke, and he was incapacitated for the last years of his life. That was a few years back, so Mai's a widow. But she still lives in Charlestown, with family all around her.

My other sisters, from me downwards, are Angela, Kathleen and Monica. Angela's married here and lives opposite the *Drum and Monkey*, in Bentley Heath. She's married to Pete O'Reilly, brother to Mick O'Reilly, the friend who first advised us to buy houses and rent them. She has four children, all grown up now; some married and some not.

Then Kathleen is married and lives in Shirley, a short distance away from *Our Lady of the Wayside*. She could walk to the church and back, she was that close. She married a lad called Frank Neary, from Bangor Erris, County Mayo. They have four very nice children – two boys and two girls; all very successful, professional people. Two girls married and two boys not married. Monica, my youngest sister, is married to John Green, from Roscommon. They have three children – two boys and a girl. The girl is a teacher and the two boys are in the construction business with their dad.

I was wrestling nearly every night, and in one of my bouts came across Harry Kendal, the deaf mute, who beat me years earlier. This time I beat Harry, but by now I was about fourteen stone, ten pounds, whereas Harry was about twelve-and-a-half stone. So I had a big advantage in weight – which made a nice change! I tried to speak to him after, but I don't know if he remembered me or not. He could not speak, only sort of grunt, and you had to stand before him, so that he could lip – read. I was on later bills with him, but never actually wrestled him again, so I never found out what his thoughts were.

Then, one of the strangest things happened. I was booked to wrestle in the Fairfield Hall, in Croydon, just outside London. When I got there, who do you think I was pitted against? Only Timmy Geoghan, who had been Young Atlas, all those years ago! He had left Ireland and had gone to America, where he started wrestling. He was from County Leitrim, in the Irish Republic. Timmy had devised a hold called the 'sleeper hold'. Before a match, he would ask for volunteers from the crowd, and he would put this sleeper hold on them; they would be put to sleep for about fifteen seconds.

He put six or seven to sleep that night. It was extremely dangerous, as I later found out when I spoke to doctors about this. He'd put a row of people down. There was a lad called Cormac Daly from Cork. He was a hardy lad and feared nothing. Cormac volunteered, but he said he had pains in his head for a week afterwards. It's no wonder, because Timmy twisted the Carotic Artery. He used to twist the head and cut off the blood supply to the brain, which caused unconsciousness.

But we had a great chat and he was delighted that I remembered him. He wasn't that old either. I would be about twenty-five or twenty-six and he would be about thirty-six or seven – powerfully built. Well, he did not put *me* to sleep, but I won't tell you the result. You will have to find that out from the wrestling records.

At this time I had been on TV a time or two, but the first time I was seen in Charlestown was great. Pa saw me, but Mammy would not watch! I also wrestled in the *Royal Albert Hall*, which was the pinnacle for any wrestler. A beautiful venue: a circular building, with tiers and tiers of people. As you walked around the Hall you reflected: here you were. You remembered the day the bus took you out to Charlestown; your first job; your training; first match in Colne. The TV cameras were just a yard from you, as you battled, oblivious to the fact that millions were watching. But most of all, you thought of your hometown and your family... and then... here you were – in the *Royal Albert Hall*. You think of all the famous, world-class acts that had performed here, and now, *you* were on that hallowed ground. Amazing.

Wrestling had become very popular. It had come from the USA and there were a few tag teams in England. Having paired up with my brother, Mickey, we became very successful. There were also the Royal Brothers, the Cadman Brothers; the Rawlings – a father and son tag team – who were actually Vick and Peter Stewart. Then there were other non-brothers who joined up and tagged. But it meant that Mickey and I now travelled together, and that was great. He had also acquired a Morris Minor car.

At this point, Mickey and I decided to buy another house. Mary and myself were now seeing each other as often as we could. At a certain time, I used to park my car on Fulham Road, in Sparkhill, and she would walk down, after work, at the same time. I looked forward to seeing her *so* much. I suppose I was falling in love. We would go to the *Tulip Festival* in Cannon Hill Park, and in the summer we always went to Swanshurst Park. I remember one particular day when we were there. She lay down on her side. I was stroking her hair. After a while, I realised she was fast asleep! She had a lovely white, short-sleeved dress on, and she looked gorgeous... and she felt relaxed with me. The sun was shining, ducks on the lake; me, young, strong and fit; a few quid in my pocket – and a beauty beside me. Could life get any better?

Mary was always a very nice dresser. She hadn't much money, but whatever she'd buy, she'd buy it nice. She's still the same to this day. When she fell asleep beside me that day, I thought: 'This is it!' She seemed so safe and secure... and I must have been in love with her. She was just lovely – side-faced, lying there, and breathing gently away. It was a time when I was extremely happy with her and I thought: 'This could be the woman I'm going to spend the rest of my days with.'

Although, it was a big step; all the lads I was living with were single and they were all saying: "Oh, we'll never get married!" I was riding on the crest of a wave at that time too. But Mary was the one, Shirley. I liked everything about her... and I still do.

But when you think about it, with hindsight, to have met someone when I was still a young man and Mary was certainly very young; and for our marriage to have lasted as long as it has, and for me to still feel the way I do, is quite unusual. But it will definitely last until one of us dies now.

You know – this could turn out to be quite a romantic novel – like *Wuthering Heights*, or something – except that was about unrequited love, and very tragic. So somebody would have to be taking Mary away and I'd have to be chasing them, to get her back! But they were marvellous times and I look back on them today, as the best times in my life.

Chapter Sixteen

A CARRYCASTLE FUNERAL

But life changes… Seamus' mother was sick at home. So he returned home, as did most of the family. All of all his brothers and sisters had moved to England by now, except for his brother Louie, who had emigrated to New York, and met Uncle Tom Gallagher, Mammy's brother there. Mammy did not seem too bad – so they returned, once again, to England. Her health remained poor, but a few months later, Seamus had a wrestling bout at an Open Air Show, in Tolka Park, Dublin. This was great timing, because it meant that his fare would be paid, he would earn money, and he could then travel down to the West of Ireland, to see his mother, the day after the contest.

When I wrestled at Tolka Park, it was the first time I'd wrestled in Ireland. Tolka Park is a big soccer stadium, which is very well known in Ireland. We had our picture taken at that show, for the Irish papers – Ernie Riley, Masambula, (the African Witchdoctor); Eric Liedermann, Emile Poilve and myself – about eight to ten of us altogether. So we wrestled that night, because I didn't realise how ill Mammy was. A first cousin of ours, Joe Dunleavy, came to see me; he was living in Dundrum, in Dublin. He took me back to his house and I stayed with him that night. He was delighted to see me, and me to see him.

The following morning I met Paddy, on the bus to the West. He explained that Mammy was pretty bad. I'd had three or four matches, the last one being in Dublin. There'd been no contact from Charlestown that night; no one wished me well for the wrestling, but now I realised why.

We did not say much on the way down, as we were a bit sad; the inevitable was staring us in the face. As we reached Ballaghaderreen, the last town before Charlestown, Mick Swords, the schoolteacher, got on the bus. He taught in Ballaghaderreen, but lived in Charlestown. When he saw me and Paddy he came up to us, shook my hand, and said: "I'm sorry for your troubles. She was a lovely woman." You know that your mum's dead, if they say that to you. Not sick or ill or anything… dead. I said: "Mick, is she dead?" He said: "She is. She died last night."

A bit of folk-lore gets into it. It was said that Mammy waited until my wrestling match was over... and then died; because they knew I was in Dublin, at the tail-end of the tour I was on. She certainly knew I was there. It was as if she was hanging on until I'd finished. Everyone told me afterwards – that she hung on... and died after the match, on 4 July 1959. Mammy was sixty-four years of age when she died, of cancer of the rectum. I never did get her the riches I had promised her. She died a poor woman, financially, but rich in the sense that she had a family who loved her.

We met everybody that we grew up with and had not seen for years. Funerals are very big in the West of Ireland. We had the usual Wake in the house – all the old women praying around her coffin; all night long, relations and so forth; all the locals. There were always plates of cigarettes at those Wakes, as well; everyone smoked in those times. Many of the old people smoked clay pipes too. Pipes are out of fashion these days, aren't they? You don't see them. So there'd be a fog of smoke, hanging over the room. All the relations, everyone with any drop of blood, or more closely related, would be there; all sitting around and praying – all praising Mary Kate. You could be the biggest villain Shirley, but once you were dead in Ireland, everything changed! There was only one place you'd be going – and that was up there!

Everyone thinks their mother is unique. She was certainly a very special woman and she was very close to all of the family – and us to her. So that was it. We buried her in Carrycastle Graveyard. A few days later, one of the saddest sights the locals reckon they ever saw was the eight of us leaving together... and Mick, my dad, left on his own. One of her relations took a photograph of us all: the remaining family – the day my mum was buried. It was very sad.

Nowadays, we wouldn't consider sixty-four to be particularly old, but in those days, many people died in their sixties; although my Pa outlived her by twenty-six years. It's often the other way around, of course – the women outlive the men! I saw lots of lads from here Shirley, who I knew through Birmingham, and had gone back to Ireland. We were all very sad.

Every single person from Charlestown was at Mary Kate's funeral – about a thousand people. That's totally normal for Ireland, even to this present day. If anyone dies, everyone attends the funeral; although they may only have passed them in the street, one time in their life, they'd go. It's like a day out; you meet everyone – everyone's there. I mean, I see funerals here and there's sometimes just one car behind the hearse. There might be someone buried at Widney Manor Road Cemetery, and we know them; we watch them from here. But over there, you might see fifty cars! If you get there a few minutes early, there'll be a throng of people outside the church.

The service was held at the Church of Saint James, in Charlestown, but the burial was in Carrycastle, four miles away. There was an altercation at the time, which I might bring to your mind. Mammy was a very strong Republican and they put the Tri-colour on the coffin, going into the church. The priest could have been the other side and he took the Tri-colour off. That caused a bit of controversy, especially with my Uncle Tom, who was, himself, a staunch Republican. Whether the priest didn't want to involve the church in politics, I'm not sure, but it was a bit sour, at the time. Some said that he should have been harangued for doing it, but others said no. Normally you wouldn't expect a priest to countermand the family's wishes, especially on such an occasion, but they were all-powerful in those days. He wasn't like a parish priest, whom you could approach and discuss it with. Also, we had all come from England, so we didn't know him that well.

I was very lonesome afterwards… for a long time. With Mammy gone, I was getting closer to my girlfriend, Mary. On 15 July 1961, just after her seventeenth birthday, we got engaged. I was twenty-six years old. We bought a ring, which would have been very expensive at the time. That night we had a little party. Her mother, Mai, a lovely Mayo woman, from the same county, was extremely shy and quiet. Our engagement party was probably the first time I had actually spoken to her.

From then onwards, every night, when I'd finished wrestling, I would pull up outside Stoney Lane. Mary would greet me at the door, having made tea and biscuits and lovely little sandwiches, cut up in diamond shapes and everything. And I really thought: 'Well, if this is married life, it's going to be great!' She looked lovely and was very polite. In those days she was really shy. I was the only one she met who was taking her out; taking her to restaurants; it was all brand-new to her. We'd play records and sit and talk, and look at each other for hours on end – eat our sandwiches. And that was it.

It was brilliant for her and for me. I was from near enough the part of Mayo where her Dad came from – just three miles away. Her mum's family lived only twelve to fifteen miles away, so we spoke the same language and had the same accents. When I started taking Mary home to Ireland, later, to her Uncle Mat, she was as Irish as me in her ways, and knew everything about the turf bogs, potatoes; how to cook – and make an apple pie. So our relationship was near perfect for both of us, and for her mum as well; someone who could speak her own language, although she and I didn't have many conversations.

Mary and myself would sit until late, in the front room, which was their best room. We would not see her mum or any of the family; they left us by ourselves. Mary was the eldest of eight children and the only one working. Her father died when she was ten years old, so life was a bit rough for them. I was still living with twelve to fourteen people in Wilton Road, so the comforts of the front room with Mary were lovely.

We bought yet another house using the same mortgage method. So now we had two houses in Wilton Road, two houses in Fulham Road and the roads ran side by side. We put down the smallest deposit and borrowed the rest. We were very busy: away most nights and looking after four houses; so we had to be on our toes. Plenty of problems: Some not having rent and it was only £1 a week. Tenants doing runners and some filthy fellows; but they were all single lads and working on the buildings; rough and ready. We had bathrooms but as I said before, I doubt whether we ever used them, because I used to have a bath in the swimming baths in Sparkhill. You paid a shilling, 5p today, and you had a fine bath. The water was put in for you; you could not regulate it, or get any more water without asking for it. It was great though.

It was a deep, deep bath. I can see the fella now... a Scotsman. He'd fill it up for you and put his hand in, to decide whether it was the right temperature. In you'd go and you'd be immersed in water; really deep baths. We'd have a bath every week, which was the norm then, for young working lads, although some didn't have a bath at all! It was something new as well, because at home, in Charlestown, we didn't even have a tin bath – just a basin. We'd just wash our legs and face. I don't think we used to touch the rest of our body, at all. It was amazing really! My kids and grandkids have a bath every single night, without fail, and clean their teeth. I never remember a toothbrush in our house, when we were growing up.

It was the same in England in those days, amongst the working classes. Pat Roach, for example, who lived in the Ladywood area of Birmingham, had his first toothbrush and paste at secondary school, in a parcel from the Americans. He shared it with his best friend, Pete Berrington, but only allowed him a little bit of toothpaste, because it was such a rare commodity. It was the same in Ireland; to the best of my knowledge, nobody ever cleaned their teeth; we only started to do so when we came here. So to go up to Sparkhill Baths, pay a shilling, get a huge bath of hot water and stay there as long as you wanted to, was a real luxury.

I would sweep number 8 Wilton Road, where I lived, about once a month. I was still in the attic, with three other lads. When I swept the home out, you could fill about four bins with the rubbish: shoe boxes, coat hangers, waste paper, newspapers, shirt wrappings; everything that fourteen or fifteen people could generate. I never supplied sheets, except when a new arrival came. I often slept in the same sheets for six months, as did most of the other lads. We were all church-goers. No women were ever allowed in, and that rule was obeyed. Mary never went there at all. I don't think she was ever in Number 8 Wilton Road.

A fifth house came up, at 16 Weatheroak Road. It was let to six or seven people already, and was a particularly good house. It cost about £1800, making it the dearest house we had bought, at that stage. We now had five houses. The tenants were a bit harder to find, because we were looking for about fifty or sixty people to keep all of our houses full. Also, every Irish couple who got married took in five to six lodgers, so it was getting a lot harder. For some reason we only dealt with Irish – although there were thousands of English out there. We discovered that later, when we started to expand a bit; that's where the pool was. I used to advertise in shop windows, and places like that; notice-boards – and so forth.

There were two lads in 16 Weatheroak Road, for a while, in one of our rooms, who we didn't get any rent off. It transpired that they were two 'dummies' – they couldn't speak. They were living in the Front Room when we bought the house, so we inherited them! One night, late on, when Mickey and I were on the same wrestling bill, we said: "We'll have to catch the two dummies." I can't even think whether there were any locks on the door, but the two dummies were in bed. We pulled the clothes off them and we said: "Rent, rent!" But they somehow indicated to us that they had no money. So we skyed the two of them out, got their gear – away and out. We never heard from them again.

You couldn't do that these days. You'd be reported to the Authorities and you'd serve time for it. It's very serious to evict someone now, but at that time the laws were an awful lot different. Nowadays, if you simply call someone a "Bloody so-and-so," he can practically take you to court for harassment!

We were engaged for around twenty-one months, so we began to talk about setting a date for our marriage. All the houses were full, so I thought we might live with my brother, Paddy, who had a big front room in Showell Green Lane, Sparkhill. Mary did not like the idea, but I wanted to keep the income coming in. Anyway, we were only talking about it. As it turned out, we never did move in to Paddy's front room.

We decided to get married on 16 April, 1963. Phew! The date was set. So the little girl, who went to her first dance in the *Shamrock Club*, got lost and could not find her way home again, was going to be my wife. She would be, by then, just nineteen years old and I was heading for twenty-nine. Time passed, because we were very busy. When Mickey and I appeared in Brum as a tag team, in the *Embassy Sportsdrome*, we really packed the place.

April was approaching, the marriage date, but still we had no place to live. About three weeks or so before the date, another house came up, at 7 Weatheroak Road. We already owned number 16, in the same road, so we made an offer and it was accepted. I thought we were saved. We put a deposit down with the agent, when we had a look at the house. The agent gave us the keys, so we had a set cut and gave him a set back. This meant that I had access again – but totally illegally. But know nowt, fear nowt!

So we started ripping up floors and demolishing, a week before the wedding. The agent decided to look at the property and saw all the work we had done; with the place not ours at all! He went mad; threatening not to sell to us and to take us to court. We had to do a lot of back-peddling, and went to him, cap in hand. Any road up, he agreed to sell to us, if we completed as soon as possible.

This was very close to our other house, but the locks were changed and we could not get into number 7, until the mortgage came through. An old person had previously lived there, so we assumed that she must have gone to a nursing home. All of her furniture had been left there. Thankfully, the mortgage came through.

Well, the big day arrived. We got married in English Martyrs Church in Sparkhill, by Cannon Hirrell. Brother Mickey was my Best Man. The Reception was in the *Mermaid Hotel*, Sparkhill. All the family came over from Ireland. We had a great day and left about six o'clock in the evening. We had booked into the *Albany*, a newly-built hotel, in the centre of the city. In the evening we ate in the *Burlington Restaurant*, again, in the city centre. We ordered anything we wanted, from the menu. The meal was beautiful. We arrived at the restaurant at twenty past seven in the evening and we made a pact, that if anything happened between us, we would always go to the *Burlington* at 7.20pm, on 16 April. We also agreed that if we ever had any problems, we would talk, and try to sort them out.

We never drank any alcohol at that time of our lives – just coke! But the meal was lovely and we were both very happy. So with the meal over, we walked back to the *Albany Hotel*. The hotel was beautiful, with a bathroom en-suite, and a toilet in the room; no sharing with anybody. It was marvellous. Lovely marble tops in the bathrooms; scented soap – the lot.

When I was finished, Mary went into the bathroom. I put on my pyjamas – I'd never worn pyjamas before and the legs were a foot too long. I hopped into bed first. Mary told me, afterwards, that she stood against the bathroom door for ages. She was totally inexperienced, and very shy. I had never seen her like she appeared then, in a Baby Doll nightdress. She got into bed and it was wonderful.

There was a TV in the room, so afterwards we watched *Wuthering Heights*, a classic love story, with Laurence Olivier and Merle Oberon. It is now our favourite film. I read somewhere that Merle was born an O'Brien, but in order to appear more enigmatic, she changed her surname, thereby disguising her Irish origins. In the morning, Mary and I had breakfast in bed. We were like two film stars. When the two of us are joking together, I often tell her that she reminds me of the racehorse, Arkle – a slow-starter, but once she gets going – Boy!

Afterwards we drove to Liverpool and booked into the *Adelphi Hotel*. Now there was a restaurant in Liverpool called *Samson and Barlow*, which had cooked turkeys in the window. I used to look at this restaurant and say to myself: 'Some day I will dine there.' I never had turkey at home. It was always goose. So we both sashayed into *Samson and Barlow's*. We started to eat, but it was burnt soup; we both agreed that it was a horrible meal. We stayed in Liverpool for a few days, and then I dropped Mary back to 7 Weatheroak Road. I was away to London for a week and could not get back. She was glad to see me when I returned, after being in that big old house by herself and sleeping in the old bed. We found out later that the previous owner of the house had died in that bed! The mattress was covered in blood. So poor Mary had a rough introduction to marriage, but I tried to reduce the number of times that I left her on her own.

We got rid of most of the old furniture; certainly the old bed and chairs, and then set about getting gas fires in, decorating, and so forth. In those far off days, we had no experience of central heating. We made a nice job of it and then had a few lodgers in – which seemed to have become part of our culture. It was a bit of a shock to Mary, but she was a grafter and got stuck in.

Although Mary had lived with her family, the idea of having lodgers, total strangers, in the same house, was unfamiliar to her. Mickey and myself had been with lodgers and strangers all our lives, so it was nothing new to us. With hindsight, it was a bad introduction to marriage, but to her credit, she stuck with it, throughout all the years. It was hard for her. Don't forget, she was very young and she was on her own; I used to be away a lot, those times. She was also working, although she became pregnant early in our marriage, so she stopped working in the city, at that point. When you're young and fit, you don't mind things like that. But nowadays the young women wouldn't stand for that.

I suppose the fact that she was used to a fair amount of hardship, with all those younger brothers and sisters to be cared for, and being the only wage earner, made her more able to cope with the situation; rather than someone who had been 'mollycoddled', for want of a better word, and had things her own way. She was still lending a hand there with her mum, for much of the time. But it did her no harm. Hard work never did anyone any harm, but there's also got to be a lot of leisure in life too.

To be doing something, keeping yourself busy, is the right way; once you get into the rut of lounging about, you can never go back to working. But we were never that way at all; we were all grafters.

Chapter Seventeen

FROM 'TALK' TO THE LIFFEY

It's from this chapter onwards that Seamus and Mary's three children, Tracey, Shamus and Russell, add their own memories to our story, having been born in 1964, 65 and 68 respectively.

Amongst Tracey's earliest memories are her dad's wrestling bag and its contents: big, shiny black boots, black trunks, with a red border round them, and white laces that tied them up. Hanging up in the wardrobe was a large, green, corduroy dressing gown, which was very special, although they were allowed to touch it! She remembers thinking: 'Oh, that's my daddy's.' It had a large golden shamrock on the back, surrounded by tiny golden sequins. Tracey recalls: "Dad was always very funny: always lifting me up in the air and throwing me as high as he possibly could. He was very strong, and would just throw me up like a doll, and catch me all the time. I used to love that."

Seamus took Tracey and his son, Shamus, on outings to Sparkhill Park and Swanshurst Park. When Seamus opened the car door, in Swanshurst Park, the two children would jump out, and run as far and as fast as they could. They also had fun on the swings in Sparkhill Park, by the far end of Showell Green Lane. Shamus remembers his Dad, from when he was a toddler. Like most fathers and sons, he wanted to go everywhere with him, and, like Tracey, recalls visiting Swanshurst Park on a Sunday. "We were living in Weatheroak Road, Sparkhill at the time. I drive past the park now, and I think it's reasonably small, but for a three-to-five-year-old it seemed to stretch for miles. We used to run and run, as far as we could, like a pair of greyhounds! Dad was always there. Occasionally, we might have a ball of some description, and he'd kick it for us, as far as the eye could see. But that was Dad. And we'd try to get into the ice-creams, sweets, and the like."

"It was fantastic, going to bed at night" continues Tracey ,"because Dad was a brilliant storyteller and had loads of stories, such as 'Goldilocks and the Three Bears', 'Sleeping Beauty', 'Little Red Riding Hood' and 'The Three Little Pigs'. He used to say: 'I'm going to tell you a story, about Johnny McGlory. Shall I begin it? That's all that's in it!' "

The children learned about Seamus' life in Ireland, from an early age. How he grew up, who his mum and dad were; what sort of toys he had; his brothers and sisters.

So they grew up with a strong sense of their own identity and family origins. When Tracey later asked school-friends about their own family background, she was amazed to discover that some of them didn't have a clue about their grandparents, or their family history.

I was now out of the dancehall – too busy. One morning, I was driving down Wilton Road, at about half past eleven in the morning, when a lodger flagged me down. It was Martin Coleman. He was one of the first lodgers in 8 Wilton Road. I remember it very well – it was like yesterday. I was living in Weatheroak Road at the time, so I'd left Wilton Road. Martin jumped out in front of me, ashen-faced. He said: "Seamus, quick! There's been a friggin' murder in the house. Whitney is dead!" I said: "Oh Christ – a murder Martin!" So I jammed on the brakes, went into the house and headed up the stairs to Seamus Whitney's room. He lay there dead in bed. He was absolutely blue in colour and there was a desperate smell of gas. When the gas meter was opened, there was just a shilling in it. The window in the room had been taped over, so it was definitely suicide, not murder – thankfully. He used to take tablets, for depression, but we'd never bothered to think anything of it.

So I called the police, ambulance, and so forth. The police and coroner arrived and when they had done with the body, they carried him downstairs. While we waited for the ambulance or hearse to arrive, they decided to put the corpse in the front room. Now there were three beds in there. A lad called Tom Broderick, from Galway, rushed to clear some clothes and stuff of someone else's bed – desperate that it shouldn't be put on his own. It was like something out of a *Carry On* film. Tom cleared the other bed in seconds, turned to assist with the body, but it wasn't there. Whisking back round again, Tom found, to his horror, that in a matter of seconds, the two fellas had deposited the corpse on his own bed!

Tom nearly went mad, and vowed he'd never sleep in that bed again… and rightly so! He was a bus conductor, on a late shift; that's why he was off. He demanded a new bed and clothes, so this was the first new bed we ever bought, for a lodger.

Meanwhile, a very large crowd had gathered outside the house. My brother, Mickey, arrived and a lad called Pete O'Reilly, who is married to my sister, Angela. Pete was Mick O'Reilly's brother, the man who first advised us to buy properties to rent. So Mick O'Reilly is Angela's brother-in-law.

Wilton Road runs down to a junction with the main Stratford Road. Weatheroak Road is directly opposite it, on the other side of the main road.

So, if you look up from where our house was, at 7 Weatheroak Road, you can see half way up Wilton Road. While all this was happening, Mary had come home for dinner, from work. As a rule I was always there and we would eat together. But on this occasion, of course, I wasn't home, because I was dealing with Seamus Whitney's suicide.

Mary came out of the house, looked up the road and saw the large crowd of people outside 8 Wilton Road. My car was there, together with about ten police cars and an ambulance. She also saw Mickey's car, and as she approached the crowd, she heard that a big Irish lad named Seamus was dead... murdered. Poor Mary thought it was me, so when I appeared she was overcome, and burst out crying. She did not go back to work that day; but she was so relieved.

She'd never had time off work, until that afternoon. She was working in a big furniture factory called *Lawrence's*, in Digbeth. The building's still there, although it's not a furniture factory now. She had a Supervisor called Francis Adams. Mary, being very young, was scared of her; she'd never answer back or anything. So she wouldn't have a minute off work. But that day when she saw me, alive and well, she said: "I'm definitely not going back to work today."

During all the commotion, I noticed a young lad across the road, just opposite number 8, where the tragedy took place. He had a big suitcase with him. Anyone you saw coming up Wilton Road with a suitcase, would always be looking for lodgings. Now I might be wrong, but he might well have been heading for Number 8. We would get lots of young Irish lads, knocking the door – that was the way it was done mostly. Being a wrestler and a Bouncer, we had a certain reputation. Indeed, it was often said: "If you don't have the rent, or you cause any trouble in a Dunleavy house, you will be killed – or beaten to death." A joke of course, but this lad may have heard those rumours. When he got to Wilton Road and saw the body being carried out, I bet he went back to Ireland, and is probably *still* telling people how lucky he was – and how close he came to death.

I'll tell you of another funny incident arising out of this. One night, a few weeks after, I was wrestling in Cardiff, at a venue where there was no shower. So I decided I would have a bath when I got home. I towelled off and did not even take my wrestling boots off – just hopped in the car and away for Brum. When I got to Birmingham, I always used to look at the houses, just to check that the lights in the hallways had been switched off – to keep the electricity bills down. When I passed Number 8 Wilton Road, the lights were on, on the landing, so I jumped out. There was a switch, just inside the front door, which was always left open. You could also switch the landing light on or off from there – a two-way switch. The downstairs switch made no sound at all when you switched it on or off.

The door was unlocked, and the lobby door too, so anyone could walk in. But who'd want to invade a house with fifteen or sixteen fit young men living there? You'd never get out alive! Even the bedroom doors had no lock on them. We'd be sleeping two, three or four to a room. The door would open and one of the lads would come in. It wouldn't occur to you that it might be a stranger. Besides, it was easier for the lads to come and go without keys.

I was just at my car again when I saw the lights go back on. I thought that the switch might have a faulty spring, so I switched it off again. This happened about four times, until eventually I decided to leave it until the morning. But what actually happened was that there was a big lad called Paddy Coleman, who was as nervous as a kitten. He came out of his room to use the toilet. The upstairs switch was just outside the toilet, so as Paddy put the light on, I switched it off, seconds later. He did this a few times, and I knocked it off. He could not hear my footsteps, because my wrestling boots made no noise. Well, the upshot of it was, I was summoned to the house the day after, and told that the house was haunted.

Martin Coleman, Paddy's brother, said: "Paddeen was having a piss last night, when the lights went off, by their own accord – several times!" They would not have it that it was me. And… the toilet was right next door to the room where Seamus Whitney committed suicide. All the lads who lived in the house were Catholic, and some were a bit superstitious. The light-switch episode had made all the tenants even more nervous; the fact that I no longer lived there made it worse. They wanted the house blessed, so I had to contact the young Kidderminster priest, from *English Martyrs*, Sparkhill, Father Harding, and get him down to the house, so that all the lads could see him. He blessed every room in the house.

I said: "Take a bucket of Holy Water with you and sky a drop everywhere, because they're very nervous. They're sure Whitney's going to come back and haunt them!" I knew Father Harding very well. So he came down and skyed a drop round every room, which settled them down a bit. But Tom Broderick said: "Poor old Whitney, he can't be buried on consecrated ground, as he committed suicide." My brother Mickey was there with me and he said: "You can throw him on top of *J.J. Gallagher's* tip, (the big contractor), as far as I'm concerned. We just want him out and away!" But that was that. They took him off.

Soon after our marriage, Mary announced that she was pregnant. Wow! I don't suppose, at twenty-nine, you realise how important that announcement is, or was. So, ten months after we married, we had a beautiful baby daughter, born on 5 February 1964. If Mary had been pregnant after eight months it would have been a big scandal, and even after you were married, if your wife was expecting, the first question would be: "How long are they married?" That was a big thing in those times.

I remember ringing up the Sorrento Hospital in Moseley, in the morning, and getting the news. We named her TRACEY, a very popular name at the time. We took little Tracey home and life became different: bottles, nappies, getting up at night. She was born small – 6 lbs odd, and she would not eat for ages. But she was such a joy and changed our lives forever, for the best.

We were still wrestling, nearly every night, but not getting much money. We saw a lot of Irish lads who started contracting; by that, I mean doing road and sewer contracts for the Council and for big firms, like *Wimpy* and *McAlpine*, and supplying men to contractors. We saw them make a lot of money. Whereas we had all the fame, we did not have the money. So we looked around for what we could get. I eventually teamed up with a lad called Jimmy MacDonagh and we got a bit of work in Coventry, doing a big sewer; putting in the sewerage systems for a housing estate. We were working for a couple of Irish subcontractors, who hadn't much idea about work. However, after about a week or two, the subcontractors got the sack and we got the work.

My brother, Mickey, was working for MacDonagh and myself now. But he deserved better, because he was a very clever lad at work; he certainly knew a lot more than me. The more pipes we laid, the more money we made, so all of a sudden, MacDonagh and I began to make very good money. We had to lay the pipes on a bed of concrete, put daub around the joints so that you could take a pipe out if you had to. Also, we had to back-fill them. Now, if the council boss was not on site, he would only come a few times a week, we would lay the pipes without putting any concrete under them, saving a lot of time and money. We back-filled them as soon as they were laid. So we were laying them as fast as billio!

The pipes were four-foot in diameter; they needed to be pretty big, to take the sewage from a big housing estate. Then Mr. Orme, who was the council boss, would come out, when we had a rake of pipes laid. He would ask: "Have you put concrete under them?" "Oh yes Mr. Orme. We put six inches under every pipe." Then we built big manholes, where you could go down and look through the lines of pipes that we laid.

Well, one day he spent a lot of time down a manhole and he could not see daylight. So he said we would have to expose a long line of pipes, to see what happened. If he found that we had concreted under them, then we would be paid. But if there was no concrete under them, we would have to pay for the excavator. Now of course, there was no concrete under them, but just before the machine started digging, MacDonagh and myself made ourselves scarce. We just left the job and never returned! But we had done OK for a while. My brother Mickey came with us.

By this time we had bought another house, at Number 6 Wilton Road, next door to Number 8, which we already owned. Then when Mickey got married he moved out of Fulham Road to the house I mentioned earlier, in Castleford Road, Sparkhill. That was seven houses we had between us. Eventually we had eleven houses in total: three in Wilton Road, five in Weatheroak Road; two in Fulham Road and one in Castleford Road.

Before that, we got a job in a factory in Coventry. The job had to be done while the factory was closed, for the two-week holiday period. We agreed a price, to lay a line of pipes through the factory. The area was a very narrow passage, so it had to be hand-dug. The firm we got the job off was called *Pargas* and the factory was *Alfred Herbert's*: a very big components factory. We got a very good Irish JCB driver, called Brendan Mulgrew, who could turn a JCB on a sixpence. He got the JCB into the narrow passage and what should have taken us ten days to dig took just two. Piped the lot back, finished, and were away in three days. We were supposed to be there for twelve or thirteen days.

Well, we made a few thousand for the three days. When we went to collect our money, *Pargas* weren't too pleased. They'd weighed it up wrong, but we got paid! Then we got the job I mentioned earlier, in Kingswinford. It was a big sewer again, and at this time it was big steel pipes. We did all the digging with a JCB. The firm we were working for laid the pipes and then we backfilled, tampered the ground, which means compressing, or consolidating it, then put tarmac over it. My brother, Mickey, had got some work off the *Gas Board* by now. This was a very good contract, and where MacDonagh and I were subcontracting, he had it directly from the *Gas Board*. He teamed up with Angela's husband, Peter O'Reilly. They called themselves *Rildon*: bits of O'Reilly and Dunleavy. They became very successful, worked the *Gas Board* for over twenty years and became very rich.

But it was now 1965, and my life was going in another direction. Mary and I had another baby – a fine boy. We called him Shamus, after myself. Until that time, I hadn't had a drink of alcohol, of any description. But the night Shamus was born is reputed to have been the first time that I ever got drunk!

I was in charge of Shamus' haircut and used to take him to *Roger* the barber's, on Showell Green Lane. I'd say: "You can have any haircut you like son… but it's got to be a crew-cut!" That same barber operates from a shop in Acocks Green now, but he remembers Shamus since he was 'knee-high-to-a-grasshopper'. His name's Roger Ward – he runs a Fishing Tackle and Barber's shop in Fox Hollies Road.

Shamus liked to accompany me; whether I was working around the house, or going out somewhere. As he grew up, if I was wrestling in the locality, I'd take him to the wrestling – at the *Embassy* or *Hams Hall*; anywhere within a five-to-ten-mile radius of where we were living. I took him to meet all the wrestlers – the likes of Pat Roach, Les Kellett, and so on. When he started school he was amazed that all his school friends didn't know these people. Later, he met Mark Rocco; his dad was Jumping Jim Hussey. Alan Dennison was another chap.

"I remember one particular match that Dad took me to," recalls Shamus. "They were just erecting the ring at the time, and I was introduced to one or two of the wrestlers who were around. I suppose I was probably four or five at the time. And I'm looking at fellas like Jackie Pallo, Billy Two Rivers and Mike Marino. But then Dad retired from the wrestling game before I was *much* older. That was in 1970, when he was thirty-five. He just did the occasional match after that.

"There were times when Dad was out wrestling at night, but it didn't affect me, as such, although I was always very interested in it. I remember one particular event that I went to, when Dad was Top of the Bill, and was wrestling Mike Marino, who at some stage was a champion. Mike asked me to sit in his corner, and he gave me his Championship belt. Now, this thing was glistening at me, and I'm only five or six years old, so in my eyes, the belt was worth a million pounds! He said: 'Don't let anybody touch it,' – and I was scared to death! But it was great – I *know* these men. I've spoken to them.

"Meeting one or two of them later in life, they hadn't changed. I remember meeting the Royal Brothers – Vic Faulkner and Bert Royal, years later. Although age had changed their faces, they were the same *people* that I'd met as a five-year-old. I remember Dad taking me down the *Embassy*, before I'd even started school. I sat in the crowd and Jackie Pallo was wrestling. He had a bellowing voice and shouted at Dad: 'Come on Seamus, you get in here, and who'll win!' It frightened me. I thought: "Oh – don't you touch my dad!"

"I remember going to another venue with Dad. He wasn't wrestling, but some of the lads I knew were wrestling, so he said: 'Come on, we'll go along.' Giant Haystacks was wrestling this particular man, and we were sitting in the crowd. Haystacks' match finished and he was baiting the crowd as he was going out. Then he saw my Dad and gave him the Finger Wave: 'You and me next time – in the ring!' Dad stood up, baiting back at him. Then I remember pushing past Dad and kicking Haystacks in the shins – because he was having a go at my Dad. 'You leave me Dad alone' – kick! As a child, and even now, I'm *immensely* proud of my Dad. He's always been as strong as an ox. He was a very strong man in his youth, and is strong even today. I've always been in awe of him."

Work in Kingswinford had come to an end, so Mick O'Reilly and myself teamed up. There was a small licensed club called the *Queen of Clubs*, on the main Stratford Road in Sparkhill. After a lot of soul-searching, Mick and I became joint-owners of the club. We rented it off a Liverpool woman called Cath Zindini; she was married to a man from the Yemen. We paid her £75 a week for the rent, in cash, so she would not be paying much tax either.

Sparkhill was a teaming Irish quarter, so naturally we changed it into an Irish Club. There were two floors; upstairs was a bit posher than the downstairs. It was just a small shop, originally, and there would have been a flat on top. The inside was completely gutted, right out to the back – and the same upstairs. There was a small bar on each floor, so it was big enough really. After a while, when the word got around, we used to be packed. There was no other licensed club around. The *Oyster Bar*, on the same side of the road, was just a short distance away. However, it presented no real competition as it was rough-and-ready, and unlicensed.

At this time, the pubs closed at 2.30pm, so we opened at the same time, until 6.00pm. At night we opened from 10.30pm until 2.00am. The ground floor of the club was for working Irishmen from the building sites. When the rain was very heavy, the sites would be rained off, so all of the workmen would head for the club. They would be dressed in heavy digging boots, Wellingtons and rough gear. They were all hardworking men and liked a drink, on the rained-off days.

This was a complete change of life for Mary, who now had me at home at five or six every evening. None of us ever took a drink at this time of our lives. We ran the club for seven days a week. Mary never came to the club. She was afraid of seeing me in trouble. We renamed it, and it became *The Talk of the Town*. We had a large sign outside. It was hard going for Mary, but she never complained, although she had a houseful of noisy lodgers too! I would eventually own or co-own seven clubs in Birmingham, which were as follows, in order of purchase: the *Talk of the Town;* the *Speak-Easy;* the *Cascade;* the *Jigsaw;* the *Peter Rabbit;* the *Del Monica* and the *Liffey.*

People started to know where we lived at 7 Weatheroak. So instead of them going to Number 8 Wilton Road, I had them knocking on the door, at all hours. Our daughter, Tracey, had now started school, at Olton Court Convent, in Solihull. For this reason and also, to avoid being woken up at all hours, we thought that we might move out to Solihull, but we couldn't afford it yet.

My youngest son Russell's first memories date from this time, when Mary and I had the clubs. He'd be going up the stairs, to bed and we'd give each other a kiss – between every balustrade. So we'd start at the bottom and then I'd come up, and go as high as I could – and he'd be going right down! That's his first memory of me. I was coming back from the clubs, somewhere around half past six in the evening, or maybe a bit later. Russell was probably around two or three years of age.

In *The Talk of the Town* we started gambling as well. We had a roulette wheel going, as well as card games, poker and brag. The dealer was one man, who took a percentage out of every hand. This was very good; a good croupier could make you a lot of money, and of course, a lot for himself as well. Mary and other family members would do various chores there, during the day, so sometimes we'd take the children with us. Tracey remembers playing downstairs at the *Talk,* as a five-year-old, in and out of the stools, and wrought iron table legs where she could crawl underneath. It was always quite dark in there.

"It was small and there was orangey lighting, from all the optics," Tracey recalls. It wasn't a bright place. There was a smell of stale smoke and beer, and there'd be cigarette butts on the floor. We were told not to touch the ashtrays. I think either my mum or her mother would be mopping up, behind the bar – and things like that.

"Then upstairs there was another room, with a big picture of a skyline – at night. I vaguely remember a figure in it – who could have been my dad. As you came down the stairs again, there was a little cubby-hole, or a place with a little hat-stand, by the door. We'd be playing in and out of there and there were telephone books on the floor, so we'd look at those. We used to know the club very well. As we passed in the car, we'd say: 'Oh look – there's the *Talk of the Town!*' Sometimes we'd pull up on the pavement outside. Dad would go in and talk to someone for a while, then come back out."

We were becoming more affluent, so we decided to have a holiday abroad and headed for Majorca – Mary, myself and the two children. This was in the late 1960s, when not many were going abroad. I can still remember the first night, getting off the plane and that beautiful wall of heat hitting you.

We stayed in the *Alexandra Hotel* and thought it was the most beautiful hotel on earth. There was a great big swimming pool and a little one for the children; bedrooms with bathrooms en-suite. It was actually a four-star hotel, but to us it was paradise. There were lots of children there as well, so our kids loved it. Just to see them turn a different colour was brilliant. I bought Tracey a little Spanish bull, but she left it on some steps.

Tracey recalls: "I was heartbroken, although it was just a simple black plastic bull, with a felt cover on it. We went to the same hotel again around 1970/71, when I was six or seven years old. I had my first boyfriend, called Philip. We met him in the pool, with his sister, Lisa. They were from up North somewhere. We ended up doing everything together, and we had a little orange boat.

"We used to go to the hotel dining-hall every evening. The waiters served the food and I remember picking up some Spanish phrases. You'd learn how to say: 'Have you finished?', 'Buenos dias,' for hello – and so on. Dad was always very good at languages and with his encouragement we'd be practising new Spanish phrases, every day," explains Tracey.

It was the first time that I was introduced to wine and Sangria. I thought Sangria was very drinkable and got well fond of it by the time we had to leave. I was not that keen on red wine though, at that time. We used to have lovely times in the evening, when the children were up in bed; sitting under the stars, wining and dining. We met some very nice people too. I used to reflect about home and if Mammy, now dead, or Dad could see me. I had conquered the world, like James Cagney, in that film *Top of the World*: "I'm on the top of the world Ma!" Then after two weeks, it was back to wrestling, the lodging houses and *The Talk of the Town*.

My son, Shamus, recalls: "The holiday in Majorca is probably a little bit vague, due to my age. But we were also in Malta and Tangiers, in North Africa. The holiday I remember the most clearly was the one in Tangiers. Again, I was still very young, so when we used to go out walking, I was in a pushchair. We'd go out to the local bazaar. I always remember the snake charmers. I don't know what happened, but I must have seen the snake charmer charm a snake out of a basket. Then later on, I fell asleep in the pushchair, and woke up with sunburn down the one side of my face. So my face was in two halves: red on one side and white on the other! But as I woke up I saw this black thing, and I swore blind it was a snake; although it wasn't – it was a piece of pipe. So from that day to this, I have a phobia about snakes. I can watch snakes on the television and my palms will start to sweat, even though they're on the telly and they're nowhere near me! If we ever visit the zoo, I won't go near the Reptile House – just a little piece of glass between me and the snake… no way!"

My brother, Mickey, was now very busy, installing gas all over Birmingham. He was getting fed up with the wrestling, and so was I. So we cut down and would only work for Midland promoters. No more London or Scotland, or bouts where you had to be away from home. During our time in the ring, we had been on television several times and I had been to the *Royal Albert Hall* – biggest Mecca in the land. Mickey had wrestled for the *Welterweight Championship of England*, but was beaten by Jack Dempsey. I was rated third or fourth in Europe, at one point. Not bad – for two laddeens from Charlestown! We also went home to Ireland, to see my Dad and show off my two children. Pity that Mammy was not there and that she had never met Mary. But, c'est la vie. I was a bit of a celeb at home, being seen on the telly and so forth.

My son, Shamus, then started at the same school as Tracey, *Olton Court Convent*, in Kineton Green Road, Solihull. It was a private school, but very relaxed. They were taught by the Nuns and were both very happy there. Around this time, I had a blood discharge on my trunks/underpants. It was like a blind boil that used to fill up, and discharge, every so often; no pain, but a bit uncomfortable. After about twelve months I went to a second doctor, who said that I must have an operation. I thought that this was the end of the world and that I would never be able to wrestle again. It was called a pilanidial sinus, but it was not life-threatening. They had to cut a fair bit of flesh out, just at the bottom of my spine – where the cheeks of your bottom start.

It's actually an in-growing hair. It happens to hairy people, particularly lorry drivers, who sit in a fixed position for long periods of time. The hair turns round and it grows in. They packed it with cotton wool and gauze, where the flesh had been removed, because they wanted it to heal from the inside of the wound out; they did not want the wound to bridge. This was a slow job and I was going back and forth to the hospital for six months, to have the wound packed.

But time passed and I was doing a few bouts again. Everything was going well. One night I said to Mary that we were doing fine. But she surprised me by saying; "No, we are working and doing OK, but we should be doing better!" I'd always kept her out of business and never thought that she wanted an input; but she surprised me. She also said that we should not be living in a terraced house in Sparkhill; we should be out in Solihull, in a big house. I said: "That is for the rich and posh, not me, and there would be no lodgers out there." She said: "Seamus, it's time we got rid of the lodgers and lived private. We have had them all my married life. Let's expand. You are clever enough to have clubs on your own; you wrestle on your own. You and Mickey have houses between you, so you can run *anything* by yourself."

Well, it was the rude awakening! So I kept looking for a club in another area, and eventually came across an old, but large, converted cinema, next to a Gardening Club, in Alum Rock. The fellow selling it was called Len Robinson; a Bookie, who had a betting shop next door. He wanted £10,000 down and the rent was about £25 a week. It was a lease we were buying, not the freehold, but we could renew it, when it ran out. I signed for ten years and no rent review. We agreed I would put £8,000 down and the weekly rent, and the deal was done. The £8,000 I had saved was in the house. No banks. No tax. Never thought there would be a day of reckoning.

I suppose it all stems back to Ireland... and my dad. As I mentioned previously, in Chapter 8, the morning I was leaving for England, he said: "Seamus, you are only seventeen and you will not get a man's wage, when you get to England." So he took my passport, and with a piece of dry bread, rubbed out the '4' in 1934, the year I was born, and substituted a '2', so that it now read 1932, making me two years older than I actually was. Now, I never had to show my passport when I was getting a job in England, so he must have been mistaken. It's a good thing that he was, because a blind man could see that the passport had been tampered with. When he put the 2 instead of the 4, the ink spread, making the alteration obvious. I suppose that would have been a criminal offence, but until I wrote this book, no one knew about it!

However, a funny thing happened a few years ago. My accountant, understandably, thought my pension was due, two years before it really was. I'd been obliged to continue the lie, throughout my working life, as far as official records were concerned. My accountant said I was therefore not eligible for another two years, and that was that – closed! But even to this day, I have to think, whether it was 1932 or 1934, when asked my date of birth.

So that was the background I came from... and it was always drummed into us: whatever you do, don't pay any tax. Every single person who left Charlestown was told, when he got to England, to be sure and say he was married – with a rake of kids in Ireland. Now you had lads of twenty putting down on the forms that they had six or seven kids, back in Ireland. Daft as it sounds, it worked most of the time. But then, the odd one would forget his name and put different names down when filling up the next tax form… and they had to move – sharpish! It was Cat and Mouse – but deadly serious.

Well, back to the clubs. I now had one on my own, called the *Jigsaw*, on the main Alum Rock Road, which was a very rough, Brummie area. My brother Paddy, who was a skilled carpenter, became the Manager. We had a very good doorman, called Brendan Breslin, who seemed to know every person who left Dublin, so he was a fair draw. There was also a very rough Belfast crowd there. Once again, we started to do good business. We opened in the afternoon, and in the evening 'til 2.00 am in the morning.

There was a doorman, from Limerick, named Tony McGuane, who worked for me at the *Speakeasy*, which was previously a little Sheiban, or drinking club, (pronounced 'shebeen') in Stratford Place. Mick O'Reilly knew the fella who owned it – a West Indian, called Martin Reed. This was only a big room, with a small stage and toilets. Mick O'Reilly had a fixation about strippers and he said we should put strippers on. Not an idea that I fancied but he was adamant. The licence only ran until 10.00pm, but then Mick used to drink with the police, and he reckoned we would be OK; and as it happens – we were.

I think we paid Martin Reed about £1200 to get out and we moved in. We had a license for ten years. You got a license for ten years in those days; it may have changed since. The first week we opened, we cleared our money – it was unbelievable. The place was called the *Speakeasy*, after the Speakeasies in America. It was like something you would see in the Klondike or the old Wild West. O'Reilly was in charge there and I was in the *Talk of the Town*. Mick was a single man and could ply his trade anywhere. He hadn't used to give a damn, and would keep the club open all night. Mick was fearless!

The *Cascade*, a much more refined club, came later. But the *Speakeasy* was something else. It used to be packed – fellas the worse for drink, trying to jump on the stage; the strippers giving them a kick in the mouth or head. Then they would get chucked out. It was amazing! I popped in one Sunday. There was some trouble and a fella got badly cut. We could not call an ambulance because we should not have been open at this time. We had no plaster, so Mick O'Reilly got a roll of insulation tape from his van, and insulated the fellow! He'd stayed on afterwards and watched all the shows.

Now the *Talk* was doing very well, so Mick O'Reilly and myself were looking around for another club, in the same area. Shamus, recalls: "Probably the most well known of Dad's clubs was *The Talk of the Town*. I remember *The Jigsaw*, in Alum Rock, because they used to have an Amateur Boxing Club there, on a Sunday morning." Brendan Breslin ran it and describes the experience in *Auf Wiedersehen Pat*. Shamus continues: "I remember there being a fire at that club, at some stage; whether it was big or small, I don't know. There was the *Cascade*, on the corner of Showell Green Lane; the *Del Monica*, and the *Peter Rabbit*."

In all innocence, I'd named the *Peter Rabbit* after a friend of mine called Peter, who had rather prominent front teeth! Shamus recalls: "You know where the Flyover used to be, in Digbeth? Well, if you were heading out of Birmingham, on the Stratford Road, you continue up towards Camp Hill, where they've got the big island. Before you get to Camp Hill, there's a road on the left, which bears down towards Bordesley Green. The *Del Monica* was right on the corner there. It's demolished now. I remember the *Liffey Club*, in Navigation Street – going in with Mum and Dad, on a Sunday, to tidy up afterwards. I remember Uncle Paddy being there too. I think Dad's sister, Auntie Mai helped too, at one stage."

A Snooker Hall came up for sale, on the corner of Showell Green Lane and the Stratford Road; about an eighth of a mile from *The Talk of the Town*. This was an upstairs club, that ran over the top of about eight shops; very big and in a good spot. We did the place up beautifully and decided that this would not be for workers; it was more suitable for family couples and business folk.

The Opening Night was jam-packed. Mary went to this club, which we called *The Cascade*. We did not open during the day, except on Sunday, but it was open seven nights, from 10.00pm until 2.00am. It also had a smart restaurant. We let the restaurant out to a very good chef… another mistake. We had gambling too. But it was still a lonely life for Mary, because of the nights. We had a resident band – the *Rooney Brothers*, who were a very good outfit. They backed Billy Furey for a few years. It was after my time, but Mick O'Reilly knew Paul Henry, who played Benny, in *Crossroads*. He used to come to the *Cascade*, although I never met him. Paul bought a pub of his own, in Digbeth, and he ran that for quite a while.

According to Russell, my youngest son, "*The Talk of the Town* was very dark – a real drinking club. I remember going right up to the top of the very narrow stairs. You walked in the entrance, and straight away, there was a door to your right, which went into the downstairs bar. I always remember the *Cascade*, which was on the corner of Showell Green Lane. That was where you'd take your girlfriend or your wife out to – it was a lot smarter. There was a big mural on the wall: I'm not sure if it was Bridget Bardot… or someone like that. The whole side of the wall was covered by a painting of a glamorous woman's head – with the hair flowing; very kitsch, actually. It would be back in fashion now, with the 60s/70s revivals. It was that sort of style, which would have been very modern at the time. There were drums there too – and we used to play on them.

"When I was getting a bit older, Dad's last club was the *Liffey*, in Navigation Street. I'd be about five by then. I remember the stairs, going up to that. Then there was the bar, and I remember Uncle Paddy, who was a carpenter, working on it. I think Uncle Tom may have worked on it too. I definitely remember the bar being fitted out; it was like a building site – almost.

"Occasionally we'd meet Dad's friends or employees there. I remember Dad had someone on the door, called Joey O'Neill. At the time I thought he was massive; however, looking back, he was small-framed, but with a muscular physique. I remember Billy Graham, who was a good friend of Dad's. I think he managed one of the clubs and I know he managed one of Dad's betting shops. He was a Dublin fella, and a very good friend. Dad got on very well with him. He had a back injury, later on in life; but he always reminded me of Rolf Harris. He probably didn't really look like him at all, but he had a shock of black hair, a beard and thick-framed glasses. I remember meeting him, and thinking: 'Is that Rolf Harris, or not?' He'd probably be horrified, if I said that to him!

"Then there was *The Jigsaw*, in Alum Rock and I remember coming in and going *down* the stairs to that. Like my brother, Shamus, I went there one Sunday morning, which was when they let a boxing club use it. I remember the *Peter Rabbit* on Broad Street. You walked up the stairs to that and there was a stage there. That was a Strip Club. Uncle John managed that. It had an old-fashioned walkway. There was a famous fight there once. Some of the fellas from Moseley Rugby Club were there. This is funny – but I only got the full story when we had the pub – the *Royal George*, in town; because Pete Evans the *Balsall Heath Basher*, helped us out on the door. Pete was there, the night that the big 'to-do' went off. I think they'd won the *Pilkington Cup*, or something. They were on a very big 'high'.

"I love Rugby, but it's not like lads who box, or who've done amateur wrestling, or anything – because they stand on their own – and they don't have to prove themselves, and therefore have more confidence. A boxer or wrestler will sit down – and if there's trouble, he's not expecting anyone to back him up, so he's less likely to want to prove himself. If you spoke to the likes of Pat Roach or Dad, they'd actually be tougher, but more self-contained and not afraid of walking away. They knew they could do it, if they had to. I'm not knocking rugby, but that's the background to it.

"Pete and Dad told me that some of the rugby players came up and started pawing at a couple of the girls, but were told to calm down. But they didn't and a fight started. Pete was wearing a mohair suit. He had to have it dry cleaned at least a dozen times, to get the blood out of it! Mick O'Reilly was also there that night, and 'King' – a big Jamaican doorman.

"Years later, I was a pupil at *Solihull School*. It was a very strict regime. If you were picked to play rugby for the school, you *had* to play. I didn't enjoy my time at *Solihull School* at all, but I wasn't a bad rugby player, when I arrived there at twelve or thirteen. The school ethos was formal, strict and disciplined. Also, when you arrived at thirteen, you were out of it a little bit, because friendships had already been made. Some of the lads had been there since the age of six or seven, so there were groups of long-standing friendships already formed.

"Anyway, I arrived and I wasn't a bad rugby player, so I started playing rugby. But they wanted me there every Saturday. It wasn't just local teams, where you'd play at eleven and finished at one. You'd be playing lads in Public schools up in North Yorkshire, so it would take up the whole day. You'd have to meet at eight o'clock, travel up there, play your game; have your tea afterwards, then travel back home. So I started feigning injury a bit, because I just wasn't interested, and I wasn't enjoying the school.

"I remember getting in trouble, for 'wagging off' a Saturday, when I should have been playing rugby; just not turning up and feigning injury. I wouldn't 'bunk off' a day when I was having lessons, although I wasn't enjoying it, but I just didn't want to play sport for them. Then we had the first Parents' Evening. He probably doesn't even remember this, but Dad recognised one of the rugby teachers, as being one of the Moseley crowd.

"I had no trouble after that at all. The team would be announced on Thursday, but I could just stick my hand up: 'Sir, I've got a bad foot.' 'No problem Dunleavy!' All the lads wondered why it was that I got away with it. It was really funny. Eventually, I started playing hockey for the school, which I enjoyed a lot more. But I never realised what had happened at the time. It was only some years later that it actually all clicked into place. But this rugby teacher knew my name and he definitely recognised Dad, at the Parents' Evening!"

Although there was a funny side to this life, there was also a very *unfunny* and sinister side, as I was about to find out…

Chapter Eighteen

A BLINDING FLASH

Mick O'Reilly eventually returned to Cavan. Then out of the blue, after living a raucous life, he married a lovely girl, when he was about thirty-five. She'd come back from America. He opened a tyre business for himself – new and second-hand, and a supermarket. He also has land and is currently doing very well. He lives in County Leitrim, in a place called Mohill. Seamus was at Mick's niece's wedding, twelve months ago, in Cavan. He and Mick met up again, and at the hotel reception afterwards, they had a great time, talking and laughing about the old days: the strippers, insulating tape; fights with the Travellers – all sorts of things. They recalled a time when a crowd of Travellers arrived at the 'Speakeasy'. Luckily, Pete Evans, the 'Balsall Heath Basher', managed to get an urgent phone call out to Mick O'Reilly and Seamus, alerting them to the fact that he was under siege.

We went down there – me and Mick O'Reilly, from Sparkhill. We sort of ambushed them; got two or three of them in the back and gave them a right kicking. There was a whole rake of them. One of them came along with a can of petrol, threw a sjoll of petrol at us and set fire to it! We couldn't go too close to him or he'd throw more petrol at us. You had to dodge back as quick as you could. But we followed them all along the top of Moseley Road, to get the petrol off them.

There had been trouble at the *Speakeasy* and he was one of them, you see. His mates had got a bit of a dusting, so he thought: 'Right, I'll get a gallon of petrol there.' He was going to torch it. A few of them got a good kicking and a good walloping, on the day. But we all survived – me and Mick and the *Balsall Heath Basher*, although Pete was cut somewhere around the ear. Pete's still got a scrap-wagon; he worked for me quite recently. He's a very good character. I've got a lot of time for Pete.

Not a long time after, I was going to my Saturday night in the *Cascade*. Mary's friend, Angela Lammond was supposed to meet her there. At about 11.30pm Mary called me to say that Angela was not coming and she would therefore not bother to go herself, either. The night went on and at about 3.00 am. I drove down Weatheroak in Mary's new Volkswagen car. I owned the house directly across the road, which had a garage, where I kept my Jaguar. I usually drove to the centre of the road, opened the garage doors and put my car in; very little traffic about, thirty-eight years ago, especially at that time of the morning.

So there was not a sinner about, on this still, cold morning, in January 1968. Our house was two or three doors from an entry. I'd got my hand on the inside car door, and was about to open it, when I saw this fellow coming out of the entry, two houses down. I could see him coming. He had a donkey jacket pulled up to the bottom of his chin and a cap like a beret. Whatever possessed me to say to myself: 'I will let this fellow pass by', I'll never know. When I thought that he had passed me, I looked up, but there he was – looking straight at me! His donkey jacket was still pulled up around his ears and his beret-like cap was pulled down to the top of his eyes.

I hadn't actually *pushed* the car door open yet, but it was unlocked. Although I didn't see a gun, when he fired the first shot, there was a blinding flash and a mighty bang. I can still remember it – as though it were yesterday. I knew that I was being shot at straight away. The first one hit the start of the roof, just above the door. The police said the shot jerked his hand; otherwise I would have had one in the head. The second one hit the half-inch strip in the front window, which this small opening window or opening light closes against – the little quarter-light that comes down. Even if the bullet had been a *fraction* one way, from where it actually hit the car, it would have caught me on the side of the face. As this second shot hit the metal, it bent it, like a wood shaving! I quickly dived down on the seat, as another bullet went into the car, on the far door, putting a half-inch depression in it.

The fourth shot caught me just on the top of my head, the spot I've just shown you. I still remember how painful it felt…. like a sting, or a burning hot iron! By now my feet had kicked the door open and I got out. I hadn't intended to open it, at first, it was just the way I went down. He fired five shots in all; they sounded very dull, as they hit the side window. But can you see my head there Shirley? Towards the back section of the top of my head; it took the whole piece out.

The gunman ran to the centre of the road, where a car picked him up. But just as he was getting into the car, he fired again. That final bullet made a nice hole in the front of my house, at 7 Weatheroak Road. Although it was a brick house, there was a band of concrete, painted white, just below a window. The bullet-hole was in that strip, between the window and the front door, for years and years!

All of this happened in seconds. I was bleeding *profusely* from the head wound. The police and an ambulance were there within minutes. Bridie Docherty across the road called them, and administered first-aid to me. It was amazing how it happened – if you saw the car; with a chunky man in it, as I was – and the position of the bullet holes.

Mary was sleeping upstairs in the front bedroom. She heard the first shot and saw the flashes from the gun, from her room. Although it was three o'clock in the morning, because of the sounds of gunfire, all the neighbours were soon out, to see what was happening. Mary suffered a miscarriage shortly afterwards. It was a harrowing time.

Tracey, just four years old at the time, was sound asleep upstairs, in the room that she shared with her brother, Shamus. She remembers the light suddenly coming on, as two policewomen entered their bedroom, to check that the children were safe – and the words: "Are they alright?"... then seeing me afterwards, with a big cotton wool patch on my head. Russell has no recollection of it at all, being just six months old.

In hospital they could not stitch my head, because the piece was blown away. The police found five bullets and casings. They were from a '38' and would have blown a hole as big as a sixpence. We went to church the next morning, in the *Old Harp Club*, in Walford Road, in Sparkhill, which was used for Mass, as an annexe to the church itself. As I walked away with Mary, I turned to look at something and the whole congregation was looking at us. They'd obviously heard about it, on the radio. Although I had a big plaster, in the shape of a cross, on my head, none of the congregation mentioned it, because they didn't want to upset me.

If you saw the car afterwards, you would never have believed that a person could have survived that kind of attack. It was a very small car and I was fifteen stone, short and bulky. Yes, it was a miracle indeed!

The plaster cross on my head made me look like a hot cross bun! It's funny, I had great pictures of it – this is a bit macabre now – taken by the police; looking down on it and across-ways. Really, they'd be a collector's item now: "That was me – after I'd been shot!"

Shamus was younger, and a much heavier sleeper: "I probably remember people coming in the room, but had no idea who they were. My earliest recollection of the shooting was what happened, perhaps days later: again, going out and always wanting to be with my Dad. I remember him having this bandage or cotton wool, on the top of his head. To a child, it looked really strange – 'What's that Dad?' Ever since I can remember, he always had a bald head, but he varied from having no beard to a full beard. At the time he had a full beard and a bald head and I remember this bandage. I think it was when we were going to Roger, the Barber's; either for me to have a haircut, or maybe for him to have his chin shaved. But everywhere we went, people had heard about what had happened.

"I was sitting in the car, while Dad was standing outside it, describing to whomever: 'Well, one bullet went here and one went there.' He had a very narrow escape. I was listening to his conversation and trying to work out what had happened, because my recollections of that evening, as a three-year-old were sketchy. Obviously, as time's gone on, I've learnt more about it. Very young children, I find, are very visual.

"I have three young sons and they're very visual too. You can tell them something until you're blue in the face, and they won't remember it. But they'll remember that you've cut yourself, or that you've got a bandage on your finger. You'll tell them that you shut it in the door. They won't remember that, but they'll remember the bandage on your finger. So I've got this image of Dad with a beard and this thing on his head."

Well, when it got out in all the wrestling circles, about what had happened to me, Jack Atherton gave me two guns and a machete. All of a sudden, I became an expert on guns! A '38' was the heaviest gun of the two; it was three pounds in weight. He also gave me a '22', which is a smaller, hand-gun that you can carry in your pocket. They were both fully loaded – and he gave me the machete too, when we were in the *King's Hall*, in Derby. He was a lovely man – Jack – and had a Lancashire accent. He said: "Seamus, I don't know what's happened, but I've got some 'material' here for you. Take it and look after yourself." I kept that *material* from Jack, for a year or two!

I kept the guns in the house, and although I didn't keep Jack's hand-gun under the dashboard, I always carried it around with me, in my jacket, whenever I went out: that was the '22' – a lovely little gun. But a lad came to me, one evening, wanting to change a cheque. A lot of the lads used to get cheques, which they couldn't change. They always knew we'd a few quid – from the clubs, you see? So this lad came up, just as I was pulling away in the car one evening, from the house. He raised his hand to me, just as I was pulling away. I thought: 'Oh no – it's here again!' So I drove quickly away from him. That was a particularly worrying part of my life.

The apprehension took a while to pass, but Mary was the one who was affected more than anybody; she'd worry about me going out to the clubs at night, and so forth. If I'd taken the opposite view, and met violence with violence, and been convicted, then the person trying to destroy me would have ultimately succeeded.

There were one or two lads come to me, who said: "We'll do it Seamus!" As simple as that – it *could* have been arranged – very easily. But all of a sudden, Shirley, you could have been looking at a man who'd served ten to twelve years inside, if I'd taken that route. As it is, I've had a great life, which has been thoroughly enjoyable. I couldn't wish for any better life than the one I've had.

When people saw the car afterwards, they said to me: "Well, you'll definitely die in bed!" Because it was such a miracle that I'd escaped – any one of the five bullets could have killed me. He was as close to me as you are now. He just suddenly hopped up. The third one, the indenture in the car; the fourth one in the top of the head; the fifth one, I'm out of the car. There's a man out there and he definitely wants you dead. Had I hopped out of the car, to garage it, as I usually do, I'd have been dead.

There was talk of a stand-up fight, shortly before, but that's neither here nor there – I didn't expect to be shot at! I never ever dreamt it would be a shooting. Well, you wouldn't would you? Apart from this, we were a very civilised family – our parents were never in trouble. We came from a poor background, but not a *rough* one.

Although it affected Mary a great deal, it did not bother me much at all. But if it happened nowadays, a person would need counselling for months afterwards. The car that the would-be killer escaped in was found burnt out, in Shirley; the next day, if I remember correctly. Reporters called at the house and wanted pictures, but I sent them packing. All the newspapers ran stories about gang warfare breaking out. You would think they were talking about Al Capone or big gangsters. I was no gangster, nor had I ever been in trouble in my life. But I was a bit unlucky that I came up against a psychopath.

So…travellers, rivals, Birmingham or London Underworld, disgruntled punters, fellas I'd had run-ins with. They were heady times, so who was responsible for the attempt on my life, I'll never know for certain. Although it could have been any one of a number of possibilities, it was a psychopath – and I believe that I know who… to this day. And he knows that I know.

But that part of my life moved on and after about six months we moved to Solihull. We bought a fine big detached house on the main Warwick Road – 513 Warwick Road, in Solihull. Really nice: beautiful gardens, front and back. Drive in and drive out; two garages. The price was £6,000. We put down a £3,000 deposit, got a mortgage of £3,000 – and we had it. Done and dusted. We spent a few months doing it up and it was beautiful.

Russell was about one-year-old when we moved, around June 1969. I used to carry him upstairs when we were doing the new house up. There was an archway leading into the bathroom, but Russell would always cry, because he was afraid to go through the arch. It's funny, isn't it? It was quite a high archway, not a tiny one, but he was terrified! He'd walk through it alright, but you couldn't *carry* him through it.

That first Christmas, when we were in the new house in Solihull was really special, after the redecoration was finished. Mary left, to fill her car up, on Christmas Eve. When she returned, it was snowing. She says to this day, it was the best Christmas she every enjoyed – all the family healthy and fit. A beautiful house… and I must say… a beautiful wife.

My daughter, Tracey, remembers walking down to the Dovehouse Parade with Mary, soon after we moved in, alongside Russell, who was in the pushchair: "My mum was saying: 'God, aren't these shops lovely?' And I'm thinking: 'Yes – they're very nice!' We had a lovely garden – a huge one. It was a large detached house, with big bay windows in the front. There was a lot of rockery on the front and we used to have fun, climbing on the rocks. Dad was wrestling and running clubs, although at the time we had no idea what he did for a living. Sometimes we'd watch him on *World of Sport*, on a Saturday afternoon. We got very involved when Dad was wrestling. We'd shout out: 'Don't do it!' 'Leave him alone!' 'He's *behind* you Dad!'"

We continued to go abroad a lot with the kids. When we left 7 Weatheroak we did not let it, we sold it for £3,000, having originally bought if for £1700, or £1750. My brother Mickey was now a successful gas contractor and wanted to get rid of the houses, so we sold them, but really, we did not end up with a lot of money. If we had held on to them, until today, we would have done very well. But we were doing a lot better without them. Years before we sold, we put water into each room, and a small gas cooker. So all the rooms were self-contained, except for the toilet, which was communal. We did away with the kitchen, and around thirteen people using it, so we'd improved things a fair bit, for whoever came after us. But we were moving on.

All the clubs were doing OK. By now I would be around thirty-five or thirty-six. So I packed in the wrestling game. A bit sorry, but everything comes to a finish or end. Our boy, Shamus, had left *Olton Convent* and started at *Eversfield Preparatory School* and Tracey left the Convent and started at *St Martin's*, a very posh girls' school, where the emphasis was to make them into little ladies – proper little madams! Both schools were for manners, nice speech and academics. Although they were Protestant schools, Shamus and Tracey had already made their First Holy Communion, so most of the Catholic groundwork had been done with them.

Chapter Nineteen

SHAY AND RUE

*By 1974, Seamus had acquired an accountant, Mr Small, whom he describes as a
"real gentleman". He was one of the partners in a firm called Small Pearsall.
However, due to his earlier experiences in Ireland, and his Dad's advice, Seamus had
not kept his accountant fully informed about the true situation. So they never actually
got to grips with things. Mr Small was only getting half the truth. The inevitable
outcome was that his tax affairs dragged on for years, as Seamus continued to pay
very little tax – if any at all!*

Eventually, several tax inspectors shuffled my tax affairs around with
houses, wrestling and Clubs, which was all very complicated. The Enquiry
Branch therefore decided to take it on. If anybody reading this book is in
business, and has had tax problems, they will know what the Enquiry Branch
is... and what they do. They are the Gestapo of the tax system!

Well, they started, and for weeks and months they delved into
everything. One day, we had a big meeting, with Mr. Small present. One of
the Enquiry Branch officials was a man named Sullivan ... a good English
name! I can't remember the other little bastard's name – a non-descript little
get. Sullivan was a big man. Anyway, the upshot was that they obtained a
Search Warrant, to search my house. They arrived, with Mr. Small and
myself, in my car. The police did not come with them. They said that if I co-
operated, it would not be necessary.

So it was a funny old drive, from the centre of Birmingham, to my house
in Solihull. These two gentlemen went through everything, finding
documents about money I had invested in Ireland, and paying no tax on it.
They had a Field Day!

Mary knew of the meeting. I had arranged to meet her at the *Liffey*, our club
in Navigation Street, in Birmingham City Centre. The club itself was on the
upper floors. A section of the ground floor was let to a musical instrument shop,
called *Woodruffe's*. The owner, Mike Woodruffe, was a member of the legendary
rock group, *Deep Purple*. We let a smaller section of the ground floor to a café.
I had the lease for twenty years, although I don't remember what I paid for it.

We opened at 2.30 pm. in the afternoon, by which time our meeting with the Enquiry Branch, and the house raid, were over. When Mary saw Mr. Small with me, she knew that something serious was up. I said: "Mary, things have happened today that will change our lives forever." She had already opened the club before we arrived. We were expecting a beer delivery. Neither Mary nor I realised how serious the situation actually was. But the tax people were now *definitely* aware of my existence.

Mr. Small came into the club, after a while. We went upstairs and talked. We put one of the punters behind the bar section, a lad called Tommy Gillespie, so there was plenty of free beer that afternoon. But we did not care. Our world had fallen apart. We had a long chat with Mr. Small. He did not know what tax we would have to pay, but he was talking six figures, and there would also be penalties to pay. But he said it was only money. We were both young and clever and we would soon bounce back.

As well as the documents relating to a few thousand pounds that I had invested in Ireland, there were other papers telling about the monies I'd earned through the years. So we were laid bare. The first thing I thought about was bailing out of the country. I started the ball rolling first. This was after a lot of soul-searching. My children were well into their schooling and all their friends were here. Mary's family were here, her mother was here and they were all very close. So the decision to leave was not an easy one to make. The tax man took my passport, but after about three weeks it was returned to me.

I got rid of the *Jigsaw*, to my brother, Paddy, who used to look after it. Then I sold the *Talk of the Town* to Mary's brother, Tommy Griffin, who was running that. Did not get a lot for them, as it had to be done quickly. The weeks passed and the investigation continued. I wasn't sure whether a jail sentence was in the pipeline. We had split our houses in Sparkhill and I had sold my lot. Martin Coleman, the lad from Galway who I mentioned in an earlier chapter, as our first lodger, bought 8 Wilton Road and number 6, where he had started off, all them years before. I sold a club in Broad Street to Ron Williams, leasehold. I could not find a buyer for the *Liffey*, so I held on to it. There were also the tenants there – the music shop and the café. We had no idea how long this investigation would last.

Russell recalls an incident that happened to me, around 1973, when he was just five years old. During a visit to Watney's Brewery in Watery Lane, Bordesley, a drayman clipped part of our Volkswagen, with his wagon and trailer. When I hopped out of the car and had words with him, the drayman said: "We'll settle it!" Unfortunately, I misunderstood his intentions, and

Seamus and little Shamus, Weatheroak Road, Sparkhill, 1965.

Seamus, Mary, little Shamus and Tracey. Russell hadn't been born yet.

Early foreign holidays, when Tracey and Shamus were small, c.1967.

Mary and Russell on holiday abroad c. 1968/69.

A Blinding Flash:
*Seamus narrowly escapes
death. The bullet holes
in Mary's new
Volkswagen are clearly
visible. Soon afterwards,
the family moved to
Warwick Road, Solihull.*

Tracey, Shamus and Russell, outside 7 Weatheroak Road. Note the bullet hole in the white band on the wall!

Russell, Tracey and Shamus, in the garden at 513, Warwick Road, Solihull, c. 1970.

Seamus and Mary's three children. L-R: Shamus, Russell and Tracey.

Seamus and his son, Shamus, in the front garden of 513 Warwick Road. Shamus is dressed for his first Holy Communion.

Cousin Stewart Griffin, young Shamus and Russell, c. 1970.

Mary and the three children, in the new house, at 513 Warwick Road.

Russell's first Communion, over in Ireland. Photograph taken at Mary Ruane's studios, in Ballina, County Mayo.

Tracey's Confirmation, in Booterstown, County Dublin.

Photograph taken for Solihull News *article featuring Mary, following their successful planning appeal for* Homer House.

In the back garden, at **Dalworth House,** *Lovelace Avenue. Young Shamus is standing. Seated left to right are Sioban, Seamus and Mary. Sioban is brother Mickey's daughter, she now lives in Chicago.*

Bragg Brothers Ltd *built* **Dalworth House** *and the Dunleavy's present home. This is an aerial view of Bragg's Churchill Road premises in Solihull, built in 1912, and just a short distance away from the two houses in question.*

The original **Dene Hollow,** *adjacent to the premises, of* Bragg Brothers Ltd, *before Muriel Water's father, Robert Bragg, one of the three co-founders of the company, made alterations to it. It was the home of Muriel and the rest of her family, shown in the next photograph.*

The Bragg Family: Back row L-R: two of Muriel's brothers, Jack and Charles (the Baker). Sister, Joan, Robert Bragg (father); Lilian (mother); Percival Robert (PR) and Denis, two further brothers. Jack, Percy and Denis all went into the family construction business. Front row: Christine, Mary, Muriel and Betty. All three photographs are by kind permission of Muriel Waters, Robert Bragg's last surviving daughter.

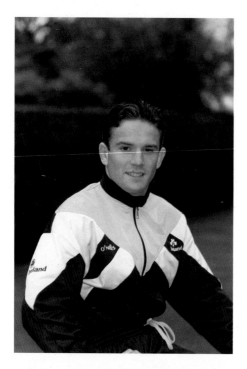

Russell Dunleavy, 1992. He has won International Competitions for Ireland, wrestled all over the World and trained in the States at the Naval Academy.

Poised for action, Russell is a three-time winner of the World States Wrestling Tournament.

Delta Airlines Olympic Awards 1992. Awarded to the Outstanding Sports Person in each of the 24 Olympic Sports in which Ireland competes: Back Row - (all standing). Harold Kyle (Clay Pigeon), Delta Airline Employee, Keith Gough (Judo), Michael O'Brien (Fencing), Conor Henry (Cycling), Russell Dunleavy (Wrestling), Rep. Spanish Olympic Committee, Jimmy Kirkwood (Men's Hockey), Athlete unknown to us, Anna Mervelot (Equestrian), Eamon Byrne (Weight - lifting), Denise Lyttle (Sailing), Barry MacDonald (Gymnastics), Sandie Fitzgibbon (Basketball), Pat McDonagh (Bobsleigh), Represented by his mother?, Wotizit' Mascot for Atlanta 96 Olympics, Michael Corcoran (Canoeing), Derek McGrath (Football), Claire Samways (Women's Hockey), Ciara Doheny (Badminton), David O'Brien (Archery), Front Row - (all seated): Ian Molloy (Target Shooting), Member of Olympic Council of Ireland, Judy Jordan President of Delta Airlines, Michael Carruth (Olympic Boxing Champion 1992), Owen Casey (Tennis), John McGrath (Rowing), Gina Galligan (Swimming), Pat Hickey President of Olympic Council of Ireland, The Lord Killanin Former President of the International Olympic Committee, Wayne McCullough, (Boxing Olympic Silver Medallist 1992), Colum Slevin (Table Tennis), Sonia O'Sullivan (Athletics) Represented by her father, Pat. These award winners had gained sponsorship and funding to represent Ireland, in the forthcoming 1996 Olympics, which were held in Atlanta.

Russell Dunleavy and boxing legend Mike Tyson met at a function at the Metropole Hotel, *Birmingham, in November 2005. Russell is a former Amateur Light - Middleweight Wrestling Champion of Ireland and ex-captain of the Irish team.*

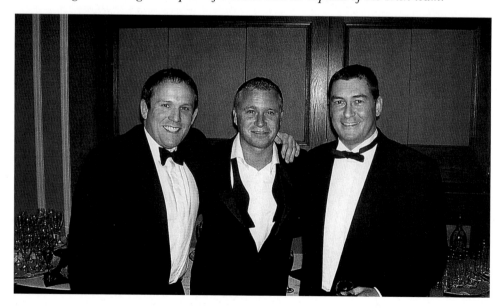

L-R: Russell Dunleavy, Steven Arnold, who plays Ashley Peacock, in Coronation Street, *and Russell's friend, Ben Griffiths.*

GREAT DAYS RECALLED AS 'SAC' CLOSES

THE "Sac" is no more. The Sacre Couer Hotel in Salthill will close its doors for the last time this coming weekend after more than forty years trading as one of Galway City's leading hotels. More than fifty years ago the Dunleavy family, parents Agnes and Jim, together with the ten children moved from Sinolane, Kilmovee, Co. Mayo, to Salthill.

In Sinolane the family ran a small dance hall, shop and Post Office. At that time, it was a major decision to move to Salthill and Galway from East Mayo. Sean Dunleavy who was 18 years old at the time and the second eldest of the family went on to manage the Hotel in the early sixties and continued to do so up to this week.

The parents built a house that became a guest house in 1951 and after that as they say "I was married here forty years ago" and indeed there have been instances where the sons and daughters of people who were married in hotel have also had their reception in the Sac.

Sean retired from driving around the roads of County Galway to take over management of the Hotel in 1963 and he married Vera. A marriage made in Heaven that saw the pair combine to lead a great team that brought the Sacre Couer to the top in Galway. Vera (nee Jennings) whose brothers John and Joe wore the Green and Red of Mayo, is a native of Ballinrobe. The Hotel exuded kindness, efficiency, cooperation, family values, and attention to detail at all times. The hotel was very popular for weddings from all over Galway and further afield. Sean tells us that before you could book the marriage in the church you had to be sure that the date was available in the Sacre Couer Hotel. In the sixties and seventies, weddings were held early in the day and were finished by 7pm. Then it was time to get ready for a function that night. Sean and Vera say that it was extremely hard work but that they were young, well able for it and that times were good. They have always paid tribute to the staff for their great work too. Four members of the staff, Bennie, Patsy, John and the great and affable Georgina have more than 140 years service between them. Tommy Hinks who retired as Chef a few years ago was also there from the start. Many more are there for long periods also. Sean and Vera have had four children, Sean Og, Aoife, Ciaran and Deirdre and they too have worked in the Hotel.

It has always been a family run hotel and one always felt at home there.

The Sacre Couer has been the scene of many great occasions. Galway football and hurling teams have come back to the Scare Couer for the victory celebrations after winning the McCarthy and Sam Maguire Cups. One remembers the thousands outside the Hotel meeting the hurling team when they won the All Ireland Final in 1980. It was two a.m. before the team sat down but the meal was hot and wholesome. That was an exciting night. People in their endeavour to get in for the night climbed drainpipes and got in windows to the surprise of guests in a room. Galway Football teams at all levels came there too when they brought back the Sam Maguire Cup. Last Sunday saw the last final G.A.A. function in the Hotel. It was the occasion of the Connaught Club games between Caherlistrane and Castlebar and Salthill and Crossmolina.

Presidents of Ireland Eskrine Childers, Paddy Hillery, Mary Robinson and Mary McAleese were in the Hotel. Taoisaigh, Liam Cosgrave, Jack Lynch, Garret Fitzgerald, Charlie Haughey, Albert Reynolds and Bertie Ahern were also visitors. Many Presidents of the G.A.A. attended functions there as did the Presidents of the F.A.I. Of those, two Mayo men were there Mick Loftus from the G.A.A. and Pat Quigley of the F.A.I. Most of Galway's G.A.A. Meeting were held in the "Sac".

One group that will miss the Hotel is Muintir Mhaigh Eo. Founded in 1970 it has had its home there and always used it as the address of Muintir Mhaigh Eo (the Association is now holding it's meeting in the Galway Bay Hotel, Salthill). Muintir Mhaigh Eo have held 35 Annual Dinner dances there and great nights were had by all and the Mayos always had a home in the "Sac". People were always sure of an outstanding meal. Muintir Mhaigh Eo were glad to be in "The Sac" as it and many other organisations treated the Hotel as home from home. Were there charges for meetings? there may have been but no one in any organisation has ever paid. Indeed one member of

Pictured is Sean Dunleavy of the Sacre Couer Hotel, Salthill, receiving a presentation from Dr. Maureen Langan Egan, Chairperson of Muintir Mhaigh Eo, Galway. The presentation took place last week on the occasion of the last official visit of Muintir Mhaigh Eo to the Hotel after 35 years. On the right of the photograph is Mrs Monica Heneghan, Secretary of Muintir Mhaigh Eo.

Muintir Mhaigh Eo has visited the premises twice per day for many years and he does not have a hungry look about him . He too,Then you have the similar to many more will miss 'The Sac" and Deirdre's greeting and kind hospitality.

Then you have the "Meeting of the Minds" group that gather on a Sunday morning - in that gathering you have Tim Kirby the man who worked with the E.S.B. at home and was seconded for his expertise to other countries, Andy Dunleavy who travelled the roads of Ireland for Kit Kat Products, Pat Mullins who is the Sacristan at Christ the King Church nearby and managed visits between Masses through the rear door of the Hotel to tell all of his exploits in his vintage cars both in Ireland and England, the Chairman and Medical adviser to the group Dr. Jim Fitzgerald who demands a special seat, Frank Gaughan on occasions will give a song and tell all of his Championship wins with Parnells in London, Ronnie Burke who played music in the Sacre Couer for forty years will tell of all the fine musicians he knows and has taken the occasional photograph. Tom Burke, of course, is there too. The Castlebar native who has retired from his Pharmacy business always has great plans for the Mayo team and then Bert Quigley gave the Galway perspective on all matters. If any group, such as Government, Church, G.A.A., F.A.I., Racing Board or the Rugby Union ever sought good advice then the Sac on a Sunday morning was the place to be and the advice would be given loudly and free. There are many other such groups that will miss the Sac.

NEW OWNER

The Managing Director of the Development Company who has purchased the Hotel is Bernard Duffy He is one of Galway's biggest and well known developers. Bernard's father Brian who also came from Kilmovee has announced that planning permission has been sought for offices and car parking to be put in place where the "Sac" now is.

HAPPY RETIREMENT

What will Sean and Vera do now? One can be sure that they will lead active lives. For more than forty years Sean rose at 6.30 to make sure that all was in readiness for the day in the Hotel, then he went to Mass and played nine holes of golf and was back for a long day's work at 10.30 a.m. Now he will rise a bit later and play 18 holes of golf. There will be no rushing to and from games because of business. These pleasant trips will be completed at a leisurely pace. Vera too will resume her golfing activities and take longer walks. We wish them health and happiness for many years to come.

NEW VENUE

Last Thursday night Muintir Mhaigh Eo in Galway moved to a new location for meetings. As has been well chronicled the organisation has been holding their meetings in the Sacre Couer since 1970. On Thursday last the Galway Bay Hotel was the venue and a General Meeting was held. The manager Dan Murphy was on hand to meet the group and similar to the previous venue refreshments were available. Muintir Mhaigh Eo look forward to their visits to the Hotel, the fact that the manager is from Cork and a great Cork supporter will not deter the attendances from being there.

SWINFORD LINK

Dr. Donnacha O'Connell, a Law Lecturer at NUIG, gave a talk at the Muintir Mhaigh Eo General Meeting last Thursday night. Donnacha from Swinford chose the topic "Exile" to talk about. It was indeed a most interesting subject and he gave of his experiences throughout the world and talked about the many thousands that have come to Ireland in the past ten years. Muintir Mhaigh Eo have Guest Speakers on two occasions each year and if we might say so he has been one of the best.

NEW PRESIDENT

The new President of the

Seamus' cousin, Sean Dunleavy, featured in a Galway News *article about the closing of the famous* Sacre Couer Hotel, *founded by Seamus' Uncle Jim, over forty years ago.*

Mary, Seamus and daughter, Tracey.

Celebration in a marquee, at Dalworth House, *hosted by Maggie Moone and Colin Davies.*

A recent photograph of Seamus, on the bridge, at Charlestown.

Another recent photograph, at the top end of Barrack Street, outside the Library and the Fire Station. Those of you with magnifying glasses should be able to read the green signposts!

The four Dunleavy grandsons: three are the sons of Shamus and his wife, Denise. Seated, from L-R: Daniel Patrick, James, (Tracey's son), and Thomas. Behind them is the eldest of the four, Seamus.

Not exactly *the* Princess Maud: *Seamus and Mary, about to embark on the* Queen Mary 2, *bound for New York.*

Seamus and Pete Roberts at a Wrestling Reunion, outside Bill Bridges' Greenwich pub, the Prince of Orange.

An early Northern Wrestlers' Reunion, in Seamus' pub, the Royal George, *in 1994, before the venue moved to Ellesmere Port. L-R: Pat Roach, Seamus, referee Max Ward, and Sparkety Clarkety - who'd gate-crashed!*

Seamus and Mary, on London Bridge.

the drayman ended up on the floor. Although I subsequently tried to help him, the drayman's union accused me of deliberately injuring his earlobe, which needed four stitches. Another young employee, witnessed the event, and testified against me, when I was summoned before two magistrates. I was fined £25 and the union decided to deliver no further beer to me. Steelhouses of the Black Country, after making a few deliveries to me, were persuaded to desist, so I had to drive to Liverpool for a while, to obtain beer for my clubs. The union's top official said: "We're going to put you out of business!" However, after help from a few friends, plus a generous contribution to the union, the ban was eventually lifted.

Some time ago, before all of this happened, I had bought a little schoolhouse, in a beautiful, scenic area of West Ireland, for £4,500. We had converted it into a nice two-bedroom cottage, on the edge of a fishing lake, called Lough Conn. So if push came to shove, we could go there. The children, of course, were not aware of any changes in our lives. I didn't have the Title Deeds because the land had belonged to the Lucan Estate. As Lord Lucan had recently disappeared, his affairs were in turmoil.

But now, preparations were being made, to leave. We took the kids out of their lovely schools. It was heartbreaking. There was a big St. Martin's Commemoration Dance held every year, but we decided not to go this time. It was a good job that we did, because on the Thursday night of 21 November, 1974, two pubs in Birmingham City Centre were blown up. IRA bombs had been planted there, killing 21 people and injuring 120. And we were the only Irish family with a daughter attending St. Martin's. Thankfully, we didn't attend the dance. Buidheachas le dia – thanks be to God!

The day after the bombings, Friday, Mary was buying a tumble dryer, to take to Ireland. She gave in an AIB card – an *Allied Irish Bank* credit card. Boy, did she get some abuse! The backlash was deadly, although we were not there to catch much of it. It was a lot worse than the papers let on. But it was a terrible act. And a terrible time to be Irish, in Birmingham.

Tracey recalls: "513 was the first house we moved into in Solihull, before we moved to Ireland. The numbering on the Warwick Road is all upside-down. Next door to 513 was something like 402. 514 was right up by 306. They're all up and down; only a few numbers follow in normal sequence. 513 and 514 are at completely opposite ends of the Warwick Road and on opposite sides."

On the Sunday evening after the bombings, a cold, November, winter's evening, we started to pull the house apart. We took all the oak doors off, they were solid Japanese oak, took out the marble fireplaces and anything that could be taken. All the carpets were taken up – it was a sin. The day after, *Robinson's Removals* were to call and take the stuff to Dublin. We packed our two family cars with our clothes and everything we could carry. Just before we pulled out, John Griffin, Mary's brother, took us to the Chinese Restaurant, in Solihull, where we all had a meal. The kids thought we were going on holiday.

Shamus elaborates: "We were leaving and my mum's mum and her brother, together with the rest of mum's family turned up, to see us off. We had two cars at the time: a white Mercedes CHA 123L, and a Volkswagen Passat. Me and Dad were in the Passat, and Russell, Mum and Tracey were in the Mercedes. We'd got 'The World and his Wife': all the possessions; bicycles, the lot, in the two cars. It was an adventure for us kids. I suppose it was explained that we were going on holiday; which was even better – not going to school! My Uncle John, my mum's brother, gave me some money. He gave us £18, which in those days in 1974, was a fortune – and he was giving it to an eight year-old! I split it between the three of us, not knowing then, the reason *why* he'd given me the money. Because we already had the house in the West of Ireland, it wasn't alien to us; it wasn't as though we didn't know where we were going."

We left the Chinese, about five o'clock in the evening. It was teeming down with rain. As we headed for Liverpool, we lost each other on the motorway. Shamus and I were ahead, in the Passat, so we waited by the end of the motorway and, luckily, Mary saw me. It was still lashing down with rain. Well, we got on the boat, with our laden-down cars, and all the kids' bikes on top. After something to eat, we settled down for the night, in a cabin for the five of us, with bunks. Before that we'd had a walk on deck, but it was very rough. When we got up in the morning, Russell, our youngest, said: "We are still in Liverpool Dad!" I said: "No, we are in Dublin." He said: "That sign was there last night – and it's still there!" He was right. It had been too rough to sail and we were still in Liverpool!

God – the night after that we *did* sail. It looked a bit calmer, but a few miles outside of port, a great gale broke out and the boat was up and down like a fiddler's elbow. Mary and the kids were very sick, but I was OK. I was too worried to be sick. The cabin floor was about two inches deep in vomit. In the morning I apologised to the staff for the condition of the cabin. When we got off the boat, we went to the *Royal Dublin Hotel*. We decided to stay the night there, get our kids nice hot baths, and a good bed, and head down for the West the next day.

Russell remembers: "I was six at the time, but even at that age I remember that there was a very bad 'Vibe', after the pub bombings. But we were delighted that we were going off to Ireland, because we loved it – it was just great; all holidays. Eventually, we didn't want to come back to England, at all! After our eventual return to England, I used to get very upset then, for a long time, even up to my teens; because I couldn't get used to the change. We had a 'fab' time: it was idyllic."

It was strange coming down to the West. Would I forget England? Oh no – all the rancour about England had gone. I'd met some lovely people there. Best friends I ever had. County Mayo is about three hours or so from Dublin. Dublin is on the Irish Sea and Mayo is on the Wild Atlantic. We stopped a few times, on the way down, passing through Charlestown, my hometown; but we didn't stay there – just carried on, to Pontoon.

Pontoon was lovely when it was a holiday home, but to come and live there, the magic soon wore off – at least for us – as adults! Two bedrooms, one of which was tiny – that is where the kids slept. We had two sets of bunk beds and not a scrap of room. But the kids loved it: huge lake outside the door and a nice little beach. We did very little for a week or two. We would drive to Ballina and Castlebar every day.

"It was strange for me," remembers Shamus, "because although I was born here, in England I was known as the Irish Kid, or a 'Paddy' of some description – with my name and coming from an Irish family. But in Ireland I was always known as the English Kid.

"In the West of Ireland there was none of that class distinction, although there *was* more in Dublin – in Blackrock. I wouldn't say you were picked on more for it, but if you did get into a scrape it was one of the things used against you: 'You're not one of us – you're the English Kid,' because you acted differently.

"Our converted schoolhouse, in Pontoon, had a perimeter wall around it, and the house was set quite high up. So you came down some steps and walked down the drive, to the main road. Now, you could probably count on one hand, the number of cars that would pass, on a daily basis; it was that quiet. From Mum and Dad's point of view, there wasn't a fear of us being knocked down by a Juggernaut. Nowadays, obviously, it's different. But you crossed the road, and the beach was probably about twenty feet down from the wall, with access points that had been made: so we could hop down some rocks, and what-have-you, and we could walk along the beach."

Tracey recalls: "It was the best time of my life – I think. We had a tiny bedroom, with bunk beds and absolutely no room in there for a wardrobe or anything; basically, you could just sleep in it. But it was a fantastic, very warm little cottage inside. There was a lovely lounge, which was absolutely fantastic to go in, and it was all very cosy. Pontoon was just brilliant – I loved it! The lake was just outside the window – a huge big lake: nine miles wide, by three miles long, with a big mountain in the distance: you could see the waterfall coming down it. It was brilliant, because you could play in all the rocks and the heather.

"It was a great place for adventures," remembers Tracey. "There'd be what we used to call 'quarries'. If you smashed the stones there, you'd find what looked like tiny diamonds and gemstones inside them. It was a wilderness. Every day we used to climb over the school wall and find a totally different landscape. Russell would have been about six at the time, so he was around too. There were wild goats everywhere and we'd follow them: nanny goats with big horns. You'd see them in the distance, but when you got closer they'd run away. Then we found a place down by the lake, by a cove, where the goats used to go when they died. We used to think it was a Grotto. We'd go down there to look for bones and things. It was just a fantastic place!"

The children were too small to realise what was happening, so we enrolled the three of them in the local school. A school bus would pick them up in the morning and drop them back in the evening. I remember dropping them off the first morning. Poor Russell was in a different room to the others. When we looked back, as we were leaving, he was sobbing his heart out. Russell confirms that the first couple of days at the new school were difficult: "But it was very different to an English 'Prep' School. The children in Ireland were lovely: they were absolutely the best children you could ever mix with. They were completely different; all country people. At that time I would have had a very 'plum-in-the-mouth' accent, even though I'd been brought up in an Irish Catholic household, with the same values that they had. I hated school in general anyway, so I would have been upset at first. But then I remember settling in and it was great!

"People over there were much friendlier. For example, you'd visit each other's houses without having to be invited. Everyone would just come round and we'd take it from there. Johnny the bus driver would close the doors on us: 'Let the girls in first!' It was a big bus, and it seemed as if they picked someone up at every house; it would take a long time. As Tracey says, it was absolutely idyllic in Pontoon. You looked out and there was a glass lake and a beach with a brook and a stream running down to it. The road snaked around the edge of the lake. You'd cross the road and then there'd literally be about twenty feet down to the beach. You'd hop from rock to rock, to get down. When you were on the beach, you'd swim or do other things.

"It was a great place for adventures. You'd go running off, away from the beach, to a part where it was all cliffs. I remember the goats there too. In the summer, the lake would be just like glass – and you'd see the salmon popping up. You took it for granted; you just thought that everyone lived like that, really. The McGoverns were behind us – they were a bit younger. There were the McHales, mum's cousins, on the other side of the lake: literally, two hundred yards or so away. We used to play with Thomas and Theresa, their son and daughter. A German family lived just around the bay – the Amibecks: Elka, Cornelia and Angelika.

"It was a fantastic experience, going to a National School in the West of Ireland, and then going from there to *Willow Park*, the junior part of *Blackrock College*, which was the equivalent to Eton over here," continues Russell. "The great and the good of Irish society send their kids there. We settled into both schools straight away. It was very easy to do that."

Shamus explains: "The two of us were at Willow Park. I'd been to Eversfield here, then Curragh Bagan National School in the West of Ireland, which was the culture shock for me. Moving from there to Willow Park was rather like returning to Eversfield: it was much more structured. Curragh Bagan was a National School, set in the heart of the West of Ireland, near a little village called Knockmoore. It took in children from within a five-mile radius. It was a village school with three classrooms, and just three teachers.

"My teacher at the National School was a Mrs. Brogan. You sat at your desk and ate a packed lunch. Russell's teacher was Mrs. O'Shaughnessy. The Headmaster was a chap called Mr. Gunning. I remember sitting down and opening my lunch-box and Mum had put in a Scotch egg. Mrs. Brogan, who was in her early forties, I suppose, had never ever seen one. Every lunchtime afterwards she'd be hovering around me, like a hawk, to find out what Mum had put in my lunch-box." Russell had a similar experience too!

"But the weirdest part was getting into the school. Dad obviously had to contact the Headmaster, but you also had to see the local parish priest, a chap called Father Hart. He ran the local parish church in Knockmoore, where Russell later made his first Holy Communion. I remember going into the priest's house with Dad, and we were sitting down, talking to him. But at that time I didn't know the difference between capital punishment and corporal punishment.

"Just before we left England, in History, we'd learned about the guillotine and capital punishment. I can always remember sitting in this priest's house and Dad asking him: 'Father Hart, is there any corporal punishment?' To which he answered: 'Of course there is!' And I'm sitting there thinking: "If I'm naughty here, they're going to cut my head off!" It wasn't until later that I worked it out. That memory stuck with me – forever! In those days, every school I went to had some form of corporal punishment, and sometimes Shamus was in quite close contact to the items employed! I had the slipper and the cane many times, for being naughty, and such."

"I was about six or seven years old," remembers Russell. "They played Gaelic football, but I was too young to play. The pitches were sloping like that. It must have been at a 40 degree angle! In Ireland they have 'Feis', pronounced 'fesh', which are competitions of songs and poetry – rather like a Welsh Eisteddfod. I remember I had to recite a poem, in Irish, at a local feis. They start them young, and they have the children singing, at that age too. You'd start learning Irish straight away, so all of the children would be fluent at quite an early age. I loved it! Father Hart, the local priest at Curragh Baggan, had coached the Irish Boxing team, at the Rome Olympics, in 1960; the same Olympic Games where Muhammed Ali won gold, as a Light Heavyweight."

While the kids were at school, Mary and I had nothing to do… we were not used to that. Also, Mary missed her mother desperately. She wanted to get back to England badly, and so did I. When we left our accountant, Mr. Small, he had no idea what was in our minds, so he had quite a shock when I rang him from the West of Ireland! But he still kept in touch with our case and we did not fall out. Thirty-eight years on, he is still our accountant, although I never paid him for years!

The case was progressing very slowly. The Revenue was aware that I was in Ireland and indeed wrote to me several times. When we'd been there for a few months, and I was proper browned off, we'd go down to a place called Corroy, where there was a public telephone box, to ring England. We had no phone of course, and you could not ring direct; you had to go through the operator. She would connect you…. and listen to your conversation as well, I'm sure!

"We'd left England in November '74," Russell continues. "People forget that 1975 and 76 were just wonderful summers. I remember arriving there and Nan coming over about Christmas. Her name is Mary – but everyone calls her Mai. It's funny – I always remember that Christmas of 1974, in Ireland. You know how you're excited on Christmas Eve? In England, Mum and Dad would have put the Christmas presents from Father Christmas in our bedroom, but it *was* a very small room. I was on the top bunk and Shamus and Tracey were on the two bottom bunks. I remember waking up in the night: 'Has he been yet?' 'No, no,' so we thought that he hadn't been. But when we went into the lounge, everything was laid out in there. It was just magical: like … 'Oh my God!' I remember that Christmas so well."

Shamus agrees that as children, life in Ireland was: "… absolutely fantastic! We were probably a bit wild, while we were living there. It was such a change, from here to there. At the time, like Russell, I'd been going to *Eversfield Prep School*, where you wore school uniform, had a sports kit, and went to a dining hall for your dinner; that had been the norm, as I knew it. Then we left and went to the West of Ireland, which was a very different place – a beautiful part of the world.

"Our nearest neighbours lived half a mile away from us, although you could see the place quite easily; you could almost read the number on the door. Their son was a friend of mine, a lad called Thomas McHale; he was in the same class as me at school. I could go round to Thomas and we'd be out playing football. It was that quiet that Dad could stand at our wall and call me for dinner, and it would be as close as we're talking now. That's how crystal clear it was."

Our TV that we bought in England would not work in Pontoon. When we did get a new one, we could not get a picture, because of the mountains. The only station we could get was RTE. *Batman* was all the rage in England and we could not get it. God – the kids missed it! Russell got sick at the St. Patrick's Day Parade, in Swinford and was still sick next day, so we kept him off school. But he was complaining of a stiff neck and didn't like daylight. So we rang from the public telephone box and the doctor came out. Mary said to the doctor: 'I think it is meningitis.' When the doctor had examined him he said: 'I think so as well. You must be a nurse.' Russell was rushed to hospital in Dublin. Straight away, we said we would drive him. We took the other two children out of school, and headed for Dublin. It was the longest drive of my life. Russell was getting steadily worse and he seemed to feel every bump in the road. "That's one of the most vivid memories of my childhood," Russell confirms. "I remember we were playing around the lake, on the morning of St Patrick's Day. We had egg and chips for lunch, and I felt great. We were going to see the parade in Swinford and I remember the drive there. Then the very next memory I have was me saying: 'I've got a headache.' Mum was surprised by that; it was almost: 'But kids don't *have* headaches.' I wanted to go home, because I really felt terrible.

"I remember, Charles Kelly drove down the street; we were on one side and Charles and his family were on the other. Charles is the family solicitor. He's very well known, not only in that part of the country, but throughout Ireland. The parade was quite short, because it was only a small town. Dad wound down the window when the parade had gone past and said to Charles: 'Where's the parade Charles?' Charles started laughing: 'Ah –

you're only codding!' Codding means joking. So they were having a laugh and a joke between themselves; but I remember feeling really terrible.

"When we got home I went straight to bed, but only slept for half an hour. When I woke up mum called Doctor Grimes, from Foxford. He came out and the next thing was, mum had the car packed and we were going to Dublin, just after the doctor had been. So we drove up there on the morning after St Patrick's Day. I got steadily worse. They took me to *Our Lady's Hospital for Sick Children*, in Crumlin, Dublin. My doctor was a Mr O'Donoghue, who became very good friends with the family afterwards. They gave me a lumbar puncture, to relieve the swelling on the brain. I remember screaming with the pain. I've seen it since, and they actually give people anaesthetics for them now. They didn't get it right to start with. Then they drained it, and the pain was completely gone. I was in hospital for five or six days, followed by antibiotics for a week or so, but then I was fine." As Russell explained, we became very good friends afterwards with his doctor, Mr. O'Donoghue. He had a holiday cottage in Westport, so he called a few times, when he was passing. Ironically, he eventually bought our holiday home in Pontoon.

Russell's illness brought something home to me. We could not live down the West – it was too isolated. It had to be a city and then it had to be Dublin. The kids were back at school and Russell was fine, so I started to go to Dublin, on and off, for to see if we could buy something there. But the prices were above us. Don't forget, I had left my house in England. The mortgage people sold that to get their money back. So I hadn't much and it was a good job that we bought the schoolhouse, all those years ago. After a lot of looking, I found a site, having decided that it would be better to *build* a house. If things went according to plan, it would be a lot cheaper. So I bought the site. I think it was about £8,000. It was in Bray, County Wicklow, about eight miles from Dublin. My money was getting very tight, but I thought I would have enough to build. There was planning permission on the site, so I could start whenever I wanted to. But the next thing was to get the family up to Dublin. So I hunted around and got a three-bedroom semi, in a place called Blackrock.

There was a girl who we used to know in Liverpool, called Eileen Sheehy, and her husband John, from Limerick. We would see them off and on, when we were on holiday, a few years before. John worked for *Murphy* for years and they bought a fine bungalow for the holidays, in Ireland. It was in a village called Parke, very near to where Mary's mother comes from. I think John had some tax problems in England. He had to bail out and ended up living in Parke, in the holiday home that they had built. They had a daughter about the same age as our Tracey. So they started coming down to us and then we would go up to them. We had done this for about six months. They had plenty of room, so we would go up, have dinner and stay the night. We also had plenty in common, because John, Eileen's husband, was a tax exile, the same as ourselves. The best nights we spent down in the West were with them.

Nevertheless, we were ready to head for Dublin. So on the 14 August 1975, we pulled out. We had a house rented in a place called Hyde Park Avenue, Blackrock. We got there and unloaded our stuff. But our main furniture was still in storage, in Birmingham. I took it back to Ireland later, when my house was built. According to Mary, "The first evening we arrived, we were awake all night, listening to the people talking. We thought it was very noisy."

It was a beautiful evening and Shay and Rue got their bikes out for a bit of a spin on the concrete footpaths. But they came in straight away. So I had a look outside and at the end of the avenue there were about twenty kids, all chatting; nearly all had bikes and footballs. My lads could not face a strange crowd, so they went out again and stayed just beside the house. When they had not come in after ten minutes, I went to investigate – and there they were – in the middle of the gang, all laughing and swapping bikes and so forth. When bedtime came, they did not want to come in, so we left them to it.

In the morning, before we were up, we must have had eight, nine or ten kids knock the door, looking for 'Shay' – that was what the Dublin lads called Shamus. Russell was 'Rue'. The Avenue was full of kids of their age, so they loved it and wanted to live in Dublin for ever. The Dublin kids were a lot friendlier than in England. They would just walk into our rented house, and our boys would do the same with them.

"The 15 August is a very big Holy Day of Obligation," explains Mary, "so the bells were ringing. There were people talking outside and lots of kids in the road. Although our kids were very shy at the beginning, I'd safely say, it turned out to be the best time of their life. They were out all day. Coming from England, they had all the latest toys, like Chopper Bikes, Tonka Toys – all the best that we could possibly buy. I don't think they ever came in the house. They'd throw their bags in and they'd be out! They did that every night, every day – they had a wonderful time!"

"It was 'fab'," confirms Russell. "We arrived somewhere towards the end of the summer. There were just loads of bikes around, when we arrived. There was no attitude of any kind; we just got to know everyone straight away. Gordon Norton, an ex Irish Rugby International, lived in the road. We were friends with his lads. There was an old woman who used to live around there, in a cul-de-sac of semi-detached houses. She was old widow, who lived in the end house. We used to call her 'Blacksie'; her real name was probably Mrs Black. She had a big house and we'd always be messing about there; hopping over into the gardens; we were all terrified of her," continues Russell.

"She was probably lovely really! It was a large Gothic type of house. I think her family had owned the land, and then sold it, to have the cul-de-sac built. But it was the perfect setting. We would all be in the road. She had a Triumph Herald, and it would suddenly be: 'Get out of the road. Old Blacksie's coming!' We were just *terrified*. There was one time when we all jumped over a brook, to get away. I was the smallest and I couldn't make it, so I had to hide behind a tree... and she was looking round for me! She certainly *looked* the part, although, as I say, she was probably a lovely person. All the locals would remember her."

"Hyde Park Avenue, Blackrock, was just off Mount Merion Avenue," Shamus elaborates. "It was a cul-de-sac, but as you came up, there was another road off it, just literally around the corner, called Hyde Park Grove. Blacksie lived in the end house there. On that road there were probably half a dozen kids of our age. Most of them went to Willow Park, although one or two of them went to what you might loosely class as a Comprehensive School. But we all got on; we each had a bicycle, so there's be a train of between eight to ten lads, riding up and down the road.

"Blacksie lived in what was probably the original house in the area, because it had a long wooded driveway, up to the house. It was the only place on that road area where you could get conkers. So of course, the conker season comes round and every child in the avenue wants conkers. Where did you go? Blacksie's! She had two daughters, who were probably in their fifties. Blacksie would have been nearer seventy. We were forever getting caught up the trees, getting conkers down. It was the last house on your left, but as you turned into it, there were trees on one side, and just at the back of the first two trees was a brook and some land, or a field, so that you could get away from there, if you were lucky.

"If she caught you she'd call the police. The local Garda would come up and give you a telling off. There were no arrests, or taking you down the police station. More often than not it was the scare factor: 'If you get caught again, I'll come down to see you mother and father.' With my generation, you did not want the police, the Garda, anywhere near the house. Even if your Dad saw you speaking to the Gards on the street, it would be: 'What's he done?' My Dad was of the generation – first of all, you don't bring the police to the doors of your house: 'You don't do anything naughty, and if you do, I'll give you a clip round the ear-hole anyway, but then I'll give you a clip for getting a clip off the Garda, and *another* one, for bringing him to the door!'"

"There was the milk float as well," adds Mary. "They were mannerly kids though; full of confidence. Do you remember that they used to jump on the milk float? It was a quiet road and the kids got to know the milkman. So when he took off a crate, they'd jump up and sit on the float – and just go along with it. Not a word was said to them – it was absolutely lovely."

The bed we slept in was useless: very narrow, and there was a big dip in the middle; so the next day we bought a new one. The kids loved the road – English TV with good, clear reception and loads of mates – boys *and* girls. This was summer, so all the kids were off school; our gang had a great month. Then it was time to sort out a new school for the boys. *Blackrock College* was where most of the lads in the road went to, but it was impossible to get in, because they were all the sons of former Old Boys. So we arranged an appointment to see a Father Stanley, who was a lovely man, but he explained the situation. Mary had approached him, unofficially, several times before that. We discovered he was from Galway, Mayo's neighbouring county, so that carried a bit of clout. Also, the fact that my Uncle Jim had a small hotel in Salthill, Galway, and that one of the family was a priest carried two additional bits of clout. Father Stanley had a nephew called Bobby Molloy, who was a TD, a Member of Parliament – of the *Dail Eirean*. He was always in Uncle Jim's hotel when he was not in Dublin, and was very good friends with him.

When Father Stanley heard all of this, and with a little donation and the promise that they would play nothing except Rugby, they were in. The local Dublin people could not believe how we managed it. Tracey was at the sister school, called *Sion Hill*. She was very happy there. Our sons already knew quite a few boys at *Blackrock* because they lived in our road.

We were still in Hyde Park Avenue, sitting by the fire one night, when we got a phone call from our friends in the West, John and Eileen Sheehy. They had packed up and were in Dublin, staying at the *West Country Hotel*. We went out, to pick them up and they explained that they had had enough of living down the West, and were selling up. Now they had a very big bungalow, a shop they had bought; also a nice bit of land, with plenty of cattle. So they were a lot better off than we were.

We put them up in our rented house, for about a month. Their daughter, Eileen, was with them as well. They then rented a house in Blackrock, not far from where we lived. Mary and I were delighted to see them and we carried on from where we left off, when we were down in the West. Eileen got into the same school as Tracey. Eventually, when our house in Bray was finished, John and Eileen bought a site near us in Bray, and built a house there. He sold that house in Bray and bought two sites, close to his rented accommodation in Blackrock. So when the two houses were finished, he moved into one and sold the other.

By this time I had started building my house in Bray, where I had bought the site. It was very hard, because whereas I knew many people in the building industry in England, I was a complete stranger in Dublin, so I had to find all the trades and get used to Dublin. Although the kids were fine, Mary and myself wanted to get back to England. The tax saga was still going on, as it would be for years. But Mr. Small was still my accountant and was working on my behalf; we were in contact all the time. The house that I was building was finally finished in the following February. I started in late August, so it took about seven months to build.

"But we had a break in, at the new house in Bray, which Seamus was working on," Mary explains. "There was no way we could look after it. So we moved from Hyde Park Avenue, and like everything else we've done in our lives, it was about seven o'clock on a February evening. We went down Mount Merion Avenue. It was freezing cold – with three young kids in the car. Oh God – that was hard!"

Yes, if you've any sort of problems, you should confront them in the morning, not at the dead of night. And any bad news, you shouldn't try to sleep on it. We got bad news the other night, but I didn't tell Russell until the following morning, or I knew he'd never sleep a wink that night. I told him the morning afterwards, because it didn't seem half as bad as it did the night before.

"There were a lot of people out of work at the time," elaborates Mary. "During this break-in in Bray, they'd take bathroom suites and radiators. So we got the furniture out of storage and just moved in to the new house, which Seamus was building, to protect it. It wasn't ready, but we were all together and it stopped them from doing it again."

The kids were so afraid, the night we moved into the unfinished house, because there were no curtains up and there was a tree outside their room. It was a very blustery night. You could see the tree branch, making a shadow, every time it moved. The three of them were in the bed and you could see their eyes; they were terrified! They called us into the room and pointed to the window. There were a lot of trees in Bray.

Mary agrees: "It was very rural. There was a family living opposite us in Bray, called the Quinns. The father of the family, Pat, had started *Quinnsworth*, one of the largest supermarket chains in Ireland. There were a lot of children in the family and they became friendly with our kids. They'd go across the road together. Eventually, when we came back to England, two of the children, Lisa and Gavin, visited us. They were particular friends of Shamus. They had a Pool Room. The father was a bit of an entrepreneur. I remember he took them once, around Christmas, to see *Joseph and the Amazing Technicolour Dreamcoat*. He also had a bus, and each seat had a small television. They were a lovely family."

He'd take people on trips to Race Meetings, on his bus. He could sell drinks on the bus, because he was licensed to do that. It was his own charabanc – like an old-fashioned coach. Mary recalls: "We had a lovely dog named Warwick. There was no fencing in front of the house, and that dog never ever left his spot, in front of the garage door. He'd never stray. He was guarding it. He was an Alsatian dog – absolutely brilliant."

Mary asks: "What about your worst nightmare – in Old Connaught Avenue? The kids used to go over to the Quinns. It was a very busy cut-through. You were bad after that. There was like a back-way, up to the *Christian Brothers*, where there was a priest's house. All the kids used to go up the back-way and they'd be playing. Seamus called out to our son Shamus, for some reason; it could have been for lunch. He ran down this back-way and never looked across the road. He didn't get run down or anything, but Seamus used to dream about that. You were bad after that, for a long time."

All the kids had their own rooms, but it was a fair distance from the schools, so either Mary or myself would take our lads, every morning. Tracey was getting bigger, so she used to catch the bus at the bottom of the road. The site I had bought was very wide. There was a small graveyard next to us; no one had been buried there for years. There were big gates on it, always locked; it was so old there were no visitors. It was surrounded by a very tall, granite wall; you could just see the odd cross and tombstone, peeping out over it. Believe it or not, it was quite attractive. I owned the land behind it, which was part of my site. So I came in a different way to my house, and used the original entrance to make another site, behind the graveyard.

I managed to get planning permission for the graveyard and I had a free site. I bought it off a lady doctor called Dr. Curtain. She owned a lot of land around there. She wasn't very pleased when she saw me get a site for nothing. Now I had the idea of selling our new house and building again and maybe I could make enough money to settle up with the Inland Revenue. But this was all in the future. Then we discovered another problem. Directly in front of my new house was a huge big wall, twelve to fourteen foot high. It was part of a big old estate. We heard all sorts of rumours that it was going for up-market housing and flats. But to my horror, it turned out to be a school for tinkers. Well, in no time the place was flooded with them. I had a wall built in front of my house, but we would get a row of them sitting on it. They had horses – all piebald and thin. They established a camp, just below the back of our garden; dogs, big as hounds, roaming everywhere. In the summer, they all disappeared. They would be gone for a few months, roaming around the country. When the weather got cold, they came back. The local people formed a committee, to try to police them, but I had made up my mind that I was getting away from them.

Tracey remembers: "It was great in Bray – being able to go over the road, to a quite old fashioned shop – to get something to eat. You had to walk round the steps inside, and some of the stuff in the window had been there for a long time. We lived on a very long road. As Dad said, I had to get the bus every day. I don't think they realised how long the walk was! It was probably about two miles or so to walk home, after I got off the bus. I had to walk up Old Connaught Avenue, which was a lovely road, with beautiful houses along it. But then all of a sudden, there was this land at the top, which tinkers had moved on to. The Government had made this land an official site and told them that they could stay there. Sister Consillio, their spokesperson, would come round and say: 'Give these people a home.' But they didn't actually *want* to be kept in this place: in the summertime they wanted to be out travelling.

"They used to be hanging around, when I was walking back, and I'd think – 'Right – the next bit – I hope the tinkers aren't out.' There was a young lad there called 'Baldy', who had a completely bald head; he was probably only about my age. He seemed to have a reputation for being one of those who might attack you, but if you went up to him and said: 'Hello,' he was fine then – he just walked on. As children, we were completely happy over in Ireland and would have preferred to stay there, for the rest of the time really. We had lovely schools, lovely friends, but we all came back to England."

Russell remembers: "At the time, they were filming *Flight of the Doves*. It was just after we moved into the new house in Bray. It was a very good film, with Willie Rushton and Ron Moody. The graveyard scenes were filmed in the graveyard on Old Connaught Avenue. It was a story about an uncle taking two children away from a wicked step-father, to Ireland. Willie Rushton was the wicked stepfather, and Ron Moody was the uncle, although he also played others characters in it. It's a very good film. The lead role is played by the guy who was the Artful Dodger, in *Oliver* – Jack Wild. Jack played the older brother; there was a younger sister."

Now my house was finished and lived in. So I started the second house, behind the graveyard, and put the first one, our house, on the market for auction. Well, the day of the auction arrived and we did not get one bid. But the auctioneer said it was a bad time. My friend from down the West, John Sheehy, was there at the auction. When no bid came forth, he said, in his Limerick accent, "I have never before seen anything like it!"

I'd definitely decided, by this stage, that I was returning to England, and would try to pay what I owed. Mr. Small said that whatever I owed the Inland Revenue could be made in staged payments, which was more encouraging. I got buyers for the house that I never got a bid on – a Welsh couple, who were being transferred to Ireland. We got about £39,000 for it. I therefore made a big decision, and bought a house along the Warwick Road, again, in Solihull, with the proceeds. This new house, number 514, cost just £30,000, because a tremendous amount of work had to be done on it. So I moved the kids and Mary back, and I stayed, to finish the house behind the graveyard.

Somewhere along the line, I'd bought yet another site, in a place called Killiney, the most upmarket place in Dublin. I paid £13,000 for it, which was very cheap. I was borrowing a fair bit of money from the AIB Bank in Swinford, County Mayo. Before I had finished the house behind the graveyard, a man called Mr. Gracie came along and decided he would have it. But I had to finish it. So with Mary and the kids in England, I rented another house in Booterstown, Dublin, returning to England every weekend.

Russell was about eight, when we returned. "It was nice being back at Eversfield again, because all the lads I'd been at Nursery with were there. It was unusual, because I was straight back in. But I missed Ireland terribly. I think we all did; we'd changed in those two years. We'd taken to the relaxed way over there; it's the difference between being brought up in England and in Ireland. There was the easygoingness of it all. Then you come back, and suddenly you're in Solihull on a Saturday afternoon – just ready to go out on your bike, to your friend's house – but you can't. Why not? Because the roads were too busy, and with some of the parents, you'd have to let them know that you were coming, beforehand. Had I been older, I would probably have understood better, but I couldn't grasp that, and it was very difficult to adjust." For Tracey and Shamus it wasn't too bad. Being older than Russell, despite having to re-adapt to changing circumstances, they didn't experience the same 're-entry crisis'!

Shamus concludes: "I had a fantastic time in Dublin and maybe, looking back with rose-tinted glasses, I would live there tomorrow, but it's almost thirty years since we lived there and times have changed. I took my wife and children back to the West of Ireland, last year. I tried to explain what it was like as a kid, when we lived there. But nowadays, between where we lived and the next house, there are probably fifteen additional houses, within that space."

Chapter Twenty

COPPERFIELD AND HOMER

Seamus' tax affairs were in a deplorable mess and there was no light at the end of the tunnel. Jim Small had no idea what they would have to pay, or what penalties and interest there would be. So maybe they'd move back and might be cleaned out and lose their house? Maybe even jail... so it was a very uncertain time for the Dunleavys. But anyway, they were back. The house at 514 Warwick Road needed a terrific amount of renovation, but at least they were in and Mary and the kids were happy. The boys had returned to the familiar surroundings of Eversfield and Tracey was back at her old school as well – Saint Martin's. So, in a way, it was 'as you were before'.

But the weight remained squarely on Seamus' shoulders. Time passed and he finished the second house in Bray; eventually Mr. Gracie moved in. This was the second of two houses that had been broken into. Work on the Killiney house was under way too.

Their Warwick Road house had no central heating, so Seamus tackled that as well. All in all, he was extremely busy. Some weekends were particularly sad, when he was unable to get a flight across to England. When he was successful, he'd find Mary and the children waiting outside the Exit, as he came through Customs, so those were the great weekends. Once the heating at 514 was installed, they were warm and cosy. Seamus battled away on his Killiney site. After a further six or seven months' grafting, the house there was almost complete.

Then a fellow came along called Mr. Copsey, an English accountant. We agreed a sale of the Killiney house, at £65,000. It took me a few weeks to finish, but then I hit a snag. For any property that was being sold for more than £60,000 you had to have a tax certificate, to show that your tax affairs in Ireland were all clear, and that all your tax was paid to date. Well I'd paid no tax at *all* in Ireland. What were we to do?

So we came up with the idea of £59,000 for the house and £6,000 cash. I thought the idea was original and brilliant, but it has actually been done since time immemorial! I finished the house, got all my stuff together, and left my rented house. I had taken my car across for the last week; packed it with tools and all sorts of bits and pieces. My boat was the late evening one, from Dun Laoghaire to Holyhead, but not the *Princess Maud*, on which I'd made some of those earlier crossings, because we were now in the 1970s; twelve years before, in 1965, she had been sold to Greek interests, and renamed *Venus*.

The *Princess Maud*, I later discovered, had come into the world the same year as myself. She had been built in 1934, by William Denny of Dumbarton, for the LMS: the London, Midland and Scottish Railway route, sailing from Stranraer to Larne. She was 330foot long, 2917 gross tons and carried 1458 passengers. *Princess Maud* travelled at a speed of twenty-one knots and was the first British-built ship to be equipped with an automatic sprinkler and fire alarm system. Throughout the Second World War, she served as a troop ship and was attached to the US Task Force for the D-Day landings.

After the war, she was reconditioned and moved to Holyhead. On the port side they added an additional flying bridge, to assist docking. She acted as a spare and relief vessel, on the Holyhead-Dun Laoghaire sailings, during the summer months. In 1951, shortly before I first left my homeland for England, she was employed on the Southampton to St Malo route. She also did relief runs on other Irish Sea routes, whilst regular vessels were being overhauled. So the *Princess Maud* had a very busy thirty-one years of service, taking countless passengers, myself and my fellow countrymen included, back and forth, before she became the *Venus*. Think of all the tales she could tell. No wonder she became a legend!

I remember the drive from Holyhead so well. I was coming home. It was magic. All the tough times with the kids in that little rustic school; all of us living in that cramped, converted schoolhouse. The lonely, dark nights, as the winter arrived. No TV for the kids. Ducking and diving – then to Dublin, and Mary badgering the priest, Father Stanley, to get them into *Blackrock*. I met Father Stanley afterwards, at a sports do, where I shook hands with him and gave him a hundred pound note. At the time, he thought it was ten pounds, but he contacted me later, saying that he couldn't believe it was a hundred pound note, and thanking me for my generosity. But it was all behind me now. All done and dusted.

There was very little traffic that night, on the road back to Birmingham. It was getting late so I stopped at a public phone box in Bettws-y-Coed, in Wales, and rang Mary. She was not sure what night I was coming. Although it was about 11 pm when I phoned, she would wait up for me, no matter what time I arrived home. The exhaust on the car was busted, and Mary reckoned she could hear me coming a mile away! But I was home. Home.

It was marvellous being back, but what was I going to do, to make a living? I got stuck into our house: there were a few walls to knock down and a few lintels to put in. You pick a wall that's not load-bearing, very carefully pull two or three bricks out, and stick an acro underneath, to hold it. After removing additional parts of the wall in this way, you then put an RSJ in to support it. I was on my own, so it was hard graft.

When I all the alterations were done, I got a decorator in. We kept the old carpets that came with the house, but when it was finished it was comfortable.

Tracey remembers: "514 Warwick Road was a beautiful house, with a very big, dark hall; but it was kind of interesting – all oak-panelled and oak on the floor. The previous owners had a large piano in there. It was wonderful, really. The only thing was, I remember going into the lounge and the previous owner had been a JP, with several dogs. I don't think he had been very good at letting them out to go in the garden, so the lounge carpet absolutely stank; we had to have that ripped up – or cleaned up!

"It was a fantastic lounge and a beautiful garden. We did a lot of renovation on the kitchen, because it was very old and small. We extended it out into the verandah and built a sloping ceiling kitchen, completely out of wood. It was very nice and cosy. They renovated the dining room and nicknamed it the 'King Henry Room', because the décor was very regal.

"I lived up on the third floor, in the attic; it was a fantastic bedroom, with brilliant views – right down the Warwick Road, because it was very high. It was a very interesting room, with a sloping ceiling and I was allowed to paint it a terrible colour – a sort of fuschia-pink; you know? Really mad! It had black beams, a private bathroom and my own little landing. It was a huge bedroom – as big as this lounge. At that age I thought my colour scheme was great! It was so interesting going in. You went up two steps, had to duck your head, and then you were in the room. It would have been difficult for an adult to use it. I loved all of that."

I was *still* racking my brains to see what I could do for a living – the clubs were all gone, but I had a lease on a place in John Bright Street, which was still let, and the club on the upper floors was empty. So we tried to open a members club, but we failed: it was turned down by the Magistrates.

An old British Rail hostel came up for sale, in a place called Selly Park – a pleasant suburb of Birmingham. It had eight or nine big rooms, plus other accommodation. We decided we would open if we could turn it into a small hotel. So we went to the auction and with the help of the AIB, managed to purchase it for £18,000. Out of eight rooms, Mary got nineteen, with a bathroom, toilet and washbasin in each; although they were very small bathrooms. We had a *desperate* job to find a plumber. Looking back, it was a very big project and we should have employed a proper firm, but finances did not permit it. Three or four plumbers came and left, each one blaming the other. Eventually we got it finished, but we did not have a *clue* how to run a small hotel.

My son, Shamus, recalls: "The *Copperfield* was in close proximity to the main Bristol Road and the Pershore Road. Selly Park is before you get to Selly Oak. It was a large building, right on the corner of Upland Road and Selly Park Road. Literally, its car park entrance was right on that junction; it had a triangular-shaped driveway. It was before I went to *Princethorpe*, so I would have been about twelve. We were living at 514 Warwick Road, so I was just going to and from it. It was advertised in the local newspapers and the like. We'd go round to the large businesses, which were likely to employ people travelling to and from the area. We also went to the BBC Studios at Pebble Mill and gave our particulars to them.

"From time to time we had the odd actor: the likes of Peter Sallis, the chap from *Last of the Summer Wine*; Wendy Craig; Lewis Collins from *The Professionals*. Those are the ones I can remember immediately. From time to time we'd have tennis players staying there, because we were close to the *Priory Lawn Tennis Club*.

"I remember coming home from school one day and Dad said: 'We're going to be on telly!' I looked at him – blankly: 'Yes? Go on – tell me.' We'd been approached by the BBC to use the *Copperfield Hotel* as the backdrop for a one story-line, two-part episode of a Police Drama Series – *Juliet Bravo*. They used the upper floors as a Children's Home. I think the episode was called *Coins*. The cellars were used as some kind of caves. But both parts of the building were used. We didn't advertise or approach the BBC ourselves. It was just that somebody came up and said: 'Oh – that will work' – and away it went.

"I didn't actually meet any of the actors involved in it – just the Props Guys. But I saw the place in the morning, as a normal hotel. Then I came back and it had completely changed," continues Shamus. "It looked just like a Children's Home and there was no way of telling that it was normally a hotel; they'd been in so quickly and converted it. The weekend would have been the most convenient time for them to film, from our point of view, because the Bed and Breakfast business was at its busiest during the week, as our guests were mainly business people.

"I don't remember any other guests in particular from the *Copperfield*, because we weren't in such close proximity to it. I remember the housekeeper there, Miss Spillane – I can see her face now. She was a little woman, black-haired; about five-foot six inches tall; greying dark hair – probably in her early fifties. Mum was tied up with us going to school, so we had the housekeeper to give Dad a hand with the morning breakfasts. As soon as we were all whisked off to school, Mum would go up and help Dad sort things out. The Bed and Breakfast business is hard in one way and easy in another. There's a rush in the morning, but then, after everybody's left and gone to work, or whatever they're in Birmingham for, you'd have a lull period, where you have to clean and tidy rooms, and what-have-you; but it's not as intensive as trying to get all the breakfasts served.

"I helped with the cleaning, making beds and vacuuming, at weekends and half terms. As Dad will tell you: 'There's no such thing as a free lunch.' In whatever business we're dealing with, there's always something to do. I'm a dab hand with a vacuum cleaner, but don't tell my wife!"

Russell recalls: "There were always German students there, who came over from *Bosch* every year. I remember one particular guest who was about six foot four. He used to say: 'Hello Mr Dunleavy. I'm Heinrich Muller.' He spoke absolutely perfect English. I'm not certain if he was the head of this particular company. Mum asked him if he'd like a full English breakfast and he said: 'Oh yes. I love being in England, because it's so important.' I asked him: 'Heinrich, how did you come to have such a good English accent?' He started laughing and said: 'I received excellent training from the German Government… in 1939!' So it turned out that he'd been a spy, who'd been shot down, and became a prisoner-of-war in England for five years. But that's just one example of the sort of guests you'd come across. He always stuck in my mind, more than anyone. He'd been in the Luftwaffe and had been trained as a spy. Whether or not he was still 'under-cover', I don't know!

"I remember Dad having a bit of trouble once," Russell continues. "There was a 'Half-way House' across the road and a chap came in, from there. He booked in as a guest at the *Copperfield*, for a few nights. This chap finished his breakfast on the last morning, then said: 'Look, I haven't got a penny, so I can't pay you – but I don't care what you do to me.' Dad was cleaning one of the tables and all of the German students were there. I could see Dad weighing him up. Then he came over, and he hit him, flush on the jaw, took him into the kitchen, and threw him down the back stairs. I remember thinking: 'Good on you Dad!' We were tight for money at the time and even though I was young, I was becoming more aware of the business side of things. I knew that although Mum and Dad were trying to expand, things were very tight. They had school bills to pay too.

"Mum and Dad were working very hard, and I remember thinking: 'Bloody Hell – what a bastard!' (Excuse my French). He'd just come in and taken advantage of us. The German students were very quiet, when that happened! But they got on great with us. I remember a team of footballers coming over, from Northern Ireland. Peter Sallis stayed there, and Wendy Craig. I remember ever so well when they took the hotel over, to make *Juliet Bravo*. They used the cellar and the gardens, to make that. They did two episodes; one using the cellar, and the other, the gardens."

All the beds were bought in *Rackhams* and we went to Whitney, for the blankets, so everything was of good quality. We had cards printed and put them all around Selly Park, and many other places in the area too. We also contacted the *NEC* in Birmingham, although we were a good distance from there. We put an advert in the *Birmingham Mail*, for a housekeeper, and were very lucky. Miss Spillane, who Shamus described earlier, was from Cork. She lived in a very smart council flat, in a big posh house, converted into four flats. It was next door to our hotel, which was ideal. She was a single mother but her son had gone to Australia, so the job suited her down to the ground.

We started to get a few people in, slowly, at first. Then we heard about a big tennis tournament at the *Priory Tennis Club*, in Edgbaston, so we advertised there. We got four tennis players to begin with, then a few more, the following day. We ended up with every room full, so we had twenty people in, for about two weeks. It felt as if we had won the Pools, but of course, they were freak weeks and the quiet times returned. *Pebble Mill*, the BBC Headquarters, in Birmingham, was about a mile from our hotel. We placed a card in there and met their Accommodation Officer, a lady named Sheila Brown. She sent us a few clients and then we started to get a few actors.

All of a sudden, if they were making a film or play, we seemed to get the whole cast: directors, producers and everybody connected with the production. We were very cheap- just £6 a night, so it suited all the actors. Amongst the famous faces were Stratford Johns; Shirley Ann Field; Peter Sallis; Jim Broadbent; Alan Cuthbertson; Wendy Craig; Geoffrey Palmer; Katherine Apponavzich, Brian Glover and almost everybody connected with TV. They did the programme *Angels*, at *Pebble Mill*, and a host of other stuff, including *Juliet Bravo*. So the hotel was becoming successful. We were making a living, but every now and then, Mr Small would want 3K, 5K, or perhaps 8K, for something or other. So the big bill was still looming and we were always broke.

Tracey recalls: "The *Copperfield* was a big, rambling building. It had a gravel drive, which made the wheels of your car crunch, as you drove up it.

I used to like going up there, to help make the bookings and clean the rooms. I don't remember making the breakfasts, or anything like that, because this was more like dad's hotel. The three of us children would often be down there. We had a big contract with *Lucas* at the time. The apprentices coming over, on an exchange between *Lucas* and *Bosch*, were regular bookings. I'd go down every now and again and speak a bit of German with the guests.

"Dad saw them more of the guests than we did," continues Tracey. "I remember seeing Katherine Apponavzich, Richard Whitely's partner (the guy from *Countdown*), because *Angels* was on at that time. Katherine played one of the nurses in it. When they filmed scenes for *Juliet Bravo*, there was a proper catering van there too. We went up to have a look at what was going on. You realise then that everything on the telly is fixed; even the woman walking along in a scene is an 'Extra' – so that was quite exciting. Dad used to come over and he might say: 'Oh, I've just had Geoffrey Palmer in.' Leon Ariss was a guest there too – Brian Glover was his real name wasn't it? It was a very busy hotel. It was nice to see the guests and so on. I'd go over there every other day."

One day I came across a derelict house, in Homer Road, right in the centre of Solihull, but had no idea who owned it. So it put me to thinking. It was all overgrown; windows broken and rusted, galvanised, corrugated iron, nailed all over the windows and doors. It was a huge site and a very big, old house. I had two friends called Ted and Maureen Scarrott. I'd known Ted for thirty years and had done a bit of sub-contract work for him. That was before the tax man and the problems. I was having a meal with Ted one day and happened to tell him that I was looking at an old house in Homer Road – Number 8. To my surprise Ted said he knew the derelict house well and had been interested in it years ago, with a view to building about twenty flats. But he had gone bankrupt in the meantime, and had forgotten about it. He knew the owner, a man called Frank Murray, a former accountant, who was long retired and living down the Cotswolds, in a place called Oddington.

So down went myself and Mary and we found him. I told him I would like to buy the house, if he had an inclination to sell it. He kept referring to it as a site. He thought the house was unliveable and that it would have to be demolished. So he agreed a price of £27K, which was very cheap, even in those times, for what was essentially a good house. There were trees growing all around it, but the structure was sound. So we agreed to have it. When we got back from Oddington, I got a chippy to put a few locks on the doors, so it was more secure. Most of the windows were broken and of course, we did not yet own the property. We had only agreed to purchase it and Frank Murray had agreed to sell it.

My own house, number 514 Warwick Road, was almost finished so I decided to put it up for sale. I figured I could then move into 8 Homer Road. Although it was totally derelict, all the timber windows were sound; so apart from a few broken doors and a small tree, growing in the place where the kitchen used to be, it was fine! All the bathrooms were ripped and destroyed, and the garden had not been looked at for years, so you could not walk a yard past the back door. It was a jungle. But it had a great feel about it, and I loved it – or I *thought* I would love it. It was a great big old Victorian house – better even than this one we're living in now! Big bay windows and as solid as a rock; you could jump up and down upstairs – the joists were that thick.

So we put 514 Warwick Road on the market for £65K (£65,000) – the same price that we had got in Killiney, Dublin. We had bought 514 for £30K and had lived there for just over two years, so we got a good price. As it seemed to be on the market for a long time I thought that it might be too dear, but the agent said that it was worth that amount.

Eversfield Preparatory School, where my sons went, is just before you come to what used to be the *St John's Hotel*, but is now the *Renaissance Hotel*, on the Warwick Road. The school had an open air swimming pool, which the parents and pupils could use every Sunday. One fine Sunday this woman commented: "Was that your house in the paper, for £65,000? You must be mad; there isn't a house on the Warwick Road that is worth that sort of money!" The same house was sold in 2002, just four years ago, for £550,000; the time that silly woman was talking was 1979 or 1980.

After a while a surgeon called Dr. Holl-Allen and his wife and children called to view it. I was rather lukewarm with them, when we first met, because the kids seemed rather boisterous, but we have since become very good friends. We heard no more and then one day, again at the pool, we got talking to another of the mothers, a doctor's daughter named Avril Embley. She said the Holl-Allens still wanted to buy our house, but they thought we were not interested in selling it, because we'd been a bit off-hand with them.

We contacted them again and they did indeed sign the contract, but could not finalise for a few months, because they had to sell their flat. We started work on Homer Road, even though we had only signed the contract and put very little money down. We left the bushes, in what is now the driveway, so that anybody driving down the road would think there was no activity, and would have no idea that anyone was working on the house. We took a chance that the owner would never visit it. Had it gone back on the open market, it would be snapped up, because it was right in the middle of Solihull, just a minute from the High Street.

The Holl-Allens finally sold their flat and we moved out ourselves – no furniture removers, and pulled into Number 8, Homer Road. We got a few brooms and swept the whole house, from top to bottom. Before that, I had hired a plumber, so one toilet was working, but we had to flush the others with cold water, from a tap that we managed to get working. Although we had no kitchen, we took the cooker with us from 514, and connected it up, so we had a means of cooking, and a toilet.

After Mary and myself had swept it out, I found some wood and firelighters, and lit a big fire. It was lovely – and we knew then that we were home. It's amazing how a cosy fire can change a situation. We got the kids beds upstairs sorted out. There were bits of furniture left from the previous owners, so we were able to manage. We used the bottom of a big old wardrobe for our grub; that's where we had our food stored. We'd done this on several occasions by now – making do with the basics, but ending up with a really special property. But when you've got a toilet, running water, food, a comforting fire, and the windows fixed – you're home, aren't you? You can hang your gear on whatever comes to hand!

There were eleven bedrooms in the house; we'd made two bedrooms out of one: out of the cold room and we re-jigged another out of the Butler's Pantry. We got a couple of good plumbers and started to pipe water to every room, putting a bathroom, toilet and washbasin in each one. That was a dreadful time for the kids. Dust, grime and cold; all the floorboards up. My daughter Tracey, whose school was next door, used to sneak out in the morning, and in the evening had a desperate job getting back, without her friends seeing her go in. We'd left the corrugated iron on the windows, so that it still looked derelict. But actually, there should have been no embarrassment really, because if you'd a brain in your head, and you looked carefully, you'd realise that it was one of the best houses in the road.

Tracey recalls: "I would go to school from there, in the mornings and some of my school-friends would say: 'You can't live in there – it's derelict!' I tried to pretend that I wasn't: 'No I just go there for a minute, then mum picks me up!' When we first moved in, we were living out of tea-chests; our clothes and things like that, were in them.

"I was absolutely *mortified* actually! I remember one girl, Paula Hancock. She found out one day, that I was living in there. She said: 'I saw you going into that horrible, derelict house yesterday. What were you doing in there? You're not *living* in there are you?' There were birds' nests in the loft and so on, although it had been a beautiful Victorian house, with original tiles on the hall floor. In its hey-day the garden would have been fantastic; it had a beautiful little bridge and all sorts of outhouses.

"I had my own room again and the two boys shared a room, in the attic. My room was in between the second and third floor and although I've had many different rooms throughout my life, if ever I'm asleep, and I suddenly wake up, and think, 'Where am I?', I always imagine myself back in *that* room. There must have been something about it that I particularly liked. It was an attic-type room again, with a sloping ceiling on one side. It was painted a pale-blue colour and I put all my posters up. Shamus and Russell had a similar, attic-type room to the one I had in 514, with sloping ceilings and beams going across, where they had to duck. It was a tremendous workload for Mum really, but there were no complaints, no depression, or anything like that. She just got on with it."

I tried to clear the garden, but after a week or two, I gave up. However, I cleared a patch, so you could at least get out of the back door and put a line up. Eventually, after getting a small machine down the garden, it took a further week to clear and burn all the foliage.

We had two garages, running tandem, with double doors at the front and back. That's the way we got the machine down – the back doors of the garage opened into the garden. When it was cleared I seeded it, although it really should have been turfed. But it came round after a while and became a fine long garden, from Homer Road, down to the railway line. We also cleared the rest of the house and had a big drive in and out, which was there already. The pillars were amazing: beautifully built, and until then, hidden by trees, moss and grass. We levelled the front, so now we could park between fifteen to twenty cars there. The pillars are still there.

The outside still looked very rough, because a lot of the brickwork had perished and frozen in winter, causing damage. Meanwhile, inside, the plumbers and electricians were beavering away. After what seemed an eternity, we had eleven rooms, each with its own private bathroom, toilet and washbasin. Then came the decorators – woodchip all the way through, but it turned out very well; for some reason or other we never got around to painting the outside.

So now, you may have guessed it. We decided that we would do Bed and Breakfast. No planning permission. Mary and I had our own room, and if you discount Tracey and the boys' rooms, that left us eight rooms to let out.

With Mary being as hot as mustard on conversion, we did all of this without help from *Our House*, or any other TV property development programmes that you see nowadays. As before, we put cards into everywhere, and started to take in guests. We became very busy after a while and well known, being right in the middle of Solihull and so convenient for the south side of Birmingham.

The *Copperfield* was hard going. I was there every morning and Mary looked after Homer Road, or *Homer House*, as it was now called. It was tough going for her too, because she had three kids to look after; getting them ready for school; then she would have to cater for between five to ten guests. She hired a cleaner after a while – Mrs. Phillips, although she would not put her hand down a toilet bowl, or anything like that, and would never *touch* a sanitary towel! But she *was* a good timekeeper. She would be around her mid-twenties.

Tracey confirms: "I was still at school and we were all running the *Homer House Hotel*, which was like mum's hotel to look after, and dad would be at the *Copperfield*. So I was doing little bits at both of them, in between my schooling."

Paul Johnson was one of our clientele in *Homer House*. Paul was a Transport Manager for *Schweppes*. He stayed with us for two years, five days a week, going home to Nottingham for the weekends. We got lot of people from the *Inland Revenue*. God, I certainly put *them* in the book, whether they paid cash or not – (phew!). There were also a lot of people from the *Ordnance Survey* office. The group of between six and eight German apprentices from *Bosch*, on a Company Exchange here with *Lucas*, were a very lucrative booking. *Lucas* would pay the bill. Their booking would be for two months. The only downside to this was that we had to make them an evening meal. Mary used to cater for the whole group, getting up at six o'clock in the morning, then once they were on the road, taking our three kids to school. Afterwards, she'd tidy the rooms, do the shopping, and cook the evening meals. Coming from a family where her dad died when she was ten and being the eldest of eight children, she already knew what it was like to work!

The Germans stayed at *Copperfield* first, before *Homer House*. I remember a fellow from *Joseph Lucas* ringing us up one day in the summer, saying that he was looking for a place for six to ten German apprentices, for a month or two; explaining what they were prepared to pay and asking if he could inspect the hotel. He had a few other places to look at too. It would be a marvellous booking, if we could get it.

To make a long story short, I was down the garden one day, in *Homer House*, raking the garden as it was full of stones. We did not turf it, so every shower of rain exposed more stones. Mary shouted, from the back doors of the house: "Seamus, come here quick. We have got the German contract!" Boy oh Boy. A great booking, especially as things had gone a bit quiet at the *Copperfield*. So we got them at *Homer House* eventually, as well.

Our housekeeper at the *Copperfield* used to have Saturday and Sunday off. So on Sunday mornings, Mary cooked a few breakfasts for me, covered them with tin foil, then I would drive up to the *Copperfield*, as quickly as possible, make the tea and serve the guests the already-cooked breakfasts. But one morning, about halfway there, I got a puncture and was about half an hour late. So I had some explaining to do!

Another weekend night, in the *Copperfield*, a Jewish lady, called Zippora Gough, booked in, without realising that she was the only person in the hotel. I never told her that. I left at about 8.30pm that evening and she was left all alone, in that old Victorian building, with the wind blowing outside. In the morning, she asked if there was anybody in the hotel, so I explained that tomorrow we were expecting eight more guests. But she was afraid, so she left – and I can't say that I blame her! After a while, I got a fellow called Albert to stay there at the weekends, but he was deaf, could not cook at all, and was filthy into the bargain. So we dismissed him and I was back to square one for the weekends.

We were in the *Copperfield* for about three-and-a-half years, before deciding to sell up. We gave it to the auctioneer, Peter Cariss, who put it up for Public Auction a week later. One or two people showed a bit of interest. There were two 'gay' people who had great plans to do it up, but that fell by the wayside. A few weeks later, Mr. Kennedy cropped up and bought it for £73,000. We'd originally bought it at auction for £19,000, so I did quite well. We had to pay a big chunk of tax to Mr. Small, but at least we were handling some money. Our final tax bill, as things turned out, was *years* away!

We now concentrated on *Homer House*, so at least the work was a bit easier. At the *Copperfield* I had to vacuum and clean about twenty bathrooms, every Saturday, so I was not sorry to see it go. One day a police car came to *Homer House*. A tall, distinguished lady got out; she had another lady police officer with her. The policewoman introduced herself, and the tall lady with her turned out to be Chief Superintendent Pauline Wren – the first and only woman Chief Super in the West Midlands. She had sold her house, as she was retiring in six months, then planned to move down to the country with her friend, a lady from the Home Office, so she needed rented accommodation for six months. Well, she inspected the guesthouse, liked it and moved in, and was usually there throughout each week, although she used to go down the country, the odd weekend.

Russell recalls: "Miss Pauline Wren, the highest ranking policewoman in the country, stayed there for a long time. She was lovely. It's a terrible thing to say, but if it was now, she'd definitely be a Chief Constable. At the time, there was a glass ceiling; it's probably still there now, I suppose, if we're honest about it. She was a Chief Superintendent, and she would have been brilliant! To get to that level, in those days, she must have been very good at her job. I liked her. In her day she would have been very attractive. She was tall and statuesque, with a long neck, and spoke in a very clipped way. In the hotel dining room, in the morning, she had her own special chair, which we made sure was always available for her. She used to have breakfast on her own, and sat there, with her glasses on, looking over at you. I also remember *Van Hools*, a Belgium company, who were the largest bus and coach manufacturers in the world. They'd take the whole hotel over every year, for the Motor Show."

But we had a call one day from a gentleman who I thought was looking for accommodation, but in *fact* he was from the Planning Office. He had discovered that we had no planning permission. Then he found that we had eleven bathrooms, so a building inspector called, after a few days, saying that we had to have nine-inch pipes. The drains were very deep and it would have been an awful job to put right. But when they opened the manholes, fair play, this house was certainly built right. All the sewer pipes were nine inches in diameter. So we were over that hurdle.

However, we had to apply for planning permission; get the plans drawn and submitted. Remember that this house had been derelict for twenty years and had been a complete eyesore. So after two months, the word came back: refused. We had a write up in the *Solihull News* about the refusal, so Miss Wren promptly left. We put in an appeal, employing solicitors *Vobe and Company*, a Mr Murphy, would-you-believe? He specialised in planning law, so that cost a bomb – but we had to have them. We kept trading all the time, until the appeal was heard, which took about six months. On the day of the Appeal, a team of planning officers called to inspect.

The Appeal Judge was a man called Harry Kettle and he remarked to Mary that his wife had the same colour kitchen as we had; he was a nice, chatty man, but that was all that was said between us. It took a further three months before we got the good news: permission granted on appeal. I came across the picture of Mary in the *Solihull News* the other day. It says: 'Solihull lady wins her appeal'. We've included the photograph they took for the article, in the book.

Well, the price of our house nearly doubled overnight with that outcome and there were no longer restrictions about how many people we could take in. In other words, we could take in fifty if we had the room! It also meant that we could now legally advertise, which up until now, we could not. But I was still looking around for something else to do.

My son, Shamus, initially regarded *Homer* House as simply a family home. "It was very large and as we lived on site, I knew a lot more about it than the *Copperfield*. It was different for me because I was boarding at *Princethorpe*, so I was free from the snobbery that Tracey experienced. It was a rambling house, but a lovely one. Over a short period of time it was renovated and became a secondary guesthouse, which, again, did very well. Being so close to Solihull Town Centre, we had all the amenities that anyone could want, like the shops, pubs and clubs.

"So by this time, we had the *Copperfield* and *Homer House Hotel* up and running. *Homer House* is still there – it's *Wood Glaister Solicitors* now. By one of the large traffic islands in Solihull town centre, there's a small section of road that's now 'one-way'. If you turn into that road, the first large building you come to is the former *Homer House*. On the boundary wall of the property, there are two pieces of stone that have been painted white, over the years. Next door to the house was a section of *St Martin's School*; the Junior Annexe of it, after the senior section moved to *Malvern Hall*. Miss Bacon was the headmistress there. They then demolished the Annexe, which was known as *Alice House*, and put a car park there for a few years. Homer Road starts from the end of Solihull railway station. If you cross over from that, you're on the end of Homer Road. There's just one building that separates you from the main island. As we walked up, there used to be houses next to us but they were all sold to *Taylor Woodrow*; they built their office headquarters there, about three years ago.

"The guests at *Homer House*, who most spring to mind, are from when we had the junior section of *Suffolk Lawn Tennis Club* staying with us. There were eight to ten players, plus the coach and his wife. They were playing at the local *Arden Lawn Tennis Club*. It was a local Youth Tournament. The coach and his wife were called Mr. and Mrs. Bastard! As a spotty teenager, the shoulders would start shaking and there'd be tittering and what-have-you! Obviously, thinking about it now, the embarrassment factor must have been amazing! I remember, the gentleman's wife asked my mum to book a table for dinner, for herself and her husband. Mum politely said, 'What name do you want me to give?' And she said: 'Oh – Mr. and Mrs. Smith.' I thought: "Yes – there must be an enormous amount of embarrassment over the name." I think his first name was Piers. That obviously sticks in your mind. But they just looked like Mr. and Mrs. Normal.

"It was a little strange for me, because I was still away at *Princethorpe*. It's a Catholic Public School, out in the middle of nowhere. Dad sometimes jokes that he's got the best educated bricklayer and carpenter working for him, in the whole of England! With hindsight, we probably didn't appreciate the actual efforts that Mum and Dad put into our education. Russell went to *Solihull School*, which was more local. Mum and Dad had the chance to send me to *Princethorpe*. I think, on Mum's part, there *may* have been an ulterior motive there. A lot of Irish families have a child in the priesthood. This particular college was run by priests and nuns. *Blackrock* was run by the *Holy Ghost Fathers*; *Princethorpe* was the *Sacred Heart Missionaries*. I think that possibly there was a hope that I might get a calling to the priesthood, one of the days!" So *that's* why Seamus encouraged him to have short haircuts!

"Initially, I was a weekly boarder: Monday to Friday and came home at weekends; but most of the rugby matches were played on the Saturday, so I tended to end up at school from Monday to Saturday, and if I missed the lift into Leamington or Coventry, it would have been late on a Saturday afternoon, when I got home. There was always something going on at school, so I thought: 'Well, I might as well stop tonight.' So for some of the time I was actually a full-time boarder, because of school commitments, basically. Although I didn't do that well at school, academically, I enjoyed it.

"I didn't enjoy the first half term, possibly, but after that I had a whale of a time. We sold *Homer House*, and I'd been round the house in Lovelace Avenue I arrived at Solihull Railway Station. I'd spoken to Mum in the week, and she said: 'When you get to Solihull, I'll pick you up, because we'll be moving.' I'd known about the move, but I'd been side-tracked by school, so it was strange, arriving at a completely different house, for the very first time, having just travelled down from *Princethorpe*," continues Shamus.

"It was a beautiful place. It was one of those strange things, when you tell people where you live: 'Yes, we live up on Lovelace Avenue. Our house has got a lift in it.' 'Has it? Bloody hell!' How many houses do you know that have a lift in them? But the house at 514 Warwick Road had its own air-raid shelter; which was another iconic kind of thing to tell somebody: 'Our house has got an air-raid shelter!'

"Frank Graves, who was the previous owner of Lovelace, had been a surveyor. It was a great house, but again, a tremendous amount of work was needed on it. But Mum and Dad's characters are such that they can look at something and see the possibilities. Mum's the *visual* person. If this room had absolutely nothing in it, and just bare walls, she would be able to visualise where the furniture would go and how things would look. I have to see it on a photograph or on a piece of paper. Dad is similar, but on a larger scale. Mum could see fine detail in something like this room, whereas Dad would be able to stand back, probably from across the road, look at the plot and say: 'Well, if this house wasn't here, or if it was slightly to the left or the right, I could have got a house in here, a bungalow, or three garages.' I haven't got that vision, but that's the way Dad is."

Mary continued to look after *Homer House* and the kids. Meanwhile, I discovered a police station in Hay Mills, on the main Coventry Road, which had come up for sale. The police station had two terraced houses adjoining it, on both sides. It was a beautiful building – still is. This was a tricky one because it was sealed bids, and you never know what to put in. But I got to know the man who was dealing with it, and we got on well. It was for sale freehold, but then Labour took over control of Birmingham City Council, and the property was transferred to a hundred-year lease. We all put in our bids, which were nearly all the same. They told us that the guide price was around £40,000.

We all had to submit a new bid – a final offer. All this took months. You know the way the Council operates. The first time I bid I offered £45,000, so I put in a new bid of £60,000. By this time the Tories had regained control of the city again, and it was being sold freehold.

I had a decorator called Mick Green decorating a few rooms in *Homer House*. Mary and I had to go out for some reason. When we returned Mick Green said: "The phone was hopping off the wall, so I answered it" – something he should *not* have done. So it was Mick Green who told us that we had bought the police station. It was knocked down to me. Great news, but I wish I had known *before* Mick.

It was sold with outline permission for a hotel. Mary reckoned she could get fifty rooms out of it. Many of the rooms were there already, but we had to make twenty more, by separating existing ones, taking down walls and splitting other rooms. We got about fifty in all, so we had to put in fifty bathrooms, washbasins and toilets. It really was a huge job. What I did not realise at the time was that I had to put in detailed plans, that then had to be passed. I was also supposed to apply for building regulations, none of which I did.

I got a chippy from Cavan, called Joe Donohue and we started on the timberwork. Every time we let a room in *Homer House* it financed a load of timber for the police station; all second-hand, from a Reclamation Yard. A fellow called Owen Murphy owned the yard. It should have been new timber, but money was scarce. I worked very hard myself, putting in new girders and removing walls. Don't forget, it was a purpose-built government building, so it was built very well; the walls were like steel. Myself and Joe the chippy worked through the winter and got most of the partitioning done. Then I employed one plumber, although really I should have had half a dozen. But the pocket would not stand it. The work-rate was set according to how busy we were in Homer Road – every time we let a room, I bought some new materials.

The plumber was a fellow called Jeff, but he was absolutely useless – must have been the slowest plumber in history! He seemed to be there for ever. Every time he saw me he wanted a bunch of quarter-inch, half-inch or three-quarter-inch copper tubing. We used to deal with *Harris of Stirchley*, a well-known Builders' Merchants. They let me run up a fair bit of credit. They were great really, but every time Jeff the plumber wanted something, it took half a day to get up there and back. I used to pass other builders' merchants, but the credit was the main reason we always went there. We kept the doors of the police station closed, although, ironically, one or two burglars got in, from time to time! We were surrounded by council houses, and plenty of unemployed robbers about. I thought we might open for the *Motor Show*, at the *NEC*, but it came and went, with no sign of us being ready.

All of the bathrooms were in place, but they were a long way off being ready to connect. Then one day there was a knock on the door, and a man outside called Ernie Berry, from the City of Birmingham Planning Office. I knew him from other meetings here and there; a nice enough fellow. He said: "We have been watching this place for six months. I know no work has been done, because we've seen no signs of activity." We already had fifty bathrooms in place and all of the studding and removal of walls. He could not believe it! Anyway, he read the Riot Act, saying that I had to apply for detailed planning permission and building regulations – and stop work. So I contacted my architect and started the plans.

Well, Glory be! Out of the blue, a big, tall man called Mr. Wright called into *Homer House* one morning and asked if we were the owners of the police station. When we said yes he explained that he represented *Mitchell's and Butlers*, the big brewing firm, and they would be interested to buy, if we could agree a price. They wanted to turn it into a pub. Well, we were definitely interested, but the first offer they made was £100,000. We were not interested at that price, so he left us and I continued to work on the Station.

Ernie Berry, Planning Chief, said: "If the plans are in, in a couple of weeks, I'll take the block off you." So we started with a vengeance. Mr. Wright left us – and that was that.

The tax investigation was going on, all this time. Just as Jim Small was making substantial progress, the tax inspector would leave and a new one would come on board. Some of them did not want to touch it, because it was far too complicated and they didn't want to do the work. Although I was being asked for large sums of money all the time, I was still years away from a settlement.

About six weeks after our first meeting with Mr. Wright, he called us again and this time increased his offer to £150,000. Wow – the get-out clause – daylight at the end of the tunnel! Again, we said no, but I was a bit sorry when we broke the talks and I continued to work away in the Station. The architect who drew up the plans was not fully qualified at that time, so they had to be sent back two or three times for amendments and further information. His name was Ken James and he worked for Solihull Council.

My family was growing up. My son Shamus was due to leave *Eversfield*, when he was thirteen. We sent him to *Princethorpe College*, a good Catholic school. He took the entrance exam and passed it, so he was off. He boarded during the week and sometimes came home on Friday night, when he wasn't stopping over.

I remember dropping him off the first morning. He popped into school without a word. I was very sad. This was the first break-up in the family. I had dragged them to Ireland, rural schools; back again, new schools, then boarding at *Princethorpe*. Life was flying past. We used to love Friday nights. Shamus would be home about five or six in the evening. We had two German Shepherd Dogs and they had to be seen first. Shamus liked *Princethorpe* and started to play rugby for the school, so there was less pressure.

Six or seven weeks later, around 6.00pm, we had another call from Mr. Wright. We were very glad to hear from him this time, and after a bit of a chat he offered £200,000. It was always Mary who spoke to him, or met him. I would have pulled the hand off him! I firmly believe that women are smarter than men, because if it had been down to me, I'd definitely have let it go for that.

But he left it with us and asked us to ring him when we had thought it over. Although our hearts were in our mouths, Mary never rang, so he came back again, with an offer of £220,000. But this time he changed his tactics and asked us what we would sell for. Mary said £300,000. So off he went and was back a week later offering £275,000. This time he said it was his final offer and no more bargaining. So we agreed that evening to sell for an exceptional figure. He said he would give us a percentage of that, for a six-month option, while they applied for planning permission.

The following morning, as I came to the Station, Jeff the plumber shouted: "Seamus, I want a three-quarter bundle of inch and a rake of stuff!" I said: "Wait a minute Jeff. Have a few months off and I will see you in six months." He didn't like it one bit and reckoned he should have got a bonus.

I saw the planning application going in, for change of use to a pub, and waited while they went through all the procedures. The six months finally came and went and we got our money. The building was then transformed into the *Old Bill and Bull Public House*, which can be found to this day, on the Coventry Road, Hay Mills.

Now, I thought I would never be broke again, and at least I would have the tax money. We were getting fed up with the kids having to duck and dive in the house. Often they would have to leave their beds, to make room for hotel guests, when we were overbooked, and had done so for years. So we decided to move.

A big house came up in Lovelace Avenue – a really beautiful house, in a private road. It was offers over £120,000, so I bid £125,000. We got it and it was great to live private. We'd started our married life off in Sparkhill, and had lodgers then, on and off, throughout our married life. But now we would be living privately. All the kids loved it, but it meant that we all had to be up very early in the mornings. We'd take Tracey and Russell with us, all have breakfast together, then off they'd go to school.

Although our Lovelace home was lovely, it was turning out to be much harder for us, so we began to think about selling *Homer House*. There was a place directly opposite, which came up for auction and an awful lot of people bid for it. It had been a Half-way House, for kids who were in trouble with the law. Now one of the bidders was a solicitor named Tony Wood, who I knew, because his kids and mine were at the same school. But he did not get it, so I approached him and asked if he had any interest in *Homer House*. He nearly pulled my hand off, and as our previous buyer had done before, with the police station, he wanted to buy the option. He had to get permission for change of use, but we agreed to sell.

There was a group of solicitors in our house and we had practically agreed the price, but Mary turned to me and said: "Let's walk down the garden for a minute." When we got back, she put another £100,000 on the price, without warning me that she was going to do so! They did not bat an eyelid and we struck a deal. They had to get planning permission for offices, so they engaged a barrister. They gave us a deposit that was ours to keep, no matter what happened, and so another fight began.

Well, the big appeal came for *Homer House*. We were not called at all. It was the Council versus Woods Solicitors, but it was on for the day. Then the planners came down to our house with their barrister and Woods the Solicitor's barrister and the Appeal Judge. They all left and we continued to run it as a guesthouse and work on the building, for four months, until the word came: permission for offices – granted. So another chapter of my life closed, as we moved to 23 Lovelace Avenue.

Chapter Twenty-one

LOVELACE IN SPLENDOUR

*As our story draws to a conclusion, it becomes clear that a substantial part of Seamus'
life has been on the creative side; whether it be music, wrestling, entrepreneurial schemes,
storytelling, or, with Mary's help, recreating unique buildings, often out of dereliction.
Talking of which, it was time, once again, for a spot of creative money management! With
£100,000 deposit and a £30,000 mortgage from the bank, the interest rate rocketed up
to about 15%. As there was no regular income coming in, things were getting a bit scary!*

*During this period, Jim Small continued to ask for £20,000 or £30,000, to pay
their outstanding debts, so Seamus had to keep peddling. Although Lovelace Avenue
was beautiful, many of their neighbours had cleaners, gardeners, and expensive cars!
Maybe he had jumped the gun a bit? Getting there was one thing, but maintaining that
lifestyle was quite another. However, he had other irons in the fire.*

*On the strength of selling Homer House, Seamus had acquired yet another property,
for about £35,000, in Streetsbrook Road, Solihull, with a garden running down to
Broad Oaks Road. So he kept half of the garden that was fronting Broad Oaks, and put
the Streetsbrook Road house up for sale. As the old woman who sold it to Seamus was
moving out she said: "I hope you don't think you are going to get a site, in the garden,
because I have been refused." He then contacted the Planning Office, about whether a
planning application had been put in for the back of the garden and they said that
nothing had been applied for. So she had probably spoken to an office junior, who didn't
know much about the situation, and had been content with that. Thanks be to God –
Buidheachas le dia – he's got me at it now!*

*It's remarkable, that from a situation years ago, as a young man, when Mick
O'Reilly first advised Seamus to buy a property and rent it out, he and the family have
built a really thriving business. He must have had an innate talent for it; some form of
genetic memory, perhaps, from his father's side of the family?*

*The Streetsbrook house was perfect on the outside: marvellous brickwork, not a crack
or anything, but on the inside, the entire middle had sunk. Although he knew about this,
Seamus had been tempted by the extra land. A Spirit Level, placed on the mantelpiece
in the front room, showed that it was two inches out, in four foot – a clear indication of
the problem, to builder and lay man alike. But don't forget the thirty-five foot of garden,
from the brick wall of the main house, with space to build another house.*

Planning permission seemed to take ages, as it always does when your life depends upon it! But I got it, so we were again thrown a lifeline. Meanwhile, the stairs up to the second floor were so lopsided that a man with a leg-and-a-half could walk up properly! It was *bad*. I put it up for sale with an agent, although I knew I would have to cure the subsidence, to sell it. So I opened the front room floor, and took a few boards up. I got down with a lamp and saw several bags of cement, in the middle of the house. I could not weigh it up, so I took a builder friend of mine down. He said: "You lucky bugger. This house has been underpinned in the last five years and they have done a very good job – it's perfect!" Well, be talking about the Devil's children having the Devil's luck! Could you believe it? The old woman must have had it done.

Wha-heeeeeee! Wha-heeeeeee! Luck. Black cats. Red-haired woman. Crowing cocks – the lot. Rabbit's tails... four-leaf shamrocks! So up for sale it went... and I kept the garden, for a site to build a house. I popped into the house a few days later, because I saw a car outside and a surveyor for the purchaser surveying it. He said: "It's not a bad house." I said: "It's a *great* house – the subsidence is done." He said: "It's fine anyway." He was a sensible fellow, from the *Yorkshire Building Society*. So the purchaser, Mr. Humphries, got his full mortgage, we got a good price, and were away to something else. That was a very close shave, without having a proper survey done.

So there we were, living in Lovelace Avenue, still struggling, but with the lifeline of two sites: the Streetsbrook one and a tiny site, but a good one, in Lovelace. Jesus, didn't I decide to build a bungalow on it? So we started. Mary's brother, Tommy, (who has died since), was a good bricklayer, and was going to build it. Shamus, having finished school, had become a bricklayer too.

We had purchased Lovelace Avenue at a very reasonable price. It was offers over £125,000. We must have sold the police station, to buy it. It was an absolutely splendid, five-bedroom house, in a private road. It had a lift in it, which we have here too, and had been built by the Bragg family. I remember meeting one of the Bragg sisters once, who was married to a solicitor, and she knew all about our house in Lovelace Avenue.

According to Muriel Waters, *Bragg Brothers, the Builders*, one of the oldest and well-established families in the area, built many houses, usually to architects' specifications, around Solihull. According to Muriel, "Mr. Horton did most of the architectural work for *Braggs, the Builders*. My grandfather, Charles Bragg, started the company.

"The original premises of *Bragg Brothers, the Builders* were in Drury Lane, which is now one of the walkways into *Mell Square*. Around 1912, the business moved to Church Hill Road. Another architect, Mr. Weedon, also worked for the company and had a beautiful house up Hampton lane, called *St Just*. He owned the land opposite him and wanted to build houses on it. So *Bragg Brothers* built three houses there and Mr. Weedon was the architect."

One brother built our former Lovelace house, and the other, our present home. The lift, I *imagine*, would have been very handy if you'd had too many brandies, or something like that; it would save you having to climb the stairs, because our lift goes up to the main bedroom. Coincidentally, Shirley met one of the senior Braggs years ago, Tom Bragg, and his wife, at his Shirley home, when she produced a dissertation in 1972, called *A History of Shirley and Two of it's Schools*, as a student teacher. It was Tom's son, Gordon, who put us in touch with Muriel.

Mary's sister, Monica Maguire, lives in Lady Byron Lane, in a house that was also architect-designed, *possibly* by Mr. Weedon. Although it doesn't have a lift, it's an absolutely splendid house as well. By a remarkable coincidence, her parents-in-law live in *St Just*, Mr. Weedon's former home – I know it well! I understand that Lord Byron has a family connection to the Lovelace family. Next door to us, where Russell lives, is a house with a green roof, called *Widney Croft*; we believe that housed servants who worked at *Widney Court*.

Tracey recalls: "23 Lovelace Avenue, otherwise known as *Dalworth House*, had a kind of sunken garden in the front, and a beautiful front door and dining room. We had a lift although there were only two floors. The lift was beautiful inside, with the old-fashioned concertina criss-cross metal doors. The house was built for an opera singer. It was lovely, with huge gardens, which were absolutely fantastic. There were even vegetable plots too. The left-hand side, at the time, would have been just a field. On the other side were the Davidsons."

Muriel Waters remembers Barry Davidson, and confirms that he was Chairman of the *Fosters Brothers* chain of clothes shops. "Despite their affluence, all the neighbours were fine; there were no 'airs and graces'," continues Tracey. "It's a fairly long road of about forty houses: a dead end, so you have to turn round. Our house was about half-way up – the fourth house on the left, as you go up. Although it's a private road, it's also open to non-residents, because there's a Nursery there, if you want to buy plants or flowers."

"I know that Bragg Brothers built *Dalworth House* personally, for Mr. Doubleday," continues Muriel. "I believe that the architect was Mr. Horton, although I might be wrong. Mr. Horton lived in Homer Road." Yet another coincidence – *Homer House!*

Widney Court, on Widney Manor Road, has a very similar design to *Dalworth House*. They both have lifts and quite a few other features in common. Muriel's family home was *Dene Hollow*, which is on Church Hill Road. Robert Bragg, her father, lived there with herself and the rest of the family, just a short distance from *Widney Court*.

Muriel confirms: "I know that there was definitely a house built up there, by *Bragg Brothers*, on Widney Manor Road, on the right-hand side, as you're coming from the town centre. If *Widney Court* is the building I'm thinking about, it has a very large drive and parking area, with an entrance and an exit."

Russell confirms: "*Dalworth House* was built in the 1930s, by the Braggs, who are undertakers and, at the time, were also builders. Frank Graves was the gentleman we bought it off, around 1983/84. He was a surveyor. With his very good business acumen, Dad spotted its potential. It was a beautiful house, with a big garden on the side of it. He spotted the potential, because there was a chance we'd get a site in there, which would be big money, if we got permission. It had a well-landscaped cottage garden, with a beautiful vegetable garden. I remember the first time I went there; I was walking round; when we'd just bought it. It was a summer's day and I literally, startled a rabbit, which was just six-foot away. If you see a rabbit, it's usually about a hundred yards away, but this one was just a few feet away – munching on some vegetables!

"We moved into 23, in 1983/84, and got permission to build a second house. About two years afterwards, Mick Traynor, a friend of Dad's who's a civil engineer, began the footings for the new house. They were good days – it was a lovely summer. It was actually my late Uncle Tommy, my mum's brother, who did all the brickwork on it," recalls Russell.

"We lived in Dalworth House for around seven or eight years," continues Tracey. "Then we moved next door to number 21, to the house that we built, and lived there for a further three or four years. I was working at the NEC from 1986, so I was living in Lovelace Avenue during that period."

"He was a fantastic bricklayer, my Uncle Tommy – a real Master Bricklayer," Russell continues. "He had a gang of bricklayers, who did the work on it. There was Tommy and a guy who's still around Birmingham today, John Tolliday, who was labouring for Tommy. Dad was labouring on it too. It was bliss – a roasting-hot summer. We all helped, because I was an apprentice carpenter at the time. Peter, from the Black Country, was one of about four carpenters working on it, at one stage; everyone worked really hard on it.

"We were really pushing it, because we wanted to get in. I just remember it being a really good laugh and real good craic, with everyone working together. It didn't take long at all. I always remember the day the brickwork was finished. Obviously, we were living next door and they all came round to our house. We were having something to eat, so we invited all the lads round. Everyone started drinking. It was a summer's evening and John Tolliday was doing handsprings up the garden – that always sticks in my head! I wasn't drinking, because I was too young and I was training very hard, but every so often Dad would say: 'Do another handspring John!'

"I particularly remember moving in. I was wrestling at Amateur level and you never see it on Terrestrial TV, unless it's the *Commonwealth Games* or the *Olympics*. But the day we were moving the furniture into the new house, Noel Loban from Great Britain was wrestling in the *Commonwealth Games* final, in Edinburgh. It was televised on *Grandstand* that particular Saturday. So I stopped helping everyone, for fifteen minutes, so that I could watch it. Dad was somewhere else, but I said: 'Look, I'm watching this.' It always sticks in my head that Noel Loban was in the Heavyweight Wrestling Final, on that particular day.

"At the time we were doing it, I used to knock about with a lad from school; we're still good friends – Simon Lewis, and another lad – Omar Mahmood. When you work on buildings, you're used to going up and down ladders and working on scaffolding. You're fearless – because you just do it every day. I remember we went up on the new roof, with these two lads from school and they were very nervous; not because they were scared, but they just weren't used to it. It was a hipped roof, on the top of it. There are four sides to it, with tiles all the way round. A gable end is where the bricks go all the way up. Hipped roofs tend to look a lot better; although I suppose that's just personal opinion. But it was a big, solid, traditional roof, and I remember working on it.

"The new house was immediately to the left of 23. We sold our house to Colin Davies. He was a real character and was married to the singer, Maggie Moon, who was quite a big star at the time. They were a nice couple, but unfortunately they split up later in life. They moved into number 23 and made it their own. They really glamorised it, and invited us round for drinks on Christmas Day. Gary Newbon would be there, Bobby Davro; a lot of showbiz people.

"You walked into 21 Lovelace Avenue," continues Russell, "and on the left-hand side was a small sitting-room; the dining room was straight ahead. The main lounge was to your right and a cloakroom to your left. So they were all the main rooms off the hallway. The stairs went up at the back; halfway up the stairs, (it was similar to here) there was a bay window that went out. Upstairs, on the left-hand side there was a small office; mum's room on your right. Then going down the corridor, there was Tracey's room, my room at the end of the corridor, and then just before that was Shamus's. I had a view straight out onto the back garden, from my bedroom. I always remember building a fence straight down the middle of the back garden, with Dad. I was at work, but we'd do a few panels each night, when I came home. Dad wanted the posts in solidly, so we'd dig down about three or four feet, and put in plenty of concrete; it was a real solid fence.

"Although I was supposed to be very bright, I didn't settle at *Solihull School*. I think, to this day, mum regrets that she let me leave school at sixteen. But actually, it worked out for the best, for me. My brother and I both went to Public School. I left school and got an apprenticeship with *Bryant's* – and it was brilliant for me; it worked out great."

Russell was actually following the family tradition: his grandfather, father and then himself, all became carpenters. "I realised that, but I didn't take it on board, because I was getting into Sport at the time."

Russell explains: "We are now basically property investors. We're landlords. We buy any type of property with a rental income coming off it. Mum and Dad started the business and they built up a fantastic residential portfolio. To be fair, Mum and Dad always saw things before anyone else; they were buying big three-storey houses and converting them into flats and renting them out, when no one else was doing it. They were trail blazers, around Birmingham and the Midlands. At the time, it was very hard to get finance from the banks, to do this. But they managed to do that. Then, realising the way the market was going, we started to move away from the residential to commercial properties – like High Street shops and Job Centres; warehouses that are let out to Blue Chip Companies. We've got buildings that are let to government institutions, like the Inland Revenue. Sixty per cent of our lets are to government institutions. We own the offices of the biggest Inland Revenue centre in the country. We cover an area now, as far as Grimsby in the North as West as Yeovil and as East as King's Lynn. We do have some advisors, but it's just something that we've developed, as a family, over a period of time. You get an instinct for situations. You think: 'Yes, this will work.'

"When you're borrowing money from a bank and you've got to pay it back, it makes you so sharp – you *have* to get it right! You cannot afford to get it wrong. When you see a building and you know there's a very good tenant in there, you still think: 'Well, what would happen if that tenant went 'bump' tomorrow?' Can you convert that property into flats, or from flats into offices? You've always got to think one step ahead – what if something goes wrong? If that shop business failed, how would you divide it up, or convert it? You consider all the angles," explains Russell.

We had a wonderful dog called Bran, but when we moved across, from 23 Lovelace Avenue, to 21, Bran would never cross the open space, to the new house, because he'd been born in *Dalworth House*. Dogs are great, aren't they! In Irish mythology, there was a giant called Finn MacCool. He had two beautiful Irish Wolfhounds called Bran and Squelan. If you ever see any clubs with the Gaelic name Tir na nOg, (pronounced Cheer na nOgue), it means *Land of Youth*. So that's all connected with the same story that our dog, Bran's name derives from.

"I'd just finished my apprenticeship, with *Bryant Homes*, confirms Shamus. "I picked a few jobs with people, over the next few months, then the plans were passed for building the house next door and all the local builders wanted to either purchase the land, or build the house for us. My parents sat on it and thought about it. My Uncle Tommy came up with the idea of doing the brickwork for us. Myself and another apprentice, from *Bryant's*, a lad called Stuart Rigby, were going to head off for America for twelve months and make our fortunes! We talked about it in the September, and decided we were going to go the following February or March, which was exactly the time when Mum and Dad decided to start building. I was under a moral obligation then: do I finish this, or do I upset the family and go? I told Stuart to go ahead and I'd catch him up in a few months time when the house was finished.

"Sometimes there would be six or seven people working on the house – bricklayers, carpenters, labourers, and so on, including John Tolliday or *Tolly*, as we sometimes referred to him. There was my Uncle Tommy; two other brickies: Des Paisley and Mick Dempsey. They were actually two lecturers from Hall Green Technical College, who taught me my trade, when I had day-release from *Bryant's*. There was also a third brickie, whose nickname was *The Donegal Tiger*. They started in March and moved in on the 2nd August of that year, when the house was completely finished."

Colin Davies, who bought *Dalworth House*, ran a printing firm called *Standard Continuous*. It later became *Forms UK*. As Russell said, Colin and

Maggie made it really special when they moved in; they made it their own. "Well, it was very showbizy…glitzy", Shamus continues. "Some of it was to my taste but other parts were a bit 'over the top'. They invited us over on Christmas morning. I remember Gary Newbon being there and one or two Thespians. I found them slightly over the top; they stretched the word 'normality' a little bit too far! The house was beautiful. Mum and Dad had done it up and made it absolutely *gorgeous*. It was rather difficult going round, when Maggie and Colin had the house, because they had their own personal style. With certain things that Mum and Dad had done, you'd walk in and think: 'Well, they've wrecked it! No – you should have left it.' But peoples' tastes are different, of course."

My family business, *Corncrake Properties*, involves both rentals and property development. We off-loaded a lot of our rental property recently, and we now own substantial commercial properties in Yorkshire, Lincolnshire, Norfolk, Nottinghamshire, Buckinghamshire, Staffordshire and Lancashire, Warwickshire, London, Somerset, Wales, Dorset and Wiltshire. Our rental property *tends* to be more West Midlands based. This is well-documented with banks and so forth.

Eventually, we paid Jim Small a six-figure sum, to settle everything. We started as his worst clients, but ended up as one of the chosen few. He and his wife, Pat, became good friends of ours, although I still call him *Mister* Small! We continue to rely on him for advice, although nowadays, he *can* be very cautious.

Russell explains: "Dad and I have a brilliant relationship. We want the same things and, primarily, we're not afraid of taking risks. We want to borrow as much money as we can – and expand as much as we can. We're very conscious that we have to pay it back, but we're on the same wavelength. If I like a building and I show it to Dad, it's 99% certain that he'll like it as well. But if I don't like it, he probably won't either; we have that rapport between us. The day-to-day running of the business is down to me, my brother and my sister, but we go back to Dad for all the big decisions. He's actually working harder now than he ever has done, but he enjoys it."

So Shamus, Tracey and Russell all work with me in the family business. According to Russell, "The easiest way to describe it, in business terms, is that Dad would be the Chairman. I would be the Chief Executive. Tracey is in charge of the office, and she's also like the Company Secretary. Shamus is more on the practical side, so he manages the day-to-day residential side of things and he's out there organising materials and contracts." Tracey's very broad experience of exhibitions, over a nineteen-year period, between May 1986 and April 2005, is proving very useful, in the family business.

"Everything is run through as a family and Mum either likes something or she doesn't like it. And if Mum really doesn't like something and puts her foot down, it won't happen. It's very rarely that she does that, but if she really has a bad feeling... Dad will tell you this – that Mum is his greatest Council," continues Russell. "She could never tell Dad what to do, because he wouldn't stand for it. But if she's really uncomfortable about something, that we're going for – if she really doesn't like it, Dad will listen to her."

Shamus elaborates: "Tracey does 99% of the office work. I don't understand what she does, but she organises it, and it runs very smoothly. Whenever I'm interviewing a prospective tenant, for a flat, I would break it down to the division that Russell and Tracey do 99% of the paperwork for dealings with the Council Tax, Utilities such as the Water Department et cetera, but my section is known as the *Breakages and Blockages Division*!

"Strangely, I prefer that side of things. I prefer working with my hands rather than my brains. I feel ill-at-ease phoning people and trying to sort out problems verbally or with the written word. But if a washing machine's not working, you assess what's wrong, you replace the faulty part and the job's finished. No 'I'll be back in a day,' or anything like that – so that's the side of the business that I like.

"Take, for example, a one or two-bedroom flat for rent, say, at £100 a week and so forth, (the rest of the particulars). It's advertised and then, a large percentage of the time, the first interview's with me, basically, because Russell's probably tied up in the office. It's not an interview to say 'You've definitely got the flat.' I'm part Estate Agent, part Letting Agent, or whatever you want to call it. I explain the 'dos and don'ts'; the 'haves and have nots'; what you can and cannot do. Explain, from our point of view, what's expected, and then what the next stage in the process is.

"Our Residential Portfolio is predominantly around the Acocks Green, Solihull area. We did have some in Walsall and around the Erdington area, but we've kind of swapped. As the residential market became less lucrative, we've concentrated more on commercial property, and that covers a broader area. Owning the largest Inland Revenue office complex, in Kings Lynn, is quite strange – having your tax bills come from a place that you own! We have Job Centres as well, Bookmakers, High Street shops...

"Dad started the rental game in the first place, because it was the same, but different to a Bed and Breakfast business," continues Shamus. "In other words, you're providing something, for a short period of time. Renting is the next stage on from Bed and Breakfast. Twenty-five years ago, in the Solihull area, you could probably count on one hand, the amount of private landlords there were, other than the Council. But in the same area now, you'd probably need three pairs of hands to count them. From the outside, everyone thinks it's any easy game, but in reality, it's very time-consuming, because tenants will ring up with the smallest of complaints – and it needs to be sorted. Only this week I had two tenants ring up. Their washing machines were still under warranty, so I had to contact the manufacturer. One sent an engineer out yesterday to a let in Acocks Green, but there's another to be repaired in Digbeth, Birmingham. Why they don't send an engineer out to repair the two on the same day, I don't know – but – hey-ho!

"When I interview somebody, who takes on a flat, I always stipulate that I'm not a warlock, a wizard or God: I can't perform miracles – although I will try my utmost! There are times when I may forget non-urgent jobs, but if it hasn't been done within a certain period of time, remind me, and I *will* do it. On a big scale, if we're doing renovations, there is a builder that we use, and plumbers and what-have-you. But on the day-to-day, small stuff, I deal with most of that myself. It's peaks and troughs; one minute you think: 'Oh, I've got nothing to do', but then tomorrow, I could have twenty hours of work; it might all come in at once," Shamus concludes.

We eventually moved from the house we built in Lovelace Avenue, to our present home. Colin still lives in Number 23. Maggie's departed and he's got himself a new wife. We had a lovely oak-panelled hall when we lived there. You never paint oak, you French Polish it, or wax it, but Maggie painted it white. It looked ghastly. And you know the way women do themselves up at the dressing table mirror? Well she had bulbs all round hers – like a show-biz dressing room.

In descending order, Mai, my eldest sister, is now widowed. She was married to Sean McConnell, a big, handsome Cavan lad, mentioned earlier in the book. They lived at 32 Phipson Road, Sparkhill. Nice house, five children. They went back to Charlestown to live in a lovely bungalow, but they weren't back there twelve months, before Sean had a massive stroke, and ended his life in hospital. Although she's a widow, her brothers, Tom, Louie and Mickey are all there. Most of her family are here: three girls and two boys. One of the boys is out in Illinois, and the other is working in England. Joanne and Yvonne and Jackie are married.

Paddy, my eldest brother, went back to Mayo too, after living in this country for forty-odd years. He died last year, so he's the only one of my siblings who's dead. His family are here, but, sadly, his son died in Scotland, about three years ago. He has a daughter here, in Birmingham.

My brother Louie, who spent ten years in America, doing a variety of jobs, is married and living at home, with two children, in Charlestown. He was a carpenter when he was in England, but I don't think he was, in the States. He's well into cars and a great mechanical man. He bought some land cheaply in Charlestown, before he left, then built ten or twelve houses there when he returned. He kept the last one and is living there himself. He's semi-retired, but has a big shed-cum-workshop; he makes steel gates too and puts up sheds that he's patented himself. Louie could retire, but he's a worker – he wants to be dabbling.

Then there's my brother Tommy, who was a very good carpenter. He's living there and married, with two girls; one working in a bank, in Sligo; the other was a nurse at *Heartlands Hospital*, but she's packed that up and is a peripatetic phlebotomist, with the Blood Bank. Sadly, Tommy is in the first stages of Alzheimer's. I saw him three weeks ago. He knows you, but he wanders round. If he gets outside the gate of his house and wanders down the street, they won't know where he is, so his wife has to watch him. Mickey is very good to him; he takes him to an Outpatients Clinic; sometimes for a day, sometimes a full week.

Then there's Mickey, who's married to Margaret and made all of his money in the Gas business and has a very big house back in Charlestown. They've two kids: one in Chicago, the girl, and his son Michael, or 'Puggy', as we call him, who was in Chicago for years but came home about five years ago. Mickey had bought a lot of land, years before. So his son, Puggy, built an estate of about thirty-five houses on it, and has built a huge house for himself. He's doing very well, and builds a few houses a year now.

Of course, we come from a family of builders: all Dad's side were stonemasons and carpenters, blacksmiths and everything. Then there's me, then after that we've got Angela, who's married to Pete O'Reilly and lives directly opposite the *Drum and Monkey*. Then there's Kathleen, who lives on Shakespeare Drive in Shirley and was married to Frank Neary. Her husband died five or six years back. Finally, there's Monica, who married and lives in Silhill Hall Road, the one after Broadoaks Road.

So whether it be in England or in Ireland, my family live very close by each other; three sisters all around me here, and, the other way around in Charlestown: one sister, with three brothers around her. Mickey lives on the edge of Charlestown. If I shout to Mickey, from my bungalow, he can hear me! It's about from the lounge here to outside the gates. If I throw weeds over my fence, they land in my brother Louie's grounds – so I have to be careful! Dad eventually died, aged eighty-six, having outlived Mammy by twenty-six years. Like her, he also had a Carrycastle funeral.

America and England were the two countries that members of our family emigrated to.

Our Wedding Anniversary is 16 April, so we usually go to the *Big Apple* for that. We may go to Florida this year, for a change, because Mary's uncle lives there, who we haven't seen for many years now, although we talk on the phone. We fly to America once a year; for pleasure, never business. I love New York, and the buzz of America. I was wondering whether we might buy an apartment there, in Manhattan. We usually do the same thing every year – into Manhattan. I love walking up and down the streets. We know a lot of people there.

The last time we were there, we were staying in the *Hyatt*, up on 7th Avenue, directly opposite to a big Irish pub, *Rosie O'Grady's*. I know the gaffer there: he comes from fifteen miles away from me, at home. His wife was a friend of Mary's, forty years ago. She became Agnes Delaney and was *previously* Agnes Connolly. We got talking to one of the waitresses: "Does Mrs. Connolly ever come in?" The girl said: "Agnes, and Austin Delaney, the owner, are divorced now." Mary left her hotel number and said, "It's Mary Griffin, from Birmingham. We used to go dancing together, forty years ago." When we got back to the hotel, there were three messages for us – all from Agnes. She said: "Three streets down there's another *Rosie O'Grady's*, run by my son, but he won't go to my husband's place. Don't tell him. Just walk in – and then I'll come in later." When we saw this young lad, Dermot Delaney, I said: "That's Agnes' son!" We said nothing and later, in she pops. We had a meal there with her – it was lovely! Then the day after, we took the subway, down to a pub that Mary's cousins own. They invited us for a round of golf, downtown.

When Russell left *Solihull School*, he had time to spare after work. So, just like me, all those years before, he used his leisure time for sports training – with great success. "The main wrestling club was the *BAI* in Highgate Road, Birmingham, opposite the Mosque – the *Birmingham Athletic Institute*. I started going there twice a week, became very keen, and began doing weights and running, three times a week, in Tudor Grange Park, Solihull. I was doing Weights in the club and roadwork for my running: going off for five to six-mile runs on my own," explains Russell.

"I had a great Hungarian coach, called Tony David. Birmingham had a very strong wrestling club at the time. My main training partner was a young

Asian, called Ravinder Singh. He won the *Commonwealth Championships* and he wrestled in the *1988 Olympics*. He had a very good cousin, Ranjit, who was a British International. Another of his cousins, Amerjit, became a very good Heavyweight wrestler; he got a silver medal in the *Commonwealth Games* in Canada, in 1994. He competed at the *Atlanta Olympics*. So the *BAI* was a very good club."

Russell started wrestling there twice a week, then increased it to three times a week. On a Wednesday there'd just be himself, Ravinder and the coach, Tony David – a really intensive, almost a one-on-one session. As these lads were from Wolverhampton, he started to wrestle there on Sunday mornings. By now he was wrestling four times a week, training six days a week. During certain periods of the year, he often trained twice a day – before and after work.

"Mum and Dad encouraged me, but Dad said: 'It's a very hard sport, and there's more to life than wrestling.' He wanted to make me aware that you can get into your twenties or thirties and start suffering as a result of wrestling; you need other strings to your bow. But they encouraged me and I got my call-up for Ireland. Then I wrestled in the European and the World Championships. I became the Irish Amateur Light Middleweight Champion, and captained the Irish team, from 1996, and we wrestled in the European and World Championships. I was very disappointed that I never did an *Olympic Games*. At the time, with the break up of the Soviet Union, each of those individual states then became individual countries, so the competition was much fiercer."

Wrestling became much more competitive. Up until 1988, if you were a national champion and they thought you were good enough, they'd send you. But after that, they brought in very hard criteria, and reduced the number of wrestlers that they'd allow to compete in the *Olympic Games*, in each weight category. So it was just decided on qualifications. 1996 was Russell's best year. Unfortunately, he was defeated in the second round, at the *European Championships*, in Budapest, by Memet Ozturk of Turkey, a former world champion, and lost on points to him. That meant that he didn't qualify for the *Olympics*.

"I'd also been unlucky in 1988. I'd missed the trials for the Irish Team; I didn't make them, because I had my wisdom teeth out and it got infected. But there's no point dwelling on that. I won International competitions for Ireland, wrestled all over the world and in Europe. I trained in the States, at the Naval Academy in America, which was a tremendous experience. I wrestled all over the States too. My best weight was seventy-four kilos – (eleven-stone nine). I had a wonderful experience. There was a competition called the *Challenge Cup of Great Britain*, which was a big International. I came fifth in it, and there were probably about forty competitors, at my weight. It was a good placing for me. I won a few of the fights and lost in the quarter final, to a German. Then in the Repercharge I beat a Canadian. I got spotted by one of the American coaches, Jim Heffernan and he asked me to come over. He was coaching at Lehigh University, Pennsylvania. He asked me to come over and try out for the team with them.

"Wrestling is very big in the American colleges. At the time, Lehigh had just managed to get three-time Olympic Champion, Sergei Belaglasov, of the Soviet Union, to come over and coach them; it was a massive coupe. So I arrived only two days after Sergei. It was a bit daunting to be honest with you, because I'd just arrived on my own, having taken the train down from New York. It was a bit of a 'baptism by fire': good, hard wrestling. There'd be about a hundred wrestlers on the mat, twice a day and only ten spots on the team. So everyone was pushing for a spot. Sergei was taking a few sessions.

"There was one session where we were really working hard, and he said, (Russian accent): 'You guys not work hard enough. Only one man has given one hundred per cent today. He gets a Soviet Singlet.' It was one of his international singlets, with the Soviet Crest on it. I was going over to get a glass of water or something, at the end of the session. He said: 'Come here, Russell, come here!' I was looking round, because I wasn't sure he meant me, because there'd been so many on the mat. But he called me over and said: 'That's for you,' and gave me the singlet. It was fortunate, because I had a real affinity with Sergei. I got to know the other wrestlers on the team and then I left there."

After the '96 European Championships Russell carried on wrestling seriously for another two years. Then he had a competition in Malta, which the Irish went to every year. It was the *World States Tournament*, which he won three times, including that year. The reason they call it the 'States', is because any State of any country can enter, so there were an awful lot of entrants. It's become as tough to win now, as a European Championship.

"If I'm perfectly honest, at the time when I won it, it wasn't as hard as nowadays, although it was still *very* hard to win. So the last time I won it was in '98. Then we came back and I was getting more interested in my work. I was asked to go to Bolivia, for a big tournament, in La Paz. The Irish team were going over and there was a big International in Tehran in Iran. I remember being selected, but thinking: 'Oh, I've got to get training!' When you're thinking like that, it's time to hang up your boots. You should be thinking: 'Oh yes!'"

Russell was still working as a carpenter, when we bought the *George*, the pub in town. "Dad had all the flats and houses and I was getting more interested in that; I always knew I would do. I was twenty-eight and ready for a change. So I said to Mick McCauley: 'Look Mick, I don't want to be up for selection, for any more Internationals.' He offered me a job coaching the Irish team, full time. They offered to fly me over three or four times a month. I've always been very lucky – I've always had good coaches when I've been wrestling; they've always given a hundred per cent. I was really honest and I just said: 'Mick, I can't give you enough commitment at this particular time.' Mick is the Head of the *Irish Amateur Wrestling Association*. I still keep in contact with him all the time and I always go the *Irish Open* every year and try to help the lads out. So I try to look after them and still keep involved. I don't go the Birmingham Club as much as I should do. I suppose, a lot of the lads have retired now and new wrestlers have come in. I would like to get back to coaching, but I don't want to do it until I'm at a stage in my life where I can give it my full commitment," explains Russell.

If Seamus had his time all over again, he would love to have been a good saxophone player – a musician. I'd also love to have been a good dancer, of the Gene Kelly type. I'm light on my feet, with a good sense of rhythm. Mickey's wife, Margaret, who's in Ireland now, is a very famous Irish Dancing teacher. She goes all over the world – Canada, America, Australia – she's been everywhere and gets very good money. She had a Dance School here for years, not far from here, by *The Plough* – they've a farm up there, in Cheswick Green. She'd a big old barn and that's where the Dance School was. When I'm over there, she teaches her grandchildren to dance, and I'm thinking: 'If I'd been taught that, I could do it, as easy as pie!' But I was watching Gene Kelly the other day and I thought: 'I'd love to have done that: tap dancing, rather than traditional Irish dancing.'

I've had a very interesting life, and as I am today, I'm totally contented with life – the family, the grandkids and everything. No serious illness – as such – none of my family has been kidnapped or raped or robbed. So when you compare that with what's happening elsewhere; there's eleven million starving on the other side of the world. Maybe I would have liked to have a few more kids. We often talk about that. We stopped very early in life, after Mary had her miscarriage. But thank God the grandchildren are coming along; there might be a few more. But there are ups and downs, and you can't win them all!

"Dad is an unusual character," explains Shamus. "If you've done something wrong, he will say his piece – and that's the end of it. There's no raking over the same ground, hours later on. He'll be blunt or cutting, but once he's said his piece, it's 'signed, sealed and delivered'. With Dad it's a short, sharp shock. Dad has a happy knack of saying the right thing at the right time, although you may not want to hear it. When you're being told off and you know you've messed up, you don't always want someone to reinforce the fact that you have... although he's right in what he does.

"I first worked with or for Dad, probably in around 1993/94; that's about twelve years. At first it was just me and Dad. He has mellowed to a small degree – he's using more brain than brawn now, is the best way of describing it. Dad is a person who will *never* retire, although he'll tell you 'til you're 'blue-in-the-teeth' that he will!

"From a son's point of view, every father has an aspiration about what their son will be in life. The day that son is born you think: 'Right – my son's going to be an airline pilot, a bank manager and so on. Whether they reach your expectations as a father is in the 'lap of the gods'. In the early days, when it was just me and Dad working together, Russell would have been away on his Round the World Tour at the time, Dad was a lot harder than he is today – he's mellowed a lot; whether it was because I'm over-sensitive, I'm not sure.

"The best picture I've got recently is that I have three young sons: Seamus, the older one, who's six, young Tom, who's three, and Daniel, who is only one year-old. Seamus is the 'apple of Dad's eye'. Although Dad will say that he treats all of them equally, I can see that he's got a very soft spot for Seamus – he was his first grandchild. I meet them at church, but ninety-nine times out of a hundred, Dad will always bring them back on the Sunday morning, for a couple of hours. Thomas absolutely *adores* Granddad: he worships the ground he walks on; although Dad doesn't seem always to know how to handle young Tom, because he'd that much more spirited. With my eldest son, Seamus, if you tell him not to do something, automatically he won't do it. But Tom needs four of five tellings, to not do something. You can see Dad reacting to that.

"When you get to know Dad, he's actually as 'soft as a kitten' underneath. It's not a side he portrays to a lot of people. His normal persona is that he's a rough-tough character; a nothing hurts him kind of person. But deep down, he *is* as soft as a kitten, especially where my children are concerned. And I'm sure he lets them get away with more than he did with us, when we were kids."

Tracey explains: "My parents moved to this present house, fairly recently. It was owned by the Chairman of Birmingham City Football Club.

There's some stained glass upstairs, which has the *Forward* shield of Birmingham City Football Club on it. The décor here is completely new. The Blues Chairman sold it to a man called Hockham, who we bought it off. He hadn't done anything to it for about twenty years, so when we bought it, it was in quite a bad state, and we had to do a lot. I thought they were mad – but they pulled it off again!"

Russell concludes: "They're an amazing team, Mum and Dad. Mum's a Capricorn, she's on the cusp, and Dad's a Sagittarius. I read years ago, in a Horoscope article, that if a Sagittarius man and a Capricorn woman get together in a partnership, then they're Empire Builders. So it really is true. Dad's a good musician. I had piano lessons at school, but I didn't stick with it.

"Dad is really understanding – if you ever have a really important problem. If it's a more minor thing, for example if you've pranged the car, then you'll think: 'Oh, Dad's going to go mad about that!' But if you ever had a major, really deep problem, you could go to Dad and there'd be no shouting or anything like that. I have a really close relationship with him – I enjoy his company. Me and Dad would never go to the pub for a pint, because he's not a pub man, at all.

"It's very hard to explain our relationship to other people, but we're very close. We travel up and down the country together, looking at various properties. It's a joy to do, because it's all very relaxed. He'll be reading the paper: 'Look at that!' He always calls me 'Champ'. I don't know where that nickname came from; he's called me that, ever since I was a little boy. I'm very lucky, because of the confidence I've got, from my Mum and Dad. I don't understand people who lack confidence. But obviously I was lucky, because of the way they brought me up and my education. Dad always instilled into me the attitude – show respect for people, but never be intimidated by anyone.

"Dad has two sides to him. On the one hand he doesn't 'suffer fools', but on the other hand, he can be very understanding and he's a good communicator. I always think that he would have been great, working with unruly teenagers; with kids who were going off the rails – trying to sort them out. You know – 'Pull yourself together – get yourself sorted out! If you want to fight, let's do it in the gym.' If life had been different for him, he could have done that well. He's a good man."

I cannot finish this book, without acknowledging the help and support of Mick Donovan, from the *Allied Irish Bank*, not to mention Mr. J.D. Small my accountant, without whose help we could never have survived. Heartfelt thanks also, to our very good friends, in rough times: Billy Graham, Charlie

Shiels, Joe Griffin (no relative), Mary Garside, and my trusted doorman, Pete Evans, aka the *Balsall Heath Basher*.

I have a nice holiday bungalow, in Charlestown, the town I was born in, next door to Bernie Swords, and I go home there a lot, on ships other than the *Princess Maud*, since she was sold to the Greeks. But now my life is in England, and I want to see my life out here now. I like everything about England: the eccentricity of English people, and the idea of having a Queen too.

Then there's the humour – Dick Emery and *The Two Ronnies* – I could watch them all day! I love the pomposity of the English, sometimes. We've grown up with them now, so this is it! I suppose I am a bit of a traditionalist really. I love 95% of what goes on in England, but, having said that, I'm a dedicated Irishman. I come from a strong Republican background, and until the day I die I'll always be a proud Mayo man... and a Charlestown man.

SELECT BIBLIOGRAPHY

Are You Somebody? – Nuala O'Faolain, Henry Holt and
   Company, New York, 1996

Angela's Ashes – Frank McCourt, Harper Collins
   Publishers 1996

Gaelic Dictionary (teach yourself series) – Boyd Robertson
   and Ian MacDonald, Hodder and Stoughton, 2004

Gander at the gate – Rory O'Connor, The Lilliput Press,
   Dublin, 2000

It's a Long Way from Penny Apples – Bill Cullen, Hodder
   and Stoughton, 2002

Newspaper article: Property West, March 21 2006 edition:
   Charlestown remains gateway to the West. Pictures by
   Robert Cullen

Website: Mayo on the Move: www.mayo-ireland.ie/
   Mayo/Towns/Charl/Charl.htm

The ship postcard website: www.simplonpc.co.uk (Ian Boyle)

OTHER BOOKS
BY SHIRLEY THOMPSON

There's More Out Than In, Brewin Books, 1999
If, The Pat Roach Story, Brewin Books, 2002
The Original Alton Douglas, Brewin Books, 2003
Pat Roach's Birmingham, Brewin Books, 2004
Auf Wiedersehen Pat, Brewin Books, 2006